CROSSING FRONTIERS

International Developments in the
Treatment of Drug Dependence

Edited by Alex Stevens

Crossing Frontiers

International developments in the treatment of drug dependence

Edited by Alex Stevens

© Pavilion Publishing (Brighton) Ltd, 2008
Chapter 1 © Civic Research Institute, 2007

Published by:
Pavilion Publishing (Brighton) Ltd
Richmond House
Richmond Road
Brighton BN2 3RL
Tel: 01273 623222
Fax: 01273 625526
Email: info@pavpub.com
Web: www.pavpub.com

Supported by:

A catalogue record for this book is available from the British Library.

ISBN: 978 1 84196 217 7

Pavilion is the leading training and development provider and publisher in the health, social care and allied fields, providing a range of innovative training solutions underpinned by sound research and professional values. We aim to put our customers first, through excellent customer service and good value.

Pavilion editor: Kerry Boettcher
Cover and page design: Faye Thompson, Pavilion
Cover image: photographed by Jan Zajc/www.sxc.hu

Printed on paper from a sustainable resource by Ashford Press

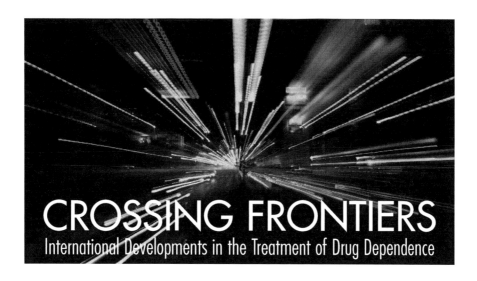

CROSSING FRONTIERS
International Developments in the Treatment of Drug Dependence

CONTENTS

FOREWORD

Lord Victor Adebowale CBE, Chief Executive of Turning Point

I welcome this much needed analysis of international approaches to the treatment of substance misuse. Building the evidence base for what works is crucial for organisations such as Turning Point, which look to push the accepted parameters of service delivery through developing new and bold approaches, and for our clients, who will benefit from better services as a result.

Turning Point is the UK's leading social care organisation, and last year our services saw over 100,000 people in 250 locations around England and Wales. We are also the largest voluntary sector provider of substance misuse counselling, treatment and aftercare, including Tiers 1 to 4 and services delivered in both community and criminal justice settings. The majority of our clients have a range of complex and overlapping needs, and substance misuse is one of the most prevalent challenges presented.

It is imperative to introduce more innovative substance misuse services that encompass the full complexity of drug users' needs and provide wraparound support to enable people to take a full role in society. Turning Point feels strongly that treatment has often been left unfinished, and has, as a result, not led to sustainable outcomes. It is imperative that on the 'conveyor belt' of the treatment journey, people finishing their treatment do not fall off the end with no ongoing support and that the next stage of their life is also considered. Further specific support is needed in employment, housing support, social exclusion, health care, and other issues such as support on leaving the criminal justice system, managing debt or rebuilding family relations. Wraparound services are stepping stones for current or former drug users out of social exclusion.

Turning Point has been involved in developing a range of innovative services that learn from the best of international and domestic approaches. These have included setting up the first English drug court in Wakefield in the 1990s, and specialist provision such as our Base Camp service, which supports parents and families with alcohol problems. From our experience, these are value-added services that are able to hold people in treatment and support them with their specific needs. It is crucial that we continue to learn from the successes (and failures) of other countries, and adapt those treatments that work for our own operating environment and our own clients.

A word on the current domestic climate. The government estimates that there are 332,000 problematic drug users in England alone; that is, those who are causing harm to themselves or others through their drug misuse. Prevalence is likely to be understated due to a hidden population of users who have little contact with criminal justice services or treatment. The Home Office estimates that Class A drug use generates an estimated £15.4 billion in crime and health costs each year, of which 99% is accounted for by problem drug users. Substance misuse represents a huge burden on the public purse and this, of course, is without accounting for its social costs: the misery, the frustration and the lives wasted by drugs and alcohol.

For these reasons, it is crucial that we re-emphasise the effectiveness of the treatment approach, in contrast with the traditional method of punishing drug abuse. The Home Office estimates that for every £1 spent on drug treatment there is a saving of £9.50 in other related costs such as crime and hospital admissions. The public health benefit of treatment and harm reduction methods are given prevalence in Turning Point's campaign report, *At the Sharp End*, which identified a new generation of injecting drug users, particularly those who are using heroin and crack together. It was found that these people are at greater risk of infection from hepatitis C and HIV, and may not have been tested or have received treatment for their illness. *Crossing Frontiers* reminds us not only of the range of treatments and harm reduction techniques out there, but also of the successes that we have seen as a result of extra money being driven into drug treatment. In order to sustain the momentum of the treatment agenda, we should strive to ensure that such insight is not lost in the future and to ensure that publications like this one will continue to highlight the range of interventions available.

As I write this, the government's Drug Strategy has just been published, and dictates the direction of substance misuse treatment for the next decade. I sincerely hope that the Strategy's framework will take into account the kind of evidence found in this publication on different and innovative ways of approaching substance misuse treatment, and that the government will continue to consider the best work from other countries for implementation in the UK. Drug consumption rooms, drug courts and multisystemic therapy are all promising developments that warrant further analysis.

Substance misuse is an ever-changing field of work, and only by staying ahead of international progress will we be able to meet the ever-changing challenges we face in service provision. And only by understanding the vast array of drug treatments available will we be able to provide an effective, holistic service for our clients.

There is an urgent need for world-class services to be replicated everywhere rather than just existing in some pockets of good practice. It can only by achieved by knowing about and sharing best practice worldwide. This is what *Crossing Frontiers* does and I commend it to you.

ABOUT THE CONTRIBUTORS

Daren Garratt is Executive Director of the Alliance, a peer-led national charity that aims to improve the quality of drug treatment via the provision of a unique helpline service, specialist, independent advocacy, training and consultancy. Daren has spoken and written extensively on the importance of user involvement since entering the field in 1998, and is frequently asked to contribute to national and international conferences, events, journals and publications. Prior to working for the Alliance, Daren was DAT Co-ordinator for Walsall in the West Midlands, and a Detached Youth Worker specialising in working with hard to reach users on the streets. Daren is a Director of the United Kingdom Harm Reduction Alliance (UKHRA), the drummer in the Nightingales, proud husband of Jez, and doting dad to Ivy and Ruby. He likes the music of Charlie Feathers, the writings of Charles Bukowski, the films of Russ Meyer and general hedonism.

Scott W Henggeler received his PhD in Clinical Psychology from the University of Virginia in 1977. Currently, he is Professor of Psychiatry and Behavioural Sciences at the Medical University of South Carolina and Director of the Family Services Research Center (FSRC). The mission of the FSRC is to develop, validate and study the dissemination of clinically effective and cost-effective mental health and substance abuse services for children presenting serious clinical problems, and their families. As such, FSRC projects have included numerous community-based randomised trials with challenging clinical populations (eg. violent and chronic juvenile offenders, youths presenting psychiatric emergencies, substance abusing juvenile offenders, maltreating families), and dissemination studies for multisystemic therapy and other evidence-based treatments are being conducted in multiple states and nations. The FSRC has received the Annie E Casey Families Count Award, GAINS Center National Achievement Award, and the Points of Light Foundation President's Award in recognition of excellence in community service directed at solving community problems. Dr Henggeler has published more than 200 journal articles, book chapters, and books, is on the editorial boards of nine journals, and has received grants from NIMH, NIDA, NIAAA, OJJDP, CSAT, the Annie E Casey Foundation, and others.

Neil Hunt is Director of Research for the treatment service KCA, an Honorary Senior Research Associate at the European Institute of Social Services, University of Kent, and Honorary Research Fellow with the Centre for Research on Drugs and Health Behaviour, London School of Hygiene and Tropical Medicine. He has a particular research interest in drug transitions and developed the 'Break the Cycle' intervention to reduce injecting, which has been disseminated nationally in the UK.

He has since completed various commissioned reviews of the evidence base for harm reduction and has recently worked as a researcher on an evaluation of quasi-compulsory treatments and a Department of Health funded project examining 'early exit' from treatment. Among his recent publications is the Beckley Foundation report *Cannabis and Mental Health: Responses to the emerging evidence* and several technical reports on drug consumption rooms that contributed to the Joseph Rowntree Foundation's independent report on this subject.

Dr Thomas Kerr is a Research Scientist with the BC Centre for Excellence in HIV/Aids and an Assistant Professor in the Department of Medicine at the University of British Columbia. In his role at the BC Centre for Excellence in HIV/Aids, Dr Kerr is a principal investigator of several large cohort studies, including the Vancouver Injection Drug Users Study (VIDUS), the Scientific Evaluation of Supervised Injecting (SEOSI), and the At-risk Youth Study (ARYS). Dr Kerr's primary research interests are injection drug use, HIV/Aids, urban health, health service evaluation, and community-based research methods. A key focus of Dr Kerr's work has been the scientific evaluation of Insite, North America's first safer injecting facility, and his research in this area has contributed significantly to academic, public, and government discussion, both nationally and internationally. Dr Kerr has published extensively in various medical and public health journals.

Charlie Lloyd's background is in criminology – studying, undertaking and publishing research at the Institute of Criminology, Cambridge, before moving on to the Home Office Research Unit in 1986. Here he undertook and published research on sex offences, prisons and probation before moving to the Home Office Drug Prevention Initiative (later the Drug Prevention Advisory Service), where he managed their research programme and undertook some of his own research on drugs prevention and vulnerable groups. On joining the Joseph Rowntree Foundation in 1999, Charlie managed the Young People's Programme and, from its inception in 2001, the Drug and Alcohol Research Programme – a programme of independent research on the social dimensions of drug and alcohol use. He is now managing a new programme of research on alcohol.

Donald MacPherson is the Drug Policy Co-ordinator for the city of Vancouver, a position the city created to bring leadership and focus to the crisis in Vancouver's Downtown Eastside with regard to drug overdose deaths, HIV and hepatitis C epidemics among injection drug users and an unacceptable level of property crime. Donald is the author of *A Framework for Action: A four pillars approach to drug problems in Vancouver*. He has worked with three successive mayors since 2000 to bring a progressive, comprehensive and evidence-based drug strategy to fruition in Vancouver.

Tina Olsson, MPA, is a PhD candidate at the University of Göteborg, Sweden. In addition to clinical work with children and families, she has 10 years' experience in evaluating programmes for children, youth and families at the local, state and federal levels in the USA as well as being a member of the research team evaluating the effects of multisystemic therapy in Sweden.

Marianne van Ooyen-Houben studied Social Psychology at the Universities of Groningen (Netherlands) and Zurich (Switzerland), with a specialisation in research methodologies in social sciences. She was a senior researcher in addiction care and quality-of-care studies at Trimbos Institute, which is a national institute for research and development in mental health care and addiction care. Since 2001, she has been Co-ordinator of Drug Research at the Research and Documentation Centre (WODC) of the Dutch Ministry of Justice. She is a part time Associate Professor in Addiction Care at Inholland University (The Hague) and teaches evaluation methods in criminology at Erasmus University, Rotterdam.

Ashli J Sheidow, PhD, is Assistant Professor of Psychiatry and Behavioural Sciences at the Family Services Research Center, Medical University of South Carolina (MUSC) and Faculty Scholar at the Center for Health Economic and Policy Studies, MUSC. She completed her graduate training in clinical psychology at the University of Illinois at Chicago, conducting research at the Institute for Juvenile Research and receiving clinical training in Cook County Hospital's adolescent division. Dr Sheidow's research interests have focused broadly on the development, prevention, and treatment of adolescent psychopathology and juvenile delinquency from an ecological perspective, with a concentration in quantitative methods. She recently completed a NIDA-funded randomised pilot to develop and evaluate an ecological outpatient treatment for youth diagnosed with co-morbid substance use and internalising diagnoses. In addition, Dr Sheidow is involved with a variety of statistical projects and economic evaluations and has been directing research for off-site US and Norwegian studies on training therapists for youth interventions.

Alex Stevens holds a PhD in Social Policy from the University of Kent (Canterbury, England) and now works there for the European Institute of Social Services. He directs the *Connections* project, which promotes research and dissemination on the prevention of drug use and related infections in the criminal justice system and is funded by the European Commission's public health programme. He led the QCT Europe study, a six-country research project on alternatives to imprisonment for drug dependent offenders. He was co-author with Peter Reuter of the *Analysis of UK Drug Policy*, published in April 2007 by the UK Drug Policy Commission. He is also Secretary of the International Society for the Study of Drug Policy and is a consultant to the Beckley Foundation's drug policy programme.

Knut Sundell is Associate Professor at the Department of Psychology, Uppsala University, and Director at the Institute for Evidence-based Social Work Practice at the Swedish National Board of Health and Welfare. His research has focused on prevalence of child maltreatment and antisocial behaviours among young people, risk and protective factors of antisocial behaviours and outcome trials of interventions in nursery schools, schools, and social work. His present work involves promoting the dissemination of an evidence-based social work practice in Sweden.

Ambros Uchtenhagen MD, PhD, trained in psychiatry and psychotherapy. He is Emeritus Professor of Social Psychiatry at Zurich University and Co-director of Psychiatric University Services, founder and President of the Research Institute for Public Health and Addiction, a WHO Collaborating Centre (associated with Zurich University), co-founder of European Addiction Research, member of the European Association on Substance Abuse Research (EASAR) and member of the WHO Expert Panel on Drugs. His main interests in the field include epidemiology of addictive behaviour, implementation and evaluation of preventive and therapeutic interventions, drug policy, education and training in the substance abuse field. He has also been involved with numerous research projects for the Swiss Federal Authorities, for the European Commission, for the Council of Europe (Group Pompidou), for the World Health Organisation (WHO), and the United Nations Organisation against Drugs and Crime (UNODC).

Evan Wood, MD, PhD, is a Research Scientist at the British Columbia Centre for Excellence in HIV/Aids and an Assistant Professor in the Department of Medicine at the University of British Columbia (Division of Aids). He has extensive research experience in the area of clinical epidemiology, especially in evaluating the treatment of HIV/Aids, addiction, and epidemiologic study design, especially among injection drug using populations. Dr Wood has published more than 200 scientific papers. National recognition of his work includes most recently the Canadian Medical Association's Award for Young Leaders. He is an Associate Editor of the *International Journal of Drug Policy* and serves on the editorial boards of a host of addiction and infectious disease journals.

INTRODUCTION
Crossing frontiers in drug treatment

Alex Stevens

Illicit drugs are globally traded commodities. Crops grown in the poppy fields of Afghanistan and the coca farms of Colombia feed rising appetites for heroin and cocaine in the developed world. The use of these drugs is at historically high levels and concern is mounting over the consequences for public health and criminality. No country can state that it is free from illicit drug use or its damaging consequences; all try to find a remedy for these problems. Some have attempted to solve the problem through penal repression of drug users, but this has little evidence to support it. In contrast, there is a rapidly growing evidence base which suggests that providing various forms of treatment to people who have problems with drugs is effective. Now there is increasing support for harm reduction measures. Some practices, such as the prescription of methadone and buprenorphine, needle and syringe exchange, residential rehabilitation, cognitive behavioural therapy and motivational interviewing, are becoming increasingly widespread as governments recognise their benefits. This book does not cover these approaches, which are well described elsewhere. Here, the focus is on newer approaches that offer the promise of reaching out to drug users who have not been able to benefit from the existing range of drug treatment services.

Before we look at the details and evaluations of these new approaches, we need to ask what we are trying to achieve when we offer treatment to a person who is struggling with their drug use. Are we trying to make them 'clean' to fit our notions of a healthy and productive life, are we satisfying our own needs to combine altruism and a professional career, or are we really empowering drug users to overcome the problems that face them? Existing methods of working with drug users have hinged on the notion that drugs stand between the user and the achievement of their full potential. In this view, drugs are seen as the causal agent that diverts users from the straight and narrow path of conventional consumption, production and reproduction. Drugs do this either by exploiting human weakness, in a view that leads to penal repression, or they do it by creating the disease of addiction, in a view that leads to the clinic. These two views, sharing a concept of drugs as the causal agent that does away with the free will of the user, structured both sides of the drug policy debate of the 20th century, between those who favoured dealing with drug use as a criminal issue and those who saw it as a problem of public health.

Both sides saw it as their duty to rescue addicts from the clutches of the drugs to which they had become unwittingly enslaved, although they used different tools for the task. Advocates of penal repression hoped that punishment and imprisonment could have a greater causal impact on the user than the drug itself. They have repeatedly been shown to be in error on this. There is very little evidence to suggest that the threat of punishment deters people from using drugs. Imprisonment is likely to extend rather than curtail the drug using career by further excluding people from social bonds (such as work and relationships with non-offenders), which support the process of desistance from drug use and crime. It is also hugely expensive for the taxpayer and damaging for the children and communities from which large numbers of young men and women have been taken (and to which they will return with even less stake in society than when they were transported to jail).

Advocates of a public health approach have tended to emphasise the disease of addiction instead of the responsibility of the user. Drugs, they say, provide such powerful sources of both negative and positive reinforcement that some users become incapable of escaping destructive patterns of drug use without the assistance of people who are far more knowledgeable than they are about the neurochemical, or even spiritual processes of addiction and recovery. This approach has been more fruitful, leading to effective approaches as diverse as methadone substitution and 12-step self-help groups. But there remains a problem at the heart of both the penal and the medical approaches. They both cede the power to overcome drug use to people other than those who are most directly affected. Drug users have to face the threat of punishment or the expertise of the doctor, keyworker or mentor if they are to overcome the attraction of the drug. Both approaches attribute such power to the drug that they are unable to explain why millions of people are able to take psychoactive substances, including heroin and cocaine, without succumbing to their awful, addictive qualities. Without understanding this, it is difficult to realise how problematic drug users can return to a state where drugs are available (as they always will be), but do not cause the personal chaos of addiction.

Critics of the dominant voices in drug policy have been arguing for many decades that the problem with drugs is one of setting as well as of substance. These critics have recognised that free will is not absolute and that drugs do not corrupt it absolutely. All of us operate within constraints that are provided for us by the society, family and space in which we live. All of us adjust our expectations and actions to the limits and resources that are available to us. The availability of psychoactive substances adds to the diverse opportunities for danger and pleasure that we all encounter, but it does not explain why some people can experience the pleasures without suffering much harm, while for others such pleasures provide just a short prelude to a life of risk and discomfort. This explanation must be sought in the limits and resources that people have before they take the drug. When the American Medical Association concluded that the emaciation typically associated with heroin use was caused by the *unhygienic and impoverished life of the addict rather than by the direct effect of the drug'* (Light & Torrance, 1929 p20), it was suggesting the importance of the material setting in which drug use occurs. More recent research has shown the importance of chemical changes in the brain, and the predisposing role of some genes. This has led to renewed attempts to find medicines that will conquer addiction (although none have yet been proven effective in rigorous clinical trials). However, even as drugs are created that can successfully target specific dopamine receptors and suppress overactive neurons, it is still vital to recognise that drug use also has a social setting. There is a range of social identities that are available to us all to perform, as long as we have the resources and abilities to 'pass' in that role. Impoverished drug users with low social capital have few roles in which they can pass, apart from the one that is often foisted upon them – that of the hopeless junkie.

This identity, which has been made available to drug users by the construction of drug use as both a criminal category and a pathological disorder, creates a set of expectations of how drug users will act, and of how they will relate to their drugs of choice. This anticipated relationship will be one of enslavement, where all remnants of free will are abandoned as the user surfs a torrent of desire for limitless consumption of the substance. The reason why some people can take drugs without becoming enslaved to them is because this relationship is not a mere product of the physical properties of the drug, nor solely of personal genetic predisposition, nor just of the material setting in which drugs are taken, but involves the question of identity. If a drug user has the wherewithal to take on other roles, then drug use is likely to remain marginal within the range of activities that they take to constitute their relationship to the outside world. If the outside world refuses to recognise any other activities than the drug use as being reflective of their true identity, then they will be thrown back on the role of the addict as their only source of social meaning and to the practice of drug use as their most effective way of coping with the troubles and barriers that face them.

Drug treatment helps to create the identities that drug users can inhabit. Some of these identities, such as the Minnesota model's recovering addict, or the methadone clinic's stabilised user, may provide a congruent source of meaning to many drug users. However, they may also clash with the expectations and hopes of others. Drug users may wish to travel from a state of impoverishment, boredom, unhappiness, insecurity or instability to a place where they are recognised and rewarded for the other contributions they can make. Existing forms of drug treatment may assist some to make this journey, but others will be unwilling to take on the particular mantle they are offered in order to move from damaging dependence to some form of normality. For these people, new forms of treatment that coincide more exactly with their own wishes and perceptions of self will be necessary. If we can create a wider range of paths that problematic drug users can use to cross the frontier that separates their world from the lives to which they aspire, then this will expand the range of opportunities and resources that are available to them. This is not about condescending to drug users by demanding that they ape the ways of conventional respectability in order to become 'clean', and it is not about indulging our own fantasies that we, personally, can heal the wretched of the earth. It is about working alongside people who have taken on identities that are so ruthlessly shunned, and jointly exploring the opportunities that we can create with them to enhance their lives and, as a secondary product, our own.

We may be able to use knowledge that has been created in other countries to help drug users to make these journeys from dependence to a fuller version of freedom. Innovations occur all over the world and often do travel across national borders. But care must be taken when importing interventions. First, there is the question of whether the intervention works, even in the context where it was created. There are some examples in the drug field where approaches have become very popular internationally on the basis of very slim evidence of effect. Perhaps the most prominent example is the use of 'zero tolerance' policing as a response to drug-related crime. This involves reducing the normal discretion that police operate towards minor crimes, such as loitering and littering, in order to prevent escalation to more serious offences. The perceived success of this approach in New York, where there were significant reductions in the crime rate after its introduction by Police Commissioner William Bratton, has often been cited as a reason for copying the approach in other cities. However, there are reasons to doubt that the zero tolerance approach can be given the credit for the fall in crime. It began before the approach was introduced, and was also seen in USA cities that used very different police tactics. Commissioner Bratton has been very active in spreading the word about zero tolerance, but even he has reported that police discretion is inevitable and that social change (not just policing) is necessary for sustainable reduction of crime and incivility. It seems that the zero tolerance approach became popular, not because it was effective, but because of its symbolic power as a slogan that resonates with perceived popular wishes to clamp down on criminals (Newburn & Jones, 2007).

If the first criteria for importing approaches from elsewhere is that they actually work in their country of origin, the second is that they will make sense in the country to which they are being transferred. North America is the predominant source of policy ideas for use in the UK, partly due to shared bonds of language and culture and the comparatively vast expenditure on evaluation research in the USA. However, the USA has a very different approach to illicit drugs. It has long been the prime proponent of drug control, with a huge influence on the global spread of prohibition. This has not prevented the growth of a domestic drug problem, which is enormous by international standards. In 2004 it was estimated that about four million Americans were dependent on cocaine, heroin or methamphetamine, or 20 people per 100,000 population. This compares to an estimated rate of nine problematic drug users per 100,000 of the UK population. The USA also has higher rates of cannabis use and of drug-related death than any European country (Reuter & Stevens, 2007). The punitive response to illicit drugs means that it now has over two million people who are in prison, on probation or on parole for drug offences. It also has a very different social and cultural context, with high levels of income and racial inequality and a deeper commitment to abstinence from all drugs (including alcohol) than many European countries. Much care should be taken in transporting interventions from this context to the UK and the rest of Europe.

A third criteria for importing approaches relates to issues of implementation. How easy is it to faithfully introduce an approach that has been used elsewhere, without falling into the trap of just copying the name? An example of this is provided by another USA export: the drug court. This is usually a court that is set up specifically to deal with drug-involved offenders. It uses the threat of imprisonment to encourage them to enter and stay in treatment. This idea rapidly spread from Florida to other USA states and then to Ireland, Canada, Australia, Scotland and England. There are significant differences between drug courts within the USA, and between the various international models. Given the range of these differences – concerning the eligible clients, the legal process, the type and length of treatments provided, the sanctions for non-compliance and the provision of aftercare – how sensible would it be to try and state whether all drug courts work?

Implementation of an evidence-based approach requires that the original approach is carefully described and evaluated. It then requires implementation of the necessary policies, protocols and procedures. But this does not guarantee that the programme will operate as intended to the benefit of its clients. Too often, implementation stops at the paper stage, with performance on the ground still dominated by the old ways of working. Both staff and service users will often be reluctant to ditch the practices that they have found to solve existing problems in favour of innovative approaches that present a whole new range of difficulties. A review of research in this area has concluded that time and money need to be devoted specifically to issues of implementation. Funding will be needed for start-up costs, for integrating the new intervention with the services that work alongside it and for ensuring ongoing fidelity with the original design of the intervention (Fixsen *et al*, 2005).

Although it is difficult to transfer approaches between countries, this is how most western countries have developed the range of drug services that they currently provide. Methadone maintenance, the 12 steps and therapeutic communities all spread from the USA, but the travel has not all been one way. Although needle exchange is not yet universally accepted as a valid approach in the USA, many states have allowed it since the Amsterdam Junkiebond, a drug user advocacy group, introduced the service in 1984. This, and the subsequent example of harm reduction measures on Merseyside and then across the world, have been repeatedly used to put pressure on reluctant American authorities. The mix of drug services that we now have in Europe is a result of the adaptation of health and criminal justice systems to the needs of the people they deal with, often using examples gleaned from abroad to meet challenges that develop rapidly. Drug use patterns are constantly changing, and so treatment systems must also evolve if they are to keep up with changing needs. The aim of this handbook is to inform such changes with evidence gained from new ways of working with dependent drug users in order to reduce the harm they experience and cause.

Of course, different groups of drug users will need different services. Until recently, there has been very little in the way of evidence-based treatment that works with young drug users. Multisystemic therapy (MST) is one of the few approaches that have good evidence of effectiveness, and its use is spreading from the USA, including new trials in both England and Scotland. In Chapter 1, a team including the leading researcher on MST, describe this approach and report on clinical trials in the USA. In this context, several studies have suggested that MST is more effective than usual services in reducing the offending and drug use of young people who have been assessed as delinquent substance misusers. It is also interesting, in the light of the importance of implementation, that studies have suggested that higher treatment fidelity is associated with better outcomes. We should also remember that the relative effectiveness of an intervention is crucially affected by what it is being compared to. The USA has relatively high rates of imprisonment of young people, and the usual services to which MST has been compared often include out-of-home placement in secure, residential settings. It is a common finding of research on effective interventions that placing delinquent youths together, away from their families and the influence of pro-social peers, can harm the prospects of desistance from crime and drug use. In Sweden, where treatment-as-usual consists of a range of comparatively non-punitive and well-developed services for youths and their families, the comparison with MST is likely to provide a stiffer test. In Chapter 2, such a test is described. In this evaluation, MST was not found to be significantly more effective than the usual Swedish services. It will be very interesting to see the results of such comparisons in the different English and Scottish contexts, where services for young offenders tend to be less punitive than the USA, but perhaps less supportive than in Sweden.

For older drug users, maintenance prescribing and needle exchange have become the most common services in some countries. However, some heroin users do not have the resources that enable them to do well on methadone or buprenorphine, or to avoid injecting. These people often pose the highest risks, both to their own health and to the safety of others. We need effective methods to help them reduce these risks. Included here are chapters that describe the state of the international art on heroin-assisted treatment and drug consumption rooms, as well as a fascinating account of the development of one of the most interesting and effective examples of a drug consumption room. Chapter 3 provides a thorough overview from the world's leading authority on heroin-assisted treatment. This treatment differs radically from the old 'British system' of providing diamorphine to registered addicts (which continues to this day in a much reduced form). Heroin is consumed on-site, rather than prescribed for home use, so much larger daily doses can safely by provided. A range of other medical and psycho-social services are also provided to patients. In at least four national contexts (Switzerland, Netherlands, Germany and Spain), such treatment has been shown to provide significant benefits to a group of drug users who had not been able to succeed in methadone treatment. They have seen significant reductions in the use of illicit heroin and other drugs, in illegal income and offending, and improvements in health and social integration. A trial of similar treatment is now under way in England, and it seems that heroin-assisted treatment is an example of an evidence-based practice that can spread internationally.

Another service that is spreading from its Swiss origins is the provision of drug consumption rooms, also known as safer injecting facilities. In Chapter 4, Hunt and Lloyd report from their work on drug consumption rooms for the Joseph Rowntree Foundation's review. They summarise their finding that such sites offer potential to reduce drug-related harms, without encouraging more drug use or social disturbance. Interestingly, they go on to discuss the political and media reception of this message. The political response was affected by the state of turmoil at the relevant department, the Home Office, at the time of the review's publication. Facing criticism on a wide range of fronts, Home Office ministers were not willing to entertain a policy idea that gained a high media profile and could play badly for them. Hunt and Lloyd conclude that such services are only likely to come into being through a long process of political negotiation. Chapter 5 describes just such a process. The Vancouver Safer Injecting Facility was not a direct response to international evidence on the effectiveness of drug consumption rooms, but required its advocates to form alliances and campaigns that could highlight both the pressing local need and the potential contribution of the safer injecting facility. The eventual success in creating a service that has since been shown to have created safer injecting practices, increased entry to drug treatment and reduced risk of overdoses, may inspire other cities to provide facilities in areas that suffer from high rates of harm to injecting drug users. However, the continuing struggle to keep the facility open in the face of political opposition should also remind us that politics are often more important than evidence in the treatment of drug dependence.

Prisoners are another group who face high risks of drug-related harm, especially with alarming rates of blood-borne viruses in the prisons of many countries. Despite the increasing availability of drug treatment services in prisons, it is still a very difficult setting for the provision of effective treatment. The social world of the prison is so dramatically different that it is hard to continue newly learnt behaviours and attitudes on release. In addition, as prisons become increasingly overcrowded, it is difficult to provide a basic regime of meaningful activity, let alone the intensive support required for successful therapy. Prison is also an extremely expensive setting in which to provide drug treatment. For these and other reasons, increasing attention is being given to the provision of alternative sentences for drug dependent offenders. These usually involve some form of coercion from the court or prosecutor, alongside the consent of the drug user. Chapters 6 and 7 focus on such quasi-compulsory treatment (QCT). Drug courts are the highest profile example of QCT, but it has been practised for longer in Europe than in the USA. The European country with the most evidence on the process of QCT is the Netherlands. Chapter 6 provides a review of this evidence, focusing on the practical obstacles to the achievement of the theoretical advantages of QCT. One such obstacle comes from what has been called the 'funnel of crime' (Russell, 1994). This refers to the fact that there are many more offenders than are ever caught by the police, and that many of them are lost or drop out at each stage of the process of completing drug treatment, including assessment of eligibility, court decision, actual entry and retention in treatment. Chapter 7 summarises results from a cross-national European study of QCT in Austria, England, Germany, Italy and Switzerland. These suggest that QCT is no less effective than similar treatments provided to people who have not come through the criminal justice system. However, the funnel of crime means that the impact in reducing overall crime from the small proportion of all offenders who complete QCT may be small. Also, the comments on page 5 on the comparability of drug courts apply at least as strongly to QCT. Legal systems differ greatly between countries, and it may not be possible or desirable to transport QCT methods directly between countries. However, the available research suggests that, in general, QCT can provide a viable and effective alternative to imprisonment for drug dependent offenders when issues of treatment quality and the co-operation between treatment services, courts and probation are properly addressed.

The final, eighth chapter of this book may look out of place here, as it does not concern the transfer of approaches between countries, but it does relate to crossing the often impermeable frontier that separates the identities of drug users from those of the people who are funded to work with them. Drug users have played a significant role in developing the drug treatment systems of several countries (the initiation of needle exchange in Amsterdam provides just one example). In addition, drug users are increasingly mobilising through organisations such as the International Harm Reduction Alliance and the International Network of People who Use Drugs to ensure, as they demand, that there is 'nothing about us without us'. The involvement of drug users in the design and management of drug services is a relatively recent development in the UK. Chapter 8 offers a personal view of the problems that have faced people who want to become more involved, not only in the management of their own drug treatment, but also in the provision of services to other drug users. It is important to recognise that any new developments should be made in close co-operation with the only people who can really make them work.

This book describes a wide range of approaches. It does not seek to set them up as better or more important than services that are already widespread. Rather, it encourages readers to think about how these and other approaches can contribute to a range of services that can be provided to meet the diverse and rapidly changing needs of problematic drug users. Their adoption will require careful processes of adaptation and implementation so that they complement existing patterns of services. They offer the opportunity to fill gaps in these patterns so that people who do not benefit from currently available services are enabled to do so. These people look to governments and treatment agencies for assistance in making the journey from the harsh world in which they have taken a provisional refuge, and from which they wish to escape with dignity and freedom. We hope that this book will make it a little more likely that these journeys can be made.

References

Fixsen DL, Naoom SF, Blase KA, Friedman RM & Wallace F (2005) *Implementation Research: A synthesis of the literature*. Tampa, Florida: University of South Florida, Louis de la Parte Florida Mental Health Institute & The National Implementation Research Network.

Light AB & Torrance EG (1929) *Opium Addiction*. Chicago: American Medical Association.

Newburn T & Jones T (2007) Symbolizing crime control: reflections on zero tolerance. *Theoretical Criminology* **11** (2) 221–243.

Reuter P & Stevens A (2007) *An Analysis of UK Drug Policy*. London: UK Drug Policy Commission.

Russell J (1994) *Substance Abuse and Crime: Some lessons from America. Harkness Fellowship report.* New York: Commonwealth Fund of New York.

CHAPTER 1
Multisystemic therapy with substance using adolescents: a synthesis of the research

Ashli J Sheidow and Scott W Henggeler

Multisystemic therapy (MST) is a well-validated, evidence-based treatment for serious clinical problems presented by adolescents and their families. Using a family and community-based treatment approach, MST targets youth with serious clinical problems who are at risk of out-of-home placement (for example detention, incarceration, or residential treatment facility). Based on an extensive body of controlled clinical research, MST has been identified as an effective treatment of youth antisocial behaviour, including substance abuse (National Institute on Drug Abuse, 1999; National Institutes of Health, 2006; President's New Freedom Commission on Mental Health, 2003; US Public Health Service, 2001). This chapter begins by outlining the empirical bases of MST for treating adolescent substance use and is followed by a brief overview of the MST treatment model. The remainder of the chapter summarises the empirical findings from clinical trials using MST to treat substance use disorders in adolescents, and describes current efforts that aim to enhance substance use outcomes with families of adolescent and adult substance abusers.

EMPIRICAL BASES FOR USING MST
Much research during the past few decades has focused on understanding the correlates and causes of adolescent behaviour problems. Indeed, several recent reviews have summarised the associations found between youth behaviour problems and variables from multiple levels of a youth's ecology (eg. Hann & Borek, 2001; Hawkins *et al*, 1998; Lipsey & Derzon, 1998; Spooner, 1999; US Public Health Service, 1999b; Weinberg *et al*, 1998). Particular attention has been devoted to delineating associations between substance use problems and individual, family, peer, school, and community risk and protective factors. In addition to direct influences on the development of adolescent substance use, risk factors are often mediated by other characteristics of the youth's ecology.

Figure 1 (Dishion & Kavanagh, 2003) summarises the current understanding of direct and indirect influences of risk and protective factors on adolescent substance abuse based upon available empirical evidence. For example, direct effects have been found for family management characteristics such as supervision, discipline strategies, consistency of parenting, parental support, and parent–child relationship quality (Barnes *et al*, 1994; Gorman-Smith *et al*, 1998; Johnson & Pandina, 1991; Peterson *et al*, 1995; Steinberg *et al*, 1994). Likewise, peer substance use consistently has been identified as one of the strongest predictors of adolescent substance use (Farrell & Danish, 1993; Newcomb & Bentler, 1989). Peers can influence an individual adolescent's substance use through a myriad of channels such as peer attitudes, beliefs, norms, attachment, access to drugs, modelling, and status (Bauman & Ennett, 1994; Dawes *et al*, 1999; Dishion *et al*, 1995; Hawkins *et al*, 1992; Kandel *et al*, 1978; Patterson *et al*, 1998). As depicted in **figure 1**, multiple factors can also exert indirect influences on adolescent substance use. For example, parental substance abuse and dependence places a youth at greater risk for substance use disorders (McGue, 1999), but this effect occurs through the impact of the caregivers' substance use on their parenting ability and other family management practices (for example, ability to reduce adolescent association with drug-using peers).

Figure 1: Parental interaction with other sources of influence in the social and emotional development of adolescents (Dishion & Kavanagh, 2003)

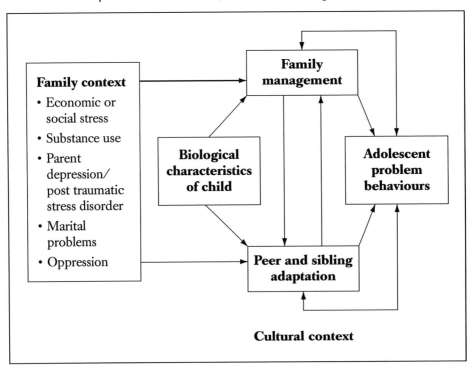

Clear evidence, therefore, exists for a relatively complex, multidetermined, ecological conceptualisation of adolescent substance use – a conceptualisation that precludes simple one-to-one causal conclusions. As explicated later in the chapter, MST interventions are based on this multidetermined conceptualisation of adolescent problem behaviours, and treatment planning within MST aims to alter pertinent aspects of the youth's ecology to effect change in these problem behaviours. Moreover, and importantly, the ecological, systemic focus of the MST treatment approach, which is based on extant risk factor research, has been supported by clinical research. Huey and colleagues (2000) used data from randomised trials with serious juvenile offenders (Henggeler *et al*, 1997) and substance abusing juvenile offenders (Henggeler, Pickrel & Brondino, 1999) to evaluate potential mediators of favourable youth outcomes. Consistent with the risk factor research depicted in ***figure 1***, results showed that MST treatment effects on antisocial behaviour were mediated by improved family cohesion and monitoring and by decreased affiliation with deviant peers. In another investigation using MST to treat delinquent adolescents, improvements in youth symptomatology were related to improvement in the marital relationship of the parents (Mann *et al*, 1990). Thus, the clinical underpinnings of the MST theory of change are consistent with extant research on the causes and correlates of adolescent substance use.

CLINICAL IMPLEMENTATION

MST clinical procedures for treating adolescent antisocial behaviour and serious emotional disturbance are described in clinical volumes (Henggeler *et al*, 1998; Henggeler & Schoenwald *et al*, 2002). Therapist and supervisory training also have been standardised, as has an extensive quality assurance protocol (Henggeler & Schoenwald, 1999) to support treatment fidelity. The MST manuals delineate the process by which youth and family problems are prioritised and targeted for change. Guided by ecological and systems theory, the assessment process and specific interventions integrated into MST treatment focus on the individual, family, peer, school, and social network variables that are linked with identified problems, as well as on the interface of these systems. Thus, MST aims to effect change in antisocial youth behaviour through altering characteristics of the youth's ecology that are linked with identified problems.

The clinical procedures used in MST programmes, which focus on youths with serious antisocial behaviour who are at imminent risk of costly out-of-home placements, and their families, are outlined briefly here.

Treatment delivery

MST is provided by full-time master's level therapists who each carry caseloads of four to six families. Three to four therapists work within a team, and each team is supervised by an advanced master's level or doctoral level supervisor who devotes at least half of their working time to the team. The clinicians provide 24-hour/seven-day-a-week (24/7) availability, which allows sessions to occur at convenient times for families and which enables therapists to react quickly to crises that might threaten goal attainment (ie. prevent out-of-home placement). Services are time-limited, entailing an average of 60 hours of direct service over three to six months.

MST uses a home-based (for example, home, school, community) model of service delivery to decrease barriers to service access. The home-based model, in combination with 24/7 availability, is particularly effective at engaging and retaining families in treatment. For example, in a trial of MST with substance abusing or dependent juvenile offenders, 100% of the adolescents and their families randomly assigned to the MST condition completed at least two months of treatment, and all but one family was retained until treatment termination at approximately four months post referral (Henggeler *et al*, 1996).

Clinical procedures

The fundamental goal of MST is to empower families to effectively resolve and manage the serious clinical problems presented by their youth, as well as the potential problems that are likely to occur subsequently during the youth's adolescence. Thus, therapists aim to help adolescents and their families develop the capacity to cope with problems that have a multisystemic set of causal and sustaining factors, often drawing on and developing resources within the families' natural ecologies to promote and maintain positive change. Rather than providing a rigid manualised plan for treatment, the MST clinical protocols provide a framework in which treatment occurs. Specifically, MST therapists and supervisors follow a set of nine core principles that guide assessment practices and the integration of evidence-based interventions within the MST framework (Henggeler *et al*, 1998).

These nine principles, noted briefly in **table 1**, opposite, are used to identify targets for intervention and to design interventions to meet the goals of treatment. For instance, principle 1 explicates the method of conceptualising identified problems. Utilising what we know about the correlates and causes of youth problems, MST practitioners conceptualise youth and family symptoms from an ecological, systemic perspective (see also principle 5). Thus, clinicians investigate and target for treatment 'fit factors', or characteristics of the youth's ecology that are maintaining the problem behaviour. This principle is implemented through the use of a specified analytical process that is dynamic throughout treatment, with regular monitoring of progress (see also principle 8) and updating of newly identified or appropriately resolved fit factors.

As another example, principle 2 denotes the optimistic perspective that is communicated clearly to the family throughout the assessment and treatment process. This optimism is supported overtly through supervision and peer consultation. Providers look for potential strengths within the various ecological contexts, investigating child factors (for example, competencies, attractiveness, altruism), caregiver factors (for example, resources, affective bonds, social support), peer factors (for example, competencies, prosocial activities), school factors (for

Table 1: MST treatment principles

1. **Finding the fit.** The primary purpose of assessment is to understand the 'fit' between the identified problems and their broader systemic context.
2. **Positive and strength focused.** Therapeutic contacts emphasise the positive and use systemic strengths as levers for change.
3. **Increasing responsibility.** Interventions are designed to promote responsible behaviour and decrease irresponsible behaviour among family members.
4. **Present-focused, action-oriented, and well-defined.** Interventions are present-focused and action-oriented, targeting specific and well-defined problems.
5. **Targeting sequences.** Interventions target sequences of behaviour within or between multiple systems that maintain the identified problems.
6. **Developmentally appropriate.** Interventions are developmentally appropriate and fit the developmental needs of the youth.
7. **Continuous effort.** Interventions are designed to require daily or weekly effort by family members.
8. **Evaluation and accountability.** Intervention effectiveness is evaluated continuously from multiple perspectives with providers assuming accountability for overcoming barriers to successful outcomes.
9. **Generalisation.** Interventions are designed to promote treatment generalisation and long-term maintenance of therapeutic change by empowering caregivers to address family members' needs across multiple systemic contexts.

example, management practices, concern, prosocial activities), and neighbourhood or community factors (for example, law enforcement, business involvement, health care, neighbour concern). Identified strengths then are utilised in interventions. For instance, if low monitoring during after-school hours is contributing to the adolescent's involvement in antisocial behaviour, then monitoring might be enhanced by empowering the caregiver to engage the youth in organised, prosocial activities available at the school or in the community. Importantly, clinicians are trained to incorporate this strength-based approach throughout their work. For example, supervisors assist clinicians in identifying 'barriers' to treatment success rather than perceiving clients as being resistant to change. The MST treatment principles are discussed more extensively in the aforementioned treatment manuals (Henggeler *et al*, 1998; Henggeler & Schoenwald *et al*, 2002).

Initially, the problem behaviours to be targeted in treatment are specified clearly from the perspectives of multiple stakeholders (for example, family members, teachers, juvenile justice authorities). Then, based on multiple perspectives (for example, opinions of stakeholders, clinical impressions), the ecological factors that seem to be driving each problem behaviour are organised into a coherent conceptual framework. Next, the MST therapist, with support from other team members, the MST supervisor, and an MST expert consultant, designs specific intervention strategies to target those 'drivers' by adapting empirically based interventions from pragmatic, problem-focused treatments that have at least some empirical support. These may include strategic family therapy (Haley, 1987), structural family therapy (Minuchin, 1974), behavioural parent training (Munger, 1993), and cognitive behaviour therapies (Kendall & Braswell, 1993). In addition, if evidence of biological contributors to identified problems is found, psychopharmacological treatment is integrated with psychosocial treatment using evidence-based prescribing practices (for example, Weisz & Jensen, 1999). As these interventions are implemented, their effects (ie. outcomes) are monitored continuously. Using a recursive feedback process, ineffective interventions are reconceptualised and modifications are made until an effective strategy is developed.

Of note, specific goals for treatment may be at the individual, family, peer, school, and social network levels. However, the MST model views the adolescent's caregivers as key to achieving desired outcomes, and interventions typically focus on empowering the family to interface with pertinent systems to realise desired outcomes.

Quality assurance

During the mid-1990s, successful MST clinical trials led numerous provider agencies across the nation to request the formation of MST teams within their organisations. It soon became apparent, however, that the development of clear, well-specified, and effective quality assurance mechanisms was needed to maintain intervention fidelity and corresponding effectiveness as MST was transported to community practice settings. The use of the quality assurance system developed subsequently is predicated on the assumption that therapist adherence to the MST protocols is critical to achieving favourable clinical outcomes. Importantly, this assumption has been supported in several MST studies that have demonstrated significant associations between treatment fidelity and favourable adolescent outcomes (Henggeler *et al*, 1997; Henggeler & Pickrel *et al*, 1999; Huey *et al*, 2000; Schoenwald & Henggeler *et al*, 2000; Schoenwald *et al*, 2004; Schoenwald *et al*, 2003). In light of these findings, the transport of MST programmes to provider organisations operating in more than 30 states across the USA and nine countries (ie. Australia, Canada, Denmark, England, Ireland, Netherlands, Norway, New Zealand, and Sweden) has relied upon the implementation of a thorough set of quality assurance procedures to optimise youth outcomes by promoting therapist fidelity to the MST intervention protocols. Indeed, Ogden and colleagues (in press) have recently described the nationwide transport of MST programmes in Norway, and Gustle and colleagues (in press) are examining MST implementation in Sweden (see also Chapter 2).

Components of the quality assurance system include: (a) extensive organisational consultation prior to and following the development of MST programmes in community-based settings, (b) manualised assessment, intervention, supervision

(Henggeler & Schoenwald, 1998), and consultation (Schoenwald, 1998) processes, (c) didactic and experiential training for clinicians, followed by regular booster sessions by MST experts, weekly supervision within the MST treatment team (consisting of therapists and MST supervisor), and weekly consultation with an MST expert, and (d) use of treatment and supervisory fidelity feedback measures including, for example, monthly caregiver-reported ratings of therapist adherence on a validated scale (Henggeler & Borduin, 1992). Thus, therapist adherence to the treatment model is monitored continuously, and intensive supports are provided to help therapists achieve optimal outcomes even when facing complex, difficult cases.

EMPIRICAL FINDINGS

MST is regarded as one of the best validated interventions in the field for youths presenting serious clinical problems, with federal entities such as the President's New Freedom Commission on Mental Health (2003), Surgeon General (US Public Health Service, 1999b; 2001), National Institute on Drug Abuse (1999), National Institutes of Health (2006), and Center for Substance Abuse Prevention (2001), as well as leading reviewers (eg. Burns *et al*, 1999; Elliott, 1998; Farrington & Welsh, 1999; Kazdin & Weisz, 1998; Mihalic *et al*, 2001; Stanton & Shadish, 1997), identifying MST as an effective treatment of youth antisocial behaviour, including substance use. Notably, the Surgeon General (US Public Health Service, 2001) reported MST to be one of only three empirically supported treatments for juvenile offenders and the Substance Abuse and Mental Health Services Administration (2005) ranks MST as one of their model programmes for this population. Findings from MST clinical trials for juvenile offenders are summarised briefly here, concluding with a summary of findings specifically for substance using delinquents.

Empirical evidence for MST with delinquent youth

MST for juvenile delinquency has been the focus of numerous published outcome studies (nine randomised and one quasi-experimental studies published) with youths presenting serious antisocial behaviour and usually at imminent risk of out-of-home placement. Four published randomised trials have been conducted with violent and chronic offenders (Borduin *et al*, 1995; Henggeler *et al*, 1997; Henggeler *et al*, 1992; Henggeler *et al*, 1993; Timmons-Mitchell *et al*, 2006), two with juvenile sexual offenders (Borduin *et al*, 1990; Borduin & Schaeffer, 2001), one with substance abusing and dependent juvenile offenders (Brown *et al*, 1999; Henggeler & Clingempeel *et al*, 2002; Henggeler & Pickrel *et al*, 1999; Schoenwald *et al*, 1996), one with substance abusing and dependent juvenile offenders in juvenile drug court (Henggeler *et al*, 2006), one with antisocial adolescents conducted in Norway (Ogden & Hagen, 2006; Ogden & Halliday-Boykins, 2004), and one quasi-experimental trial was conducted with inner-city delinquents (Henggeler *et al*, 1986).

Findings across these studies have consistently favoured MST in comparison with control conditions. For example, MST has achieved significant reductions in rates of rearrest and conduct problems across trials, with follow-ups as long as 13.7 years

(Schaeffer & Borduin, 2005). Reductions in rates of recidivism have ranged from 26% to 69% across studies for youth treated with MST compared to treated control groups. A recent meta-analysis of MST trials (Curtis, Ronan, & Borduin, 2004) included seven outcome studies (708 total participants, 35 MST therapists). Effect sizes for studies averaged .50 for criminal behaviour (based on official records), 1.01 for arrest seriousness, and .29 for substance use. Further, these studies typically have been completed in field settings and included few exclusion criteria, features that strengthen support for treatment effectiveness of MST in real-world community practice settings. In addition, juveniles in the comparison conditions for all trials received treatment (typically services usually available in the community for juvenile offenders), lending further validity to MST treatment effects.

MST treatment effects also have emerged for variables that have been identified as correlates/mediators of adolescent antisocial behaviour. For example, MST has improved family relations and functioning, increased school attendance, and decreased adolescent psychiatric symptoms. MST clinical trials also have been conducted with youth who are not currently offenders, but are at imminent risk of out-of-home placement in psychiatric or foster-care settings. Successful MST outcomes have been observed for youths presenting with psychiatric emergencies (ie. suicidal, homicidal, psychotic; Henggeler & Rowland et al, 1999; Huey et al, 2004; Rowland et al, 2005; Schoenwald & Ward et al, 2000) and for children in maltreating families (Brunk et al, 1987), populations that are at high risk for engaging in substance use.

Together, findings from clinical trials have demonstrated the capacity of MST to change key determinants of antisocial behaviour (eg. family relations) and to produce significant reductions in rearrest and out-of-home placement for juvenile offenders.

Substance use outcomes within MST clinical trials

Not surprisingly, extensive evidence supports the strong relationships among adolescent alcohol abuse, drug abuse, and criminal activity (eg. Barnes & Welte, 1986; Crowley et al, 1998; Dembo et al, 1994; Fergusson et al, 1996; Huizinga et al, 1994). Indeed, findings from the early clinical trials of MST with serious juvenile offenders showed potential for MST's positive impact on adolescent substance use, leading reviewers to note the promise of MST in treating substance abusing youths (eg. McBride et al, 1999; Stanton & Shadish, 1997).

Substance-related outcomes were examined in two of the early randomised trials of MST with violent and chronic juvenile offenders (Borduin et al, 1995; Henggeler et al, 1992), and these substance-related findings were published in a single report (Henggeler et al, 1991). Findings in the first study (Henggeler et al, 1992) showed MST treatment effects at post treatment for self-report alcohol and drug use. In the second study (Borduin et al, 1995), drug use, per se, was not assessed, but substance-related arrests at four-year follow-up were 4% in the MST condition versus 16% in the comparison condition – a significant difference. Moreover, an almost 14-year follow-up of participants in this study showed that MST participants continued to have fewer drug related arrests than did their counterparts who received individual therapy (Schaeffer & Borduin, 2005). In a meta-analysis of family-based treatments of drug abuse (Stanton & Shadish, 1997), the MST effect sizes were among the highest of those reviewed.

Subsequent to the findings from these two trials, the effectiveness and transportability of MST was examined in a study with 118 juvenile offenders meeting DSM-III-R criteria for substance abuse (56%), or dependence (44%) and their families (Henggeler & Pickrel *et al*, 1999). Participants were randomly assigned to receive MST versus usual community services, which entailed probation services, outpatient substance abuse services (typically, weekly 12-step programme meetings) or inpatient/residential treatment, and mental health services (public or private outpatient, school-based, family preservation, residential, and/or inpatient). Compared to the usual services condition, MST reduced self-reported alcohol and marijuana use at immediate post treatment, decreased days incarcerated by 46% at the six-month follow-up (ie. six months following treatment termination), decreased total days in out-of-home placement by 50% at six-month follow-up (Schoenwald *et al*, 1996), and increased youth attendance in regular school settings (Brown *et al*, 1999). Cost data from this study showed that the incremental cost of MST was offset by the reduced placement (ie. incarceration, hospitalisation, and residential treatment) of youths in the MST condition (Schoenwald *et al*, 1996).

Moreover, as noted earlier, MST was especially effective at engaging the substance abusing and dependent youths and their families in treatment. Fully 100% (58 of 58) of families in the MST condition were retained for at least two months of services, and 98% (57 of 58) were retained until treatment termination at approximately four months post referral, averaging 40 hours of direct clinical contact with an MST therapist (Henggeler *et al*, 1996). These figures would be extraordinary for any clinical population, and are especially remarkable in light of the low client retention rates traditionally attained in the area of substance abuse treatment (Office of Applied Studies, 2002; Stark, 1992).

Finally, a four-year follow-up on 80 of the original 118 participants examined several key outcomes for the substance abusing participants in this study (Henggeler & Clingenpeel *et al*, 2002). Analyses of drug tests demonstrated significantly higher rates of marijuana abstinence for MST participants (55% abstinent) compared to participants who had received usual services (28% abstinent). The young adults who had participated in MST as youths four years earlier also engaged in significantly less criminal activity than did usual services participants, based on archival and self-report indices. For example, MST participants had an average of .15 convictions per year for violent crimes versus .57 convictions per year in the usual services group.

Thus, MST began to establish a successful track record for effectively treating delinquent youth with substance use disorders.

Integrating contingency management techniques

During the aforementioned trial of juvenile delinquents with diagnosed substance use disorders (Henggeler & Pickrel *et al*, 1999), MST researchers gained their first experiences with contingency management (CM) techniques. More so than for other MST clinical trials, the MST treatment team for this trial was faced with a large number of cases in which the youth's caregiver was abusing substances, and the abuse was preventing treatment progress and/or exacerbating the adolescent's problem behaviours. Following the MST approach described earlier in the chapter, the MST supervisor and therapists were responsible for overcoming this primary barrier to achieving favourable outcomes, which entailed providing treatment to the substance abusing caregiver. A review by the principal investigator of the empirical literature at that time identified CM techniques as having success with treating substance abusing adults. In particular, the CM intervention techniques developed by Higgins and Budney (Budney & Higgins, 1998; Higgins & Budney, 1993), which include behavioural and cognitive-behavioural treatment protocols (Community Reinforcement Approach, CRA), seemed very suitable. Their method includes a functional analysis of drug use (ie. antecedents, behaviours, and consequences related to substance use incidence), a voucher system linked with results from frequent urine analyses, and development of drug refusal skills. Importantly, CM techniques have proven effective with several populations of adult drug abusers (Petry, 2000; Roozen *et al*, 2004).

Based on the evidence supporting CRA and other CM procedures, as well as the theoretical and clinical compatibility of CM with the MST model, the MST treatment team was trained in CRA techniques during the trial of MST with substance abusing juvenile offenders (Henggeler, Pickrel *et al*, 1999). However, these techniques were utilised only with substance abusing parents of the youths participating in this study. In addition, the implementation of CRA in this study was not the focus of research. Regardless, the MST treatment team and researchers for this project were impressed with the CRA techniques, finding them easy to integrate into MST treatment and a useful means for treating substance use disorders in adult caregivers. As a result of this experience, and supported by extant empirical evidence for the use of CM in adolescents (Azrin *et al*, 1996; Azrin & Donohue *et al*, 1994; Azrin *et al*, 2001; Azrin & McMahon *et al*, 1994), MST researchers began to examine the viability of integrating CM techniques with MST for treating adolescent substance use disorders.

Empirical evidence for MST with CM integration

The first integration of CM procedures within MST for use with substance abusing adolescents took place in a neighbourhood-based intervention project (Swenson, Henggeler *et al*, 2005) with 13 substance abusing youths, almost all of whom were involved in the juvenile justice system. The integration of CM required MST therapists, using a family-based approach, to help youth identify triggers that might cause them to use drugs or alcohol, practise what to do when triggers occurred, develop effective and practical drug refusal skills, and generate drug avoidance techniques. In addition to these cognitive behavioural interventions, the family and MST therapist monitored adolescent drug use through regular and random substance use testing via instant response urine cups and breathalysers, as well as targeted testing (eg. following curfew violations). Further, the MST therapist helped the family to generate a contract for effective rewards and consequences for clean and dirty screens. Based on results from weekly urine screens, all youths were abstinent for cocaine and 85% were abstinent for cannabis by seven weeks after treatment. These outcomes were generally maintained across an average of 22 weeks of treatment.

The positive experience with this integration of CM and MST for the neighbourhood-based project provided the foundation for a randomised trial conducted in collaboration with juvenile drug court (Henggeler *et al*, 2006). The study was designed to evaluate (a) the effectiveness of juvenile drug court, *per se*, (b) the effects of integrating an evidence-based treatment (ie. MST), as the community intervention component of the drug court process, and (c) whether the integration of CM techniques into the MST treatment protocol would improve substance use outcomes for MST. To conduct these comparisons, 161 juvenile offenders meeting diagnostic criteria for substance abuse or dependence were randomised to one of four treatment conditions.

- Family court with community services: youths appeared before a family court judge on average once or twice per year and received outpatient alcohol and drug abuse services from the local centre of the state's substance abuse commission.
- Drug court with community services: youths appeared before the drug court judge once a week for monitoring of drug use (urine screens) and participated in outpatient alcohol and drug abuse services from the local centre of the state's substance abuse commission.
- Drug court with MST: youths received an evidence-based treatment (MST) rather than community services in conjunction with drug court.
- Drug court with MST enhanced with CM: youths received MST enhanced with key components of CM in conjunction with drug court.

Over a one-year assessment period, measures of adolescent substance use, criminal behaviour, mental health symptomatology, and days in out-of-home placement were assessed. In general, findings supported the view that drug court was more effective than family court services in decreasing rates of adolescent substance use and criminal behaviour. Possibly due to the greatly increased surveillance of youths in drug court, however, these relative reductions in antisocial behaviour did not translate to corresponding decreases in rearrest or incarceration.

In addition, findings supported the view that the use of evidence-based treatments within the drug court context improved youth substance related outcomes. For example, during the first four months of drug court participation, 70% of the urine screens were positive for youths in the drug court with community services condition, in comparison with only 28% and 18% for counterparts in the drug court with MST and drug court with MST enhanced with CM conditions, respectively. Urine screens collected over the succeeding eight months maintained the distinction between drug court with community services and the drug court with MST conditions (45%, 7%, and 17%, respectively). Importantly, analyses also showed that substance use decreased significantly among the siblings of the drug court participants who received the evidence-based substance abuse treatment (Rowland *et al*, in press). These findings support the viability of juvenile drug courts and seem to show that CM can facilitate substance-related treatment gains when integrated into MST protocols. In addition, clinical and cost-related outcomes are being examined in a five-year follow-up.

In summary, research findings have provided clear support for the effectiveness of MST in treating adolescent substance use problems. MST provides a comprehensive framework that can efficiently integrate specific interventions into a unified, methodical strategy. Based on this approach and experience from clinical trials, CM is a specific intervention that is consistent with the MST model and can be integrated to enhance MST treatment for adolescent substance abuse.

CURRENT MST SUBSTANCE ABUSE-RELATED RESEARCH

MST substance abuse-related research is continuing in several major projects. Bridging clinical and services areas of research, these projects are evaluating adaptations of MST for different clinical populations and studying different strategies for transporting evidence-based substance abuse treatments to community practice settings.

Transportability and international replication

MST researchers currently are conducting services research to evaluate methods for ensuring accurate uptake of CM implementation within community-based MST treatment teams. One study (Henggeler *et al*, in press) compared strategies to sustain treatment fidelity to an evidence-based practice (ie. MST with CM integration for substance abusing delinquents) in community practice settings. In collaboration with community-based treatment organisations that already had adopted MST, the capacity of an intensive quality assurance system to promote therapist fidelity to CM in the treatment of adolescent marijuana abuse was examined using a design in which MST teams are randomised to CM intensive quality assurance, modelled after the intensive MST quality assurance protocol described previously, versus a two-day CM workshop with no sustained quality assurance. Consistent with findings from a small extant literature (eg. Sholomskas *et al*, 2005) and the perspectives of transportability researchers (eg. Mihalic & Irwin, 2003; Schoenwald & Henggeler, 2003), the intensive quality assurance increased therapist use of CM cognitive behavioural techniques, but increases in the use of CM monitoring techniques were not observed. This project is being replicated in Norway to examine cultural variation in the transport of evidence-based substance abuse treatments for adolescents (Ogden *et al*, in press).

Comorbid substance use and mental health disorders

The rates of psychiatric comorbidity among substance abusing youth are high (Armstrong & Costello, 2002) and youths with a dual diagnosis are (a) at particular risk for negative outcomes (Grella *et al*, 2001; Wilens *et al*, 1997) and (b) more difficult and costly to treat (King *et al*, 2000; Rohde *et al*, 2001). Given the paucity of researched treatments for this population, Sheidow has developed and is evaluating a treatment for dually diagnosed youths that relies on the MST case conceptualisation and treatment planning procedures (Sheidow *et al*, 2007). This treatment is directed toward youths in need of an outpatient level of care (traditional MST targets youths who are at imminent risk of out-of-home placement), and provides comprehensive treatment for the co-occurring disorders rather than the sequential or parallel treatments most often used with this population.

Integrating evidence-based adult treatments into family-based treatments for adolescents

As noted earlier, research and considerable anecdotal evidence suggests that parental or caregiver substance abuse attenuates the capacity of evidence-based treatments of child and adolescent psychosocial problems to achieve favourable outcomes. Rowland (see Schaeffer *et al*, in press) is integrating key aspects of the CRA model for substance abusing caregivers whose families are in community-based MST programmes. The project is specifying the parental drug abuse treatment protocols and, through a pilot study, evaluating the direct effects of the intervention on parental substance use as well as its indirect effects on youth outcomes. If results are promising, the parental intervention protocols will be adapted and tested for integration with other evidence-based treatments of childhood behaviour problems.

The Building Stronger Families project

Child maltreatment associated with parental substance abuse is the primary reason that children are taken into custody in the child protection system in the USA (Bess, 2002; US Public Health Service, 1997; 1999a). At great emotional and fiscal cost, these children frequently are removed from their families for prolonged periods of time – pending successful treatment of their substance abusing caregiver. Unfortunately, in spite of the existence of effective treatments for adult substance abuse (NIDA, 1999), few caregivers involved in the child protection system receive an evidence-based substance abuse treatment. The Building Stronger Families project, with support from the Annie E Casey Foundation, integrates an MST adaptation for child maltreatment, including, for example, the specification of child safety plans, guidelines for collaboration with child protection, and cognitive behavioural protocols for treating post-traumatic stress disorder (Swenson & Saldana *et al*, 2005), with reinforcement-based therapy (Gruber *et al*, 2000; Jones *et al*, 2005), which is a promising CM intervention for drug abusing adults. The capacity of this integration to reduce caregiver substance use and children's out-of-home placement is being tested in a small research trial (Schaeffer *et al*, in press).

Juvenile drug court benchmarking study

This project aims to replicate the aforementioned effectiveness of integrating evidence-based substance abuse treatments into juvenile drug court (Henggeler *et al*, 2006) within the context of a benchmarking study. That is, adolescent outcomes for MST with CM integration currently being provided in juvenile drug court are being tracked, and the effects will be compared to those achieved in the juvenile drug court clinical trial. As such, this study is also examining the sustainability of the MST-CM team of clinicians working with the juvenile drug court. Of particular concern is the capacity and willingness of the drug court authorities to support family- and empirically-based services outside the context of a highly resourced clinical research study.

CONCLUSION

Drug use plays a significant role in many serious adolescent problems, including suicide (Bukstein *et al*, 1993; Crumley, 1990; Fergusson *et al*, 2002), automobile accidents (Centers for Disease Control and Prevention, 1996), and drownings (Office of Technology Assessment, 1991). Youths with substance use disorders have increased rates of risky sexual behaviour, which increases their chances of contracting sexually transmitted diseases (Deas-Nesmith *et al*, 1999; Kann *et al*, 2000). Adolescents with substance use disorders also report relatively high rates of physical and sexual abuse (Clark *et al*, 1997). Socially, adolescent substance use (Mensch & Kandel, 1988) and hard drug use (Newcomb & Bentler, 1988) predict school dropout, and hard drug use during adolescence predicts decreased college involvement. Further, adolescent substance use is linked with unemployment and job instability in young adulthood (Kandel & Yamaguchi, 1985; Newcomb & Bentler, 1988). In general, drug abusing and dependent youth represent a greatly under-served population (Pickens *et al*, 1991) at high risk of presenting significant deleterious long-term outcomes and costs for themselves, their families, communities, and society. Through a well-conceived theoretical approach and a responsible programme of research, MST researchers and clinicians are developing and implementing sound, cost-effective treatment for adolescent substance use problems. Moreover, considerable research attention is being devoted to determining the most effective ways to transport evidence-based substance abuse practices to community treatment settings and to improving youth outcomes by integrating evidence-based adult substance abuse services and improving the effectiveness of existing services for adolescents.

Acknowledgements

This manuscript was supported by grants K23DA015658, R01DA08029, R01DA10079, R01DA08029, and R01DA13066 from the National Institute on Drug Abuse and by grant R01AA122202 from the National Institute on Alcoholism and Alcohol Abuse and the Center for Substance Abuse Treatment.

Correspondence concerning this chapter should be addressed to Ashli J Sheidow, Family Services Research Center, Department of Psychiatry and Behavioral Sciences, Medical University of South Carolina, 67 President Street M/C 406, Charleston, South Carolina, 29425. Electronic mail may be sent to sheidoaj@musc.edu.

References

Armstrong TD & Costello EJ (2002) Community studies on adolescent substance use, abuse, or dependence and psychiatric comorbidity. *Journal of Consulting and Clinical Psychology* **70** 1224–1239.

Azrin NH, Acierno R, Kogan ES, Donohue B, Besalel VA & McMahon PT (1996) Follow-up results of supportive versus behavioural therapy for illicit drug use. *Behaviour Research and Therapy* **34** 41–46.

Azrin NH, Donohue B, Besalel VA, Kogan, ES & Acierno R (1994) Youth drug abuse treatment: a controlled outcome study. *Journal of Child & Adolescent Substance Abuse* **3** 1–16.

Azrin NH, Donohue B, Teichner GA, Crum T, Howell J & DeCato LA (2001) A controlled evaluation and description of individual-cognitive problem solving and family-behavior therapies in dually-diagnosed conduct-disordered and substance-dependent youth. *Journal of Child and Adolescent Substance Abuse* **11** 1–43.

Azrin NH, McMahon PT, Donohue B, Besalel VA, Lapinski KJ, Kogan ES, Acierno R & Galloway E (1994) Behavioural therapy for drug abuse: a controlled treatment outcome study. *Behaviour Research & Therapy* **32** (8) 857–866.

Barnes GM, Reifman AS, Farrell MP & Dintcheff BA (1994) The effects of parenting on the development of alcohol misuse: a six-wave latent growth model. *Journal of Marriage and the Family* **62** (1) 175–186.

Barnes GM & Welte JW (1986) Adolescent alcohol abuse: subgroup differences and relationships to other problem behaviors. *Journal of Adolescent Research* **1** 79–94.

Bauman KE & Ennett ST (1994) Peer influences on adolescent drug use. *American Psychologist* **49** 820–822.

Bess R (2002) *The Cost of Protecting Vulnerable Children. Caring for children: Facts and perspectives.* Washington, DC: The Urban Institute.

Borduin CM, Henggeler SW, Blaske DM & Stein RJ (1990) Multisystemic treatment of adolescent sexual offenders. *International Journal of Offender Therapy and Comparative Criminology* **34** 105–113.

Borduin CM, Mann BJ, Cone LT, Henggeler SW, Fucci BR, Blaske DM & Williams RA (1995) Multisystemic treatment of serious juvenile offenders: long-term prevention of criminality and violence. *Journal of Consulting and Clinical Psychology* **63** 569–578.

Borduin CM & Schaeffer CM (2001) Multisystemic treatment of juvenile sexual offenders: a progress report. *Journal of Psychology & Human Sexuality* **13** 25–42.

Brown TL, Henggeler SW, Schoenwald SK, Brondino MJ & Pickrel SG (1999) Multisystemic treatment of substance abusing and dependent juvenile delinquents: effects on school attendance at post treatment and six-month follow-up. *Children's Services: Social Policy, Research, and Practice* **2** 81–93.

Brunk MA, Henggeler SW & Whelan JP (1987) Comparison of multisystemic therapy and parent training in the brief treatment of child abuse and neglect. *Journal of Consulting and Clinical Psychology* **55** 171–178.

Budney AJ & Higgins ST (1998) *A Community Reinforcement Plus Vouchers Approach: Treating cocaine addiction.* NIH Publication No. 98–4309. Rockville, MD: US Department of Health and Human Services, National Institutes of Health, National Institute on Drug Abuse.

Bukstein OG, Brent DA, Perper JA, Moritz G, Baugher M, Schweers J, Roth C & Balach L (1993) Risk factors for completed suicide among adolescents with a lifetime history of substance abuse: a case-control study. *Acta Psychiatrica Scandinavica* **88** 403–408.

Burns BJ, Hoagwood K & Mrazek PJ (1999) Effective treatment for mental disorders in children and adolescents. *Clinical Child and Family Psychology Review* **2** 199–254.

Center for Substance Abuse Prevention (2001) *Exemplary Substance Abuse Prevention Programs Award Ceremony.* Washington, DC: Substance Abuse and Mental Health Services Administration, Center for Substance Abuse Prevention.

Centers for Disease Control and Prevention (1996) Involvement by young drivers in fatal motor-vehicle crashes: United States, 1988–1995. *Morbidity and Mortality Weekly Report* **45** 1050–1053.

Clark DB, Lesnick L & Hegedus AM (1997) Traumas and other adverse life events in adolescents with alcohol abuse and dependence. *Journal of the American Academy of Child and Adolescent Psychiatry* **36** 1744–1751.

Crowley TJ, Mikulich SK, MacDonald M, Young SE & Zerbe GO (1998) Substance-dependent, conduct-disordered adolescent males: severity of diagnosis predicts two-year outcome. *Drug and Alcohol Dependence* **49** 225–237.

Crumley FE (1990) Substance abuse and adolescent suicidal behavior. *Journal of the American Medical Association* **263** 3051–3056.

Curtis NM, Ronan KR & Borduin CM (2004) Multisystemic treatment: a meta-analysis of outcome studies. *Journal of Family Psychology* **18** 411–419.

Dawes M, Clark D, Moss H, Kirisci L & Tarter R (1999) Family and peer correlates of behavioral self-regulation in boys at risk for substance abuse. *American Journal of Drug and Alcohol Abuse* **25** 219–237.

Deas-Nesmith D, Brady KT, White R & Campbell S (1999) HIV-risk behaviors in adolescent substance abusers. *Journal of Substance Abuse Treatment* **16** 169–172.

Dembo R, Williams L, Wothke W & Schmeidler J (1994) The relationships among family problems, friends' troubled behavior, and high risk youths' alcohol/other drug use and delinquent behavior: a longitudinal study. *International Journal of the Addictions* **29** 1419–1442.

Dishion TJ, Capaldi D, Spracklen KM & Li F (1995) Peer ecology of male adolescent drug use. *Development and Psychopathology* **7** 803–824.

Dishion TJ & Kavanagh K (2003) *Intervening in Adolescent Problem Behavior: A family-centered approach*. New York: Guilford.

Elliott DS (Ed) (1998) *Blueprints for Violence Prevention*. Boulder, CO: University of Colorado, Center for the Study and Prevention of Violence, Blueprints Publications.

Farrell AD & Danish SJ (1993) Peer drug associations and emotional restraint: causes or consequences of adolescents' drug use? *Journal of Consulting and Clinical Psychology* **61** 327–334.

Farrington DP & Welsh BC (1999) Delinquency prevention using family-based interventions. *Children and Society* **13** 287–303.

Fergusson DM, Horwood LJ & Swain-Campbell N (2002) Cannabis use and psychosocial adjustment in adolescence and young adulthood. *Addiction* **97** 1123–1135.

Fergusson DM, Lynskey MT & Horwood LJ (1996) Alcohol misuse and juvenile offending in adolescence. *Addiction* **91** 483–494.

Gorman-Smith D, Tolan PH, Loeber R & Henry DB (1998) Relation of family problems to patterns of delinquent involvement among urban youth. *Journal of Abnormal Child Psychology* **26** 319–333.

Grella CE, Hser Y-I, Joshi V & Rounds-Bryant J (2001) Drug treatment outcomes for adolescents with comorbid mental and substance use disorders. *Journal of Nervous and Mental Disease* **189** 384–392.

Gruber K, Chutuape MA & Stitzer ML (2000) Reinforcement-based intensive outpatient treatment for inner city opiate abusers: a short-term evaluation. *Drug and Alcohol Dependence* **57** 211–223.

Gustle L, Hansson K, Sundell K & Andree-Lofholm C (in press) Implementation of evidence-based models in local social work practice: practitioner perspectives on the MST trial in Sweden. *Journal of Child and Adolescent Substance Abuse*.

Haley J (1987) *Problem-solving Therapy* (2nd ed). San Francisco, CA: Jossey-Bass.

Hann DM & Borek N (2001) *Taking Stock of Risk Factors for Child/Youth Externalizing Behavior Problems*. NIH Publication No. 02–4938. Washington, DC: Department of Health and Human Services, Public Health Service, National Institutes of Health, National Institute of Mental Health.

Hawkins JD, Catalano RF & Miller JY (1992) Risk and protective factors for alcohol and other drug problems in adolescence and early adulthood: implications for substance abuse prevention. *Psychological Bulletin* **112** 64–105.

Hawkins JD, Herrenkohl T, Farrington DP, Brewer D, Catalano RF & Harachi TW (1998) A review of predictors of youth violence. In: R Loeber & DP Farrington (Eds) *Serious and Violent Juvenile Offenders: Risk factors and successful interventions*. Thousand Oaks, CA: Sage Publications, 106–146.

Henggeler SW & Borduin CM (1992) *Multisystemic Therapy Adherence Scales*. Charleston, SC: Medical University of South Carolina, Department of Psychiatry and Behavioral Science.

Henggeler SW, Borduin CM, Melton GB, Mann BJ, Smith L, Hall JA, Cone L & Fucci BR (1991) Effects of multisystemic therapy on drug use and abuse in serious juvenile offenders: a progress report from two outcome studies. *Family Dynamics of Addiction Quarterly* **1** 40–51.

Henggeler SW, Clingempeel WG, Brondino MJ & Pickrel SG (2002) Four-year follow-up of multisystemic therapy with substance-abusing and substance-dependent juvenile offenders. *Journal of the American Academy of Child and Adolescent Psychiatry* **41** 868–874.

Henggeler SW, Halliday-Boykins CA, Cunningham PB, Randall J, Shapiro SB & Chapman JE (2006) Juvenile drug court: enhancing outcomes by integrating evidence-based treatments. *Journal of Consulting and Clinical Psychology* **74** 42–54.

Henggeler SW, Melton GB, Brondino MJ, Scherer DG & Hanley JH (1997) Multisystemic therapy with violent and chronic juvenile offenders and their families: the role of treatment fidelity in successful dissemination. *Journal of Consulting and Clinical Psychology* **65** 821–833.

Henggeler SW, Melton GB & Smith LA (1992) Family preservation using multisystemic therapy: an effective alternative to incarcerating serious juvenile offenders. *Journal of Consulting and Clinical Psychology* **60** 953–961.

Henggeler SW, Melton GB, Smith LA, Schoenwald SK & Hanley JH (1993) Family preservation using multisystemic treatment: long-term follow-up to a clinical trial with serious juvenile offenders. *Journal of Child and Family Studies* **2** 283–293.

Henggeler SW, Pickrel SG & Brondino MJ (1999) Multisystemic treatment of substance abusing and dependent delinquents: outcomes, treatment fidelity, and transportability. *Mental Health Services Research* **1** 171–184.

Henggeler SW, Pickrel SG, Brondino MJ & Crouch JL (1996) Eliminating (almost) treatment dropout of substance abusing or dependent delinquents through home-based multisystemic therapy. *American Journal of Psychiatry* **153** 427–428.

Henggeler SW, Rodick JD, Borduin CM, Hanson CL, Watson SM & Urey JR (1986) Multisystemic treatment of juvenile offenders: effects on adolescent behavior and family interaction. *Developmental Psychology* **22** 132–141.

Henggeler SW, Rowland MD, Randall J, Ward DM, Pickrel SG, Cunningham PB, Miller SL, Edwards JE, Zealberg J, Hand L & Santos AB (1999) Home-based multisystemic therapy as an alternative to the hospitalization of youths in psychiatric crisis: clinical outcomes. *Journal of the American Academy of Child and Adolescent Psychiatry* **38** 1331–1339.

Henggeler SW & Schoenwald SK (1998) *The MST Supervisory Manual: Promoting quality assurance at the clinical level.* Charleston, SC: MST Services.

Henggeler SW & Schoenwald SK (1999) The role of quality assurance in achieving outcomes in MST programs. *Journal of Juvenile Justice and Detention Services* **14** 1–17.

Henggeler SW, Schoenwald SK, Borduin CM, Rowland MD & Cunningham PB (1998) *Multisystemic Treatment of Antisocial Behavior in Children and Adolescents.* New York: Guilford Press.

Henggeler SW, Schoenwald SK, Rowland MD & Cunningham PB (2002) *Serious Emotional Disturbance in Children and Adolescents: Multisystemic therapy.* New York: Guilford Press.

Henggeler SW, Sheidow AJ, Cunningham PB, Donohue BC & Ford JD (in press) Promoting the implementation of an evidence-based intervention for adolescent marijuana abuse in community settings: testing the use of intensive quality assurance. *Journal of Clinical Child and Adolescent Psychology.*

Higgins ST & Budney AJ (1993) *Treatment of Cocaine Dependence through the Principles of Behavior Analysis and Behavioral Pharmacology. Behavioral treatments for drug abuse and dependence*. NIH Publication No. **137** 93–3684. Rockville, MD: US Department of Health and Human Services, National Institutes of Health, National Institute on Drug Abuse Research.

Huey SJ Jr, Henggeler SW, Brondino MJ & Pickrel SG (2000) Mechanisms of change in multisystemic therapy: reducing delinquent behavior through therapist adherence and improved family and peer functioning. *Journal of Consulting and Clinical Psychology* **68** 451–467.

Huey SJ Jr, Henggeler SW, Rowland MD, Halliday-Boykins CA, Cunningham PB, Pickrel SG & Edwards J (2004) Multisystemic therapy effects on attempted suicide by youth presenting psychiatric emergencies. *Journal of the American Academy of Child and Adolescent Psychiatry* **43** 183–190.

Huizinga D, Loeber R & Thornberry TP (1994) *Urban Delinquency and Substance Abuse: Initial findings*. Washington, DC: Office of Juvenile Justice and Delinquency Prevention, US Department of Justice.

Johnson V & Pandina RJ (1991) Effects of the family environment on adolescent substance use, delinquency, and coping styles. *American Journal of Drug and Alcohol Abuse* **17** 71–88.

Jones HE, Wong CJ, Tuten M & Stitzer ML (2005) Reinforcement-based therapy: 12-month evaluation of an outpatient drug-free treatment for heroin abusers. *Drug and Alcohol Dependence* **79** 119–128.

Kandel DB, Kessler RC & Marguiles RZ (1978) Antecedents of adolescent initiation into stages of drug use: a development analysis. In: DB Kandel (Ed) *Longitudinal Research on Drug Use: Empirical findings and methodological issues*. Washington, DC: Hemisphere (Halstead-Wiley) 73–99.

Kandel DB & Yamaguchi K (1985) *Developmental Patterns of the Use of Legal, Illegal, and Medically Prescribed Psychotropic Drugs from Adolescence to Young Adulthood* (NIDA Research Monograph No. 56). Rockville, MD: US Department of Health & Human Services, National Institute on Drug Abuse.

Kann L, Kinchen SA, Williams BI, Ross JG, Lowry R, Grunbaum JA & Kolbe LJ (2000) Youth risk behavior surveillance – United States, 1999. State and local YRBSS Co-ordinators. *Journal of School Health* **70** 271–285.

Kazdin AE & Weisz JR (1998) Identifying and developing empirically supported child and adolescent treatments. *Journal of Consulting and Clinical Psychology* **66** 19–36.

Kendall PC & Braswell L (1993) *Cognitive-behavioral Therapy for Impulsive Children* (2nd Ed). New York: Guilford Press.

King RD, Gaines LS, Lambert EW, Summerfelt WT & Bickman L (2000) The co-occurrence of psychiatric substance use diagnoses in adolescents in different service systems: frequency, recognition, cost, and outcomes. *Journal of Behavioral Health Services and Research* **27** 417–430.

Lipsey MW & Derzon JH (1998) Predictors of violent or serious delinquency in adolescence and early adulthood: a synthesis of longitudinal research. In: R Loeber & DP Farrington (Eds) *Serious and Violent Juvenile Offenders: Risk factors and successful interventions*. Thousand Oaks, CA: Sage Publications, pp86–105.

Mann BJ, Borduin CM, Henggeler SW & Blaske DM (1990) An investigation of systemic conceptualizations of parent-child coalitions and symptom change. *Journal of Consulting and Clinical Psychology* **58** 336–344.

McBride DC, van derWaal CJ, Terry YM & van Buren H (1999) *Breaking the Cycle of Drug Use Among Juvenile Offenders* (NCJ Publication No. 179273). Washington, DC: National Institute of Justice.

McGue M (1999) Behavioral genetic models of alcoholism and drinking. In: KE Leonard & HT Blane (Eds) *Psychological Theories of Drinking and Alcoholism* (2nd ed). New York: Guilford Press, pp372–421.

Mensch BS & Kandel DB (1988) Dropping out of high school and drug involvement. *Sociology of Education* **61** 95–113.

Mihalic S & Irwin K (2003) Blueprints for violence prevention: From research to real-world settings – factors influencing the successful replication of model programs. *Youth Violence and Juvenile Justice* **1** 307–329.

Mihalic S, Irwin K, Elliott D, Fagan A & Hansen D (2001) *Blueprints for Violence Prevention.* Boulder, CO: Center for the Study of Violence Prevention.

Minuchin S (1974) *Families and Family Therapy.* Cambridge, MA: Harvard University Press.

Munger RL (1993) *Changing Children's Behavior Quickly.* Lanham, MD: Madison.

National Institute on Drug Abuse (1999) *Principles of Drug Addiction Treatment: A research-based guide* (NIH Publication No. 99-4180). Rockville, MD: US Department of Health and Human Services, National Institutes of Health and National Institute on Drug Abuse.

National Institutes of Health (2006) State-of-the-science conference statement: preventing violence and related health-risking, social behaviors in adolescents, October 13–15, 2004. *Journal of Abnormal Child Psychology* **34** 457–470.

Newcomb MD & Bentler PM (1988) *Consequences of Adolescent Drug Use: Impact on the lives of young adults.* Newbury Park, CA: Sage.

Newcomb MD & Bentler PM (1989) Substance use and abuse among children and teenagers. *American Psychologist* **44** 242–248.

Office of Applied Studies (2002) *National Survey of Substance Abuse Treatment Services (N-SSATS): 2000. Data on substance abuse treatment facilities* (DASIS Series: S-16, DHHS Publication No. (SMA) 02-3668). Rockville, MD: Substance Abuse and Mental Health Services Administration, Office of Applied Studies.

Office of Technology Assessment (1991) *Adolescent Health – Volume II: Background and the effectiveness of selected prevention and treatment services* (US Congress No. OTA-H-466). Washington, DC: US Government Printing Office.

Ogden T, Christensen B, Sheidow AJ & Holth P (in press) Bridging the gap between science and practice: the effective nationwide transport of MST programs in Norway. *Journal of Child and Adolescent Substance Abuse.*

Ogden T & Hagen KA (2006) Multisystemic therapy of serious behaviour problems in youth: sustainability of therapy effectiveness two years after intake. *Child and Adolescent Mental Health* **11** 142–149.

Ogden T & Halliday-Boykins CA (2004) Multisystemic treatment of antisocial adolescents in Norway: replication of clinical outcomes outside of the US. *Child and Adolescent Mental Health* **9** 77–83.

Patterson GR, Forgatch MS, Yoerger KL & Stoolmiller M (1998) Variables that initiate and maintain an early-onset trajectory for juvenile offending. *Development and Psychopathology* **10** 531–547.

Peterson PL, Hawkins JD, Abbott RD & Catalano RF (1995) Disentangling the effects of parental drinking, family management, and parental alcohol norms on current drinking by black and white adolescents. In: GM Boyd, J Howad & RA Zucker (Eds) *Alcohol Problems among Adolescents: Current directions in prevention research.* Hillsdale, NJ: Lawrence Erlbaum, pp33–57.

Petry NM (2000) A comprehensive guide to the application of contingency management procedures in clinical settings. *Drug & Alcohol Dependence* **58** 9–25.

Pickens RW, Leukefeld CG & Schuster CR (1991) *Improving Drug Abuse Treatment* (Research Monograph No. 106). Rockville, MD: US Department of Health and Human Services, National Institutes of Health, National Institute on Drug Abuse.

President's New Freedom Commission on Mental Health (2003) *Achieving the Promise: Transforming mental health care in America* [online]. Available at: http://www.mentalhealthcommission.gov/reports/FinalReport/downloads/downloads.html (accessed November 2007).

Rohde P, Clarke GN, Lewinsohn PM, Seeley JR & Kaufman NK (2001) Impact of comorbidity on a cognitive-behavioral group treatment for adolescent depression. *Journal of the American Academy of Child and Adolescent Psychiatry* **40** 795–802.

Roozen HG, Boulogne JJ, van Tulder MW, van den Brink W, de Jong CA & Kerkhof AJ (2004) A systematic review of the effectiveness of the community reinforcement approach in alcohol, cocaine and opioid addiction. *Drug and Alcohol Dependence* **74** 1–13.

Rowland MD, Chapman JE & Henggeler SW (in press) Sibling outcomes from a randomized trial of evidence-based treatments with substance abusing juvenile offenders. *Journal of Child and Adolescent Substance Abuse.*

Rowland MD, Halliday-Boykins CA, Henggeler SW, Cunningham PB, Lee TG, Kruesi MJ & Shapiro SB (2005) A randomized trial of multisystemic therapy with Hawaii's Felix Class Youths. *Journal of Emotional and Behavioral Disorders* **13** 13–23.

Schaeffer CM & Borduin CM (2005) Long-term follow-up to a randomized clinical trial of multisystemic therapy with serious and violent juvenile offenders. *Journal of Consulting and Clinical Psychology* **73** 445–453.

Schaeffer CM, Saldana L, Rowland MD, Henggeler SW & Swenson CC (in press) New initiatives in improving youth and family outcomes by importing evidence-based practices. *Journal of Child and Adolescent Substance Abuse.*

Schoenwald SK (1998) *Multisystemic Therapy Consultation Guidelines.* Charleston, SC: MST Institute.

Schoenwald SK & Henggeler SW (2003) Current strategies for moving evidence-based interventions into clinical practice: introductory comments. *Cognitive and Behavioral Practice* **10** 275–277.

Schoenwald SK, Henggeler SW, Brondino MJ & Rowland MD (2000) Multisystemic therapy: monitoring treatment fidelity. *Family Process* **39** 83–103.

Schoenwald SK, Sheidow AJ & Letourneau EJ (2004) Toward effective quality assurance in evidence-based practice: links between expert consultation, therapist fidelity, and child outcomes. *Journal of Clinical Child and Adolescent Psychology* **33** 94–104.

Schoenwald SK, Sheidow AJ, Letourneau EJ & Liao JG (2003) Transportability of evidence-based treatments: evidence for multi-level influences. *Mental Health Services Research* **5** 223–239.

Schoenwald SK, Ward DM, Henggeler SW, Pickrel SG & Patel H (1996) Multisystemic therapy treatment of substance abusing or dependent adolescent offenders: costs of reducing incarceration, inpatient, and residential placement. *Journal of Child and Family Studies* **5** 431–444.

Schoenwald SK, Ward DM, Henggeler SW & Rowland MD (2000) Multisystemic therapy versus hospitalization for crisis stabilization of youth: placement outcomes four months postreferral. *Mental Health Services Research* **2** 3–12.

Sheidow AJ, Molen LA, Navas-Murphy L & Chapman JE (2007) Stage I research evaluating an outpatient treatment for co-occurring substance use and internalizing problems. In: AJ Sheidow (Chair) *Co-occurring Substance Use and Mental Health Problems: Recent findings from transportability and clinical research.* Symposium conducted at the annual Joint Meeting on Adolescent Treatment Effectiveness, Washington, DC.

Sholomskas DE, Syracuse-Siewert G, Rounsaville BJ, Ball SA, Nuro KF & Carroll KM (2005) We don't train in vain: a dissemination trial of three strategies of training clinicians in cognitive-behavioral therapy. *Journal of Consulting and Clinical Psychology* **73** 106–115.

Spooner C (1999) Causes and correlates of adolescent drug abuse and implications for treatment. *Drug and Alcohol Review* **18** 453–475.

Stanton MD & Shadish WR (1997) Outcome, attrition, and family-couples treatment for drug abuse: a meta-analysis and review of the controlled, comparative studies. *Psychological Bulletin* **122** 170–191.

Stark MJ (1992) Dropping out of substance abuse treatment: a clinically oriented review. *Clinical Psychology Review* **12** 93–116.

Steinberg L, Fletcher A & Darling N (1994) Parental monitoring and peer influences on adolescent substance abuse. *Pediatrics* **93** 1060–1064.

Substance Abuse and Mental Health Services Administration (2005) *SAMHSA Model Programs: Multisystemic therapy.* Rockville, MD: US Department of Health and Human Services, Substance Abuse and Mental Health Services.

Swenson CC, Henggeler SW, Taylor IS & Addison OW (2005) *Multisystemic Therapy and Neighborhood Partnerships: Reducing adolescent violence and substance abuse.* New York: Guilford Press.

Swenson CC, Saldana L, Joyner CD, Caldwell E, Henggeler SW & Rowland MD (2005) *Multisystemic Therapy for Child Abuse and Neglect.* Charleston: Medical University of South Carolina, Family Services Research Center.

Timmons-Mitchell J, Bender MB, Kishna MA & Mitchell CC (2006) An independent effectiveness trial of multisystemic therapy with juvenile justice youth. *Journal of Clinical Child and Adolescent Psychology* **35** 227–236.

US Public Health Service (1997) *National Study of Protective, Preventive and Reunification Services Delivered to Children and Their Families.* Washington, DC: US Department of Health and Human Services, Administration for Children and Families.

US Public Health Service (1999a) *Blending Perspectives and Building Common Ground: A report to Congress on substance abuse and child protection.* Washington, DC: US Department of Health and Human Services.

US Public Health Service (1999b) *Mental Health: A report of the Surgeon General.* Rockville, MD: US Department of Health and Human Services, National Institutes of Health, National Institute of Mental Health.

US Public Health Service (2001) *Youth Violence: A report of the Surgeon General.* Washington, DC: US Public Health Service.

Weinberg NZ, Rahdert E, Colliver JD & Glantz MD (1998) Adolescent substance abuse: a review of the past 10 years. *Journal of the American Academy of Child and Adolescent Psychiatry* **37** 252–261.

Weisz JR & Jensen PS (1999) Efficacy and effectiveness of child and adolescent psychotherapy and pharmacotherapy. *Mental Health Services Research* **1** 125–157.

Wilens TE, Biederman J, Abrantes AM & Spencer TJ (1997) Clinical characteristics of psychiatrically referred adolescent outpatients with substance use disorder. *Journal of the American Academy of Child and Adolescent Psychiatry* **36** 941–947.

CHAPTER 2
Effective services for alcohol and drug abusing youth: perspectives from Sweden

Tina Olsson, Håkan Leifman, Knut Sundell and Kjell Hansson

As described in the previous chapter, there is increasing evidence from the USA and international studies that multisystemic therapy (MST) provides an effective method for working with young people who have a range of behavioural and substance misuse problems. This chapter gives the results of an evaluation of MST compared to the usual Swedish way of working with such young people, with a specific focus on outcomes for substance abusing young people. The results offer a very interesting contrast to other studies of MST, and suggest the value of well-developed, mainstream services for young people and the importance of social context on the prospects for importing methods from other countries.

The first MST team began operating in Sweden in 2002. This was one of the first evidence-based treatments for young people with serious behaviour problems to be used in Sweden and the first intervention within the Swedish social services to be evaluated in a multi-site study using an experimental design, allocating participants between treatment (MST) and control (treatment as usual) groups. The evaluation aimed to explore the effects of MST and treatment as usual (TAU) in the Swedish setting. This chapter begins by describing the background to MST's import from the USA to Sweden, which includes describing some changes in policies at the national level. It goes on to describe the Swedish social welfare system as it relates to substance abusing young people. The remainder of the chapter summarises the short-term (seven-month) empirical findings from the transportability trial using MST to treat young people with conduct disorders and introduces additional findings for those young people in the sample who were identified as alcohol and/or drug abusing. This chapter concludes with a discussion of cultural considerations that may be helpful in explaining the results presented here, as they are contrary to those found in other studies. The evaluation found that MST did not produce significantly better outcomes after seven months than mainstream Swedish social services.

SUBSTANCE ABUSE POLICIES: FROM NATIONAL CONTROL TO LOCALISED PREVENTION

Controlling the extent to which young people have access to alcohol and drugs has long been a public policy priority in Sweden. Most researchers would agree that national policies have contributed to the relatively low alcohol and drug consumption levels in Sweden. The restrictive Swedish alcohol policy has strong scientific support and many of its most distinguished features – measures limiting availability and high taxation – are mentioned for example, by the World Health Organisation as among the most effective and evidence-based of public health alcohol policies (for example, Babor *et al*, 1992). The United Nations has recently released a report presenting Sweden's national drug control policy as an example of a successful drug policy (United Nations Office on Drugs and Crime, 2006).

Despite the success of the national policies in reducing the prevalence of substance use and abuse in Sweden, both the alcohol and drug policies have been challenged by increased Swedish integration with Europe. In particular, the Swedish entry into the European Union (EU) in 1995 has led to a weakening of the traditional effective policy measures on alcohol consumption (for example, a decrease in tax on alcohol). As a possible consequence of this, the alcohol consumption in litres of pure alcohol increased by more than 60% among young people aged 15–16 years old during the decade 1990–2000. The lifetime prevalence of drug use for this group also increased from 3% in 1990 to around 10% in 2001 (see ***figure 1***). This trend can also be seen among older youths. In 1992 for example, 6% of men aged 18–19 years old reported having used drugs. Ten years later in 2002, 18% reported having used drugs. Other plausible explanations to the increase in alcohol and drug consumption among young people is the substantial economic recession in Sweden during the 1990s, which led to, among other things, cutbacks within the Swedish social safety net (welfare system) and fewer resources to prevention. When considering narcotics use, the majority of western European countries experienced increases during the 1990s. The increases were not, however, as dramatic as those experienced in Sweden. The increases witnessed in Sweden could, in part, be seen as a consequence of an international trend toward more liberal views on narcotics among young people, as witnessed in certain youth cultures. The rave culture is an example of this.

As a consequence of the strains put on the traditionally restrictive policies and of the increased consumption and problems related to alcohol and drugs during the 1990s, the Swedish Parliament endorsed new national action plans with the intent of reducing substance use. As opposed to being focused on control, these action plans emphasised the need to develop and strengthen preventive measures. A clear shift from earlier policies was the increased emphasis on prevention at the local level. It was argued that, since the instruments of control at the national level were weakened, the municipalities needed to take more of a responsibility in the prevention of substance abuse at the local level. As a result, Sweden's 290 local authorities were financially encouraged to employ prevention workers to work exclusively with substance abuse prevention by focusing on the development of a long-term structure and organisation of all prevention efforts. The most recent national alcohol plan (prop. 2005/06:30) has cited these prevention workers as being central figures in the success of the development of local prevention efforts.

Figure 1: Self-reported lifetime experience of any illicit drug – percentage among students (boys and girls) 15–16 years of age and among male conscripts (18–19 years of age)

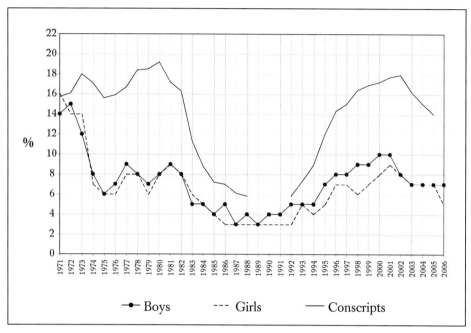

In addition to the national action plans for reducing alcohol related harm and promotion of a drug free society, the Swedish government in 2001 commissioned the National Board of Health and Welfare to implement a programme supporting development within the social services based on research knowledge. This was due to a lack of perceived effectiveness of social service interventions for service users as well as a real lack of information regarding the effects of social services interventions for service users. The programme highlighted the importance and significance of evaluation of social work practice for clients and service users.

THE WELFARE SYSTEM AND SUBSTANCE ABUSING YOUNG PEOPLE

In Sweden, children and young people presenting with alcohol or drug related problems are almost entirely treated within what has been described as a child welfare approach (Levin, 1998). This is also true for behaviour that arises out of complications due to alcohol and drug addiction. The standard procedure for prosecutors or criminal courts that come into contact with minors, for example, is to refer these young people to the social services, without any other legal sanctions imposed on the individual. During the past 10–15 years there has been a rapid increase in the development of non-residential services for children and young people receiving interventions through the Social Services Act. These services cover a broad spectrum and range from general prevention efforts to more targeted interventions. The Swedish system has been classified by Gilbert (1997) as having a family service orientation, which emphasises therapeutic interventions, as opposed to Anglo-American countries' stronger legalistic focus on substantiating referrals and reviewing evidence of allegations. The interventions provided in Sweden, however, do not normally include behaviour modification, manualised treatments or evidence-based programmes (see Socialstyrelsen, 2006a; Cederblad, 2005) and very little is known about the effects of treatment on the outcomes for young people within the Swedish social service system.

MST OUTCOMES EVALUATION

In this context of a perceived lack of effectiveness in the interventions that were used for young people with severe behaviour problems, a considerable increase in attention to the issue of prevention and an evolving interest in evidence-based programmes, the first Swedish MST team was launched in a suburb of Stockholm in 2002. The second MST team started in the spring of 2003 in the west coast town of Halmstad. Seven teams subsequently started between the autumn of 2003 and the spring of 2004, serving primarily the three largest cities of Sweden: Stockholm, Göteborg and Malmö.

Of these eight MST teams, six were included in a multi-site evaluation that compared MST with traditional services provided to young people with behaviour problems (Sundell *et al*, submitted). The study was a randomised controlled experiment within the normally operating social services. Young people were assigned to either MST or treatment as usual (TAU) with a 50/50 random allocation between the two treatment groups. For the short-term outcome analysis, data was collected prior to randomisation, and again approximately seven months after randomisation. The child welfare services in 27 local authorities from Sweden's three largest cities (Stockholm, Göteborg, Malmö), and one west coast town (Halmstad), served as the recruiting area for the study.

The target group for the study was defined as young people aged 12–17 years that fulfilled the criteria for a clinical diagnosis of conduct disorder according to DSM-IV-TR (American Psychiatric Association, 2000) and where the parents or guardians were willing to start MST. Young people were excluded from the study if they had ongoing treatment by another provider, substance abuse without other antisocial behaviour, sexual offending, autism, acute psychosis, or imminent risk of suicide, or that their presence in the home posed a serious risk to the young person or to the family.

A total of 156 families agreed to participate in the study (79 in the MST group; 77 received TAU). The sample consisted of 95 boys (61%) and 61 girls (39%) who were on average 15 years old. These young people were referred for services due to a range of problem behaviours. More than two-thirds of them were referred for services for at least three reasons. The most common presenting problem was repeated truancy (85%), followed by delinquency (47%), serious disruptive behaviour at school (37%), harm to self or other (38%) and substance abuse (30%). Of the young people in this study, nearly one-third (32%) had been placed outside of the home at some point during the six months prior to joining the study.

Almost half (47%) of the families involved in the study were of a nationality other than Swedish and spoke a language other than Swedish within the home, 13% had at least one parent that was born in a country other than Sweden, and 40% had parents that were both of Swedish descent. The majority of families with non-Swedish heritage were from Asia (n = 30), Europe outside Scandinavia (n = 25), and Africa (n = 14). A large majority of the young people (67%) lived in a single parent home. Of the mothers, 18% had a college education and 51% were unemployed. Of the families involved, 61% lived entirely or in part on social welfare grants. The young participants were therefore much more likely to come from socio-economically disadvantaged and ethnic minority groups than the rest of the Swedish population.

Data were gathered on a series of domains, including mental health, delinquency and substance use using various research instruments, including the Child Behaviour Checklist (Achenbach, 1991a; 1991b), the Self-Report Delinquency Scale (Elliott *et al*, 1983), the Pittsburgh Youth Study Bad Friends Subscale (Keenan *et al*, 1995), the Sense of Coherence Scale (Antonovsky, 1987), the Alcohol Use Disorder Identification Test (AUDIT, Babor *et al*, 1992), the Drug Use Disorder Identification Test (DUDIT, Berman *et al*, 2005) and the Family Relations Scale (Stattin, unpublished). Parental psychiatric symptoms were also measured, using the Symptoms Checklist-90 (Derogatis & Cleary, 1997).

There was very little dropout from the study. Only seven families (4%) dropped out completely. All analyses were based on an intent-to-treat approach, so the analyses included those who dropped out of treatment. All values of variables for people who were missing from the second stage of measurement were imputed by carrying forward the pre treatment measure.

INTERVENTIONS

MST: Families and young people who participated in MST in this study were provided a programme licensed by MST Services, Inc, of Charleston, South Carolina (see Sheidow and Henggeler's chapter on p11 for a fuller description of MST). Weekly expert consultation (via telephone), quarterly on-site booster sessions, and biannual implementation reviews were provided by the MST consultant in charge. The on-site MST supervisor delivered supervision and programme direction according to the *MST Supervisory Manual* and the treatment adhered to the *MST Organisational Manual*. As an additional measure of quality assurance, therapist adherence to the nine principles of MST was assessed using caregiver reports on the *MST Therapist Adherence Measure Form*.

Treatment as usual: Young people assigned to the group receiving TAU were referred to social services. The most common intervention received by the group of young people in this study was individual counselling (1–2 hours every other week) provided by the case manager or a private counsellor and financed by the Social Welfare Administration (n = 20), followed by family therapy (n = 16). In most cases, the family therapy took place for 1–2 hours per week at the social welfare office with two social workers present. In general, therapists usually have additional training in psychodynamic or systemic family therapy. Other services for the TAU group were mentoring with nonprofessional volunteers spending time with the young people (normally 10 hours a month provided at two or more occasions) in a supportive, nonjudgemental manner while acting as role models (n = 12), and out-of-home care, primarily residential care (n = 8). Less frequent services were aggression replacement training (ART) (n = 4), addiction treatment (n = 2) and special education services (n = 2). Thirteen of the young people in this group received no services.

RESULTS
Treatment outcomes
The short-term (seven-month) results of this study showed that young people in both treatment groups showed significant improvements in their psychiatric health and self-reported delinquency, as well as the number of official arrests. In addition, young people in both groups significantly improved their outlook and saw a brighter future for themselves. Parental psychiatric health was also significantly improved from study start to seven-month follow-up for the parents of young people in both treatment groups. There were, however, no significant differences in these outcomes between treatment groups. Analysis of changes in short-term alcohol and drug use outcomes revealed no difference over time and no differences between treatment groups in the extent to which young people involved in this study reported their alcohol and/or drug consumption. The young peoples' levels of drug and alcohol use were similar at the seven-month follow-up to the levels reported when they joined the study.

Treatment outcomes were also compared for the substance abusing sub-sample (n = 64) with that of the non-substance abusing group (n = 92). The substance abusing sub-sample consisted of those young people identified as having a substance abuse (alcohol and/or drug) problem at some point during the year prior to joining the study. Of these young people, 44% were girls and 56% were boys, 42% were part of the MST group and 58% were in the TAU group. The substance abusing and non-substance abusing groups differed significantly in several ways at entry to the study. First, the young people that were identified as having substance abuse problems were on average one year older than their non-substance abusing counterparts. Second, the young people with substance abuse problems were found to have significantly fewer antisocial peers than the non-substance abusing conduct disorder young people. Third, the substance abusing young people had significantly more psychiatric symptoms, familial problems, and antisocial behaviour problems than those young people that were not substance abusing. Substance abusing young people had more problems in parent-reported family functioning and in self-reported externalising problem behaviour. In addition, their sense of coherence was significantly lower than their non-substance abusing peers.

As would be expected, alcohol and drug use was also significantly higher among those young people identified as having a substance abuse problem than the non-substance abusing young people in this sample. Of those young people identified as having had a substance abuse problem, 52% had used illicit drugs during the six months prior to study inclusion. In comparison, only 10% of the non-substance abusing group reported using drugs during the same time period.

Table 1, overleaf, presents a comparison of treatment outcomes for those young people with substance abuse problems to those for non-substance abusing young people. There were no significant differences between treatment outcomes between these groups. Similarly, there were no interaction effects found between type of intervention and whether a substance abuse problem was present. This was true for parental reported family functioning, self-reported externalising problems and self-reported sense of coherence as well as for all measures related to alcohol and drug use. This suggests that MST and TAU were equally effective in helping both substance abusing and non-substance abusing young people to improve their behaviour problems and family relationships, even if they did not reduce their actual levels of alcohol and drug use.

Economic evaluation: The impact of MST on the short-term economic outcome of intervening in youth problem behaviour was also investigated. All interventions received by the young people in the MST and TAU groups during the first six months following study intake were identified. All the costs of social service intervention in youth problem behaviour were estimated and included. They are not limited to those costs associated with placement of the young people outside of the home, family preservation services, substance abuse treatment and tests, but include all services and interventions provided by social services from study intake to six months following study intake. Direct costs borne by the young people and families involved in this study (such as the costs of transportation) were not included. Furthermore, indirect costs, such as productivity losses associated with lost or impaired ability to work or to engage in leisure activities were not included.

Resource use is based on the number of days a young person's case was open for intervention during the six-month follow-up period. Information on type and duration of intervention received by young people in the study was collected from the participating social service agencies and validated through unit supervisors and providers. As this study is concerned with differences in costs, those costs that are common for participants in both groups are not included in the calculations.

All cost calculations were based on average unit cost estimates. When available, these estimates were taken directly from social services records and are equal to the

Table 1: Means and standard deviations (SD)[1] in treatment outcome (change scores) and resource use for youth with a substance abuse problem and youth without a substance abuse problem in multisystemic therapy (MST) and treatment-as-usual (TAU) groups

Outcomes	Substance abusing youth		Non-substance abusing youth		Treatment[2]		Substance abuse[3]		Interaction[4]	
	MST (n = 27)	TAU (n = 37)	MST (n = 52)	TAU (n = 40)	F^5	p^6	F	p	F	p
Family relations	.20 (.50)	.35 (.62)	.21 (.63)	.05 (.43)	.01	ns	2.59	ns	2.93	ns
CBCL – psychiatric health problems	-10.38 (12.60)	-10.62 (12.94)	-7.64 (13.05)	-4.80 (14.56)	.27	ns	4.00	ns	.58	ns
CBCL – internalising problems	-5.39 (12.05)	-9.05 (17.51)	-4.78 (11.66)	-2.36 (14.04)	.10	ns	2.68	ns	1.89	ns
CBCL – externalising problems	-11.96 (17.86)	-9.76 (12.29)	-8.60 (15.60)	-6.31 (14.99)	.70	ns	1.98	ns	.01	ns
YSR – psychiatric health problems	-1.27 (7.37)	-3.86 (10.54)	-4.38 (12.35)	-5.65 (11.92)	1.14	ns	.12	ns	.18	ns
YSR – internalising problems	.49 (7.61)	-4.72 (12.90)	-3.73 (13.19)	-2.35 (10.80)	.99	ns	.22	ns	.09	ns
YSR – externalising problems	-11.78 (18.11)	-11.63 (19.98)	-19.07 (18.92)	-12.60 (18.15)	1.13	ns	1.75	ns	1.03	ns
alcohol consumption	132.5 (950.1)	-54.4 (1144.2)	-20.9 (1138.7)	-153.4 (894.3)	.84	ns	.53	ns	.02	ns

Measure					F		F		F	
AUDIT – problem drinking	-096 (6.34)	-0.17 (6.53)	0.27 (4.23)	1.15 (2.60)	1.04	ns	2.40	ns	.00	ns
Narcotics use (%)[7]	0	0	2%	12.5%	-	-	-	-	-	-
DUDIT – problem drug use	0.48 (10.68)	-0.18 (9.66)	0.95 (4.17)	-0.01 (4.74)	.46	ns	.07	ns	.02	ns
Sense of coherence	0.96 (12.07)	4.85 (11.27)	2.96 (14.11)	1.23 (10.69)	.28	ns	.16	ns	1.91	ns
Number of interventions[8]	1.50 (.76)	1.63 (1.01)	1.51 (.67)	1.38 (.61)	.00	ns	.82	ns	.96	ns
Intervention days[8]	157.85 (31.45)	137.03 (48.10)	144.86 (38.03)	143.78 (45.51)	2.34	ns	.19	ns	1.90	ns
Total costs[8,9]	16,000 (10,800)	13,200 (19,300)	14,200 (10,300)	8,000 (9,400)	1.84	ns	1.11	ns	-	-
Days placed outside of the home[8]	13.54 (30.02)	25.03 (56.96)	11.06 (27.81)	14.09 (39.83)	1.14	ns	.97	ns	.39	ns

1. The standard deviation (SD) is the average difference in the individual scores from the mean.
2. Treatment refers to the effect that can be attributed to either MST or TAU.
3. Substance abuse refers to the effect that can be attributed to a young person belonging to either the substance abusing or non-substance abusing groups.
4. Interaction refers to the effect that can be attributed to an interaction between treatment and substance abuse.
5. F is the statistical test used in these analyses and refers to the distribution with which we have compared our results.
6. p represents the significance level and is an indication of the likelihood to which the results obtained can be attributed to chance alone. In these analyses $p < .05$ was considered significant.
ns = non significant.
7. $\chi^2(6) = 8.25$, $p > .05$
8. Only those young people in receipt of at least one intervention ($n = 141$) during the study period are included in the resource use analysis (SA/MST = 26; SA/TAU = 32; N-SA/MST = 51; N-SA/TAU = 32).
9. The standard t-test was used to explore differences in cost between treatment groups and substance using groups as it has been identified as the most appropriate hypothesis test for cost data from randomised trials. Due to the lack of main effects, interaction effects were not explored as this increases the familywise error rate (Howell, 2002).

cost paid per intervention day to the relevant provider. Cost estimates unavailable through the participating social service agencies were taken directly from those organisations responsible for providing the interventions received by study participants and based on annual operating costs and annual workload measures. Costs were calculated in Swedish crowns (SEK) for that year in which the costs were incurred and inflated when necessary to 2005 real values using the change in producer price index of 0.045% (Official Statistics of Sweden, 2006). Intervention costs were then converted to Euros using the exchange rate of 1€ = 9.29 SEK (Central Intelligence Agency, 2006).

Of the 156 young people involved in this study, 90% received at least one intervention during the follow-up period. As non-receipt of services equates to negligible costs, only those young people in receipt of services are considered here. The participants received a combined total of 220 interventions from 101 providers. In addition to MST, 19% of the young people involved in this study were placed in an institution at some time during the follow-up period, 17% received mentorship services, 17% received counselling services, 14% received intensive/needs-based services, 9% were placed in foster care, 4% received an ART intervention, 2% received special education services and 1% of participating young people received addiction treatment services at some time during the first six-months following study intake. In addition to these services, five young people received periodic drug screening, the family of one young person received respite care services from two providers concurrently, and two young people were involved in day camp activities.

On average, the young people were considered active participants in some sort of intervention during 145 days, or 79% of the study period. Young people were placed outside of their homes for an average of 35 days and received an average total of 1.5 interventions. More than one-third of the young people involved in this study received more than one intervention during the period under review and at least one young person received five interventions during the study period.

Considering both resource use and total intervention costs, there were no differences found between that group of young people who received MST and the group of young people that did not receive MST. Young people in both groups were re-referred for new interventions, were actively participating in an intervention (as measured by open case days), and were placed outside of their homes to the same extent. The total cost per young person to the public social services system was the same for those young people in the MST group as for the young people in the TAU group.

Resource use comparisons for the substance abusing and non-substance abusing sub-samples can be found in **table 1** on the previous page. There were no differences found in the extent to which young people used social services resources when comparing substance abusing young people and non-substance abusing young people. Those young people that were identified as having a substance abuse problem were re-referred for intervention and received an equivalent number of days of intervention as the non-substance abusing young people. There were also no differences in the extent to which young people were placed outside of the home. In addition, there were no differences found in the costs associated with treating young people with substance abuse issues as compared to those young people without substance abuse issues. The public social service system's economic outlays were on average the same for both groups of young people during the period under review.

DISCUSSION

These findings suggest that, in the short-term at least, MST is no more effective than the services usually available for young people in Sweden. In most cases, young people in both MST and TAU groups significantly decreased their problem behaviour, showed improved relations within the family, and improved their social skills. These improvements were not statistically significantly different between groups. For substance abuse outcomes, there were no significant differences between MST and TAU groups, and no significant changes over the period of the study. Since young people included in this study were at the age that they usually progress from abstinence towards use, the lack of increase in substance useage could be interpreted as a positive result of the services provided. The extent to which these young people used social services resources, including the total costs associated with intervention were the same for both groups. The lack of significant between group differences cannot easily be accounted for by site effects, programme maturity or treatment fidelity. These are all potential influences on outcome that have been identified in previous research (Henggeler, 2004), but which did not appear to be present in this study.

In addition, there were no significant differences in treatment outcome when comparing substance abusing young people to non-substance abusing young people. Although this result is in line with the general conclusion of this evaluation, it should be noted that the study was not designed to test the different effectiveness between substance-users and abstainers. In the inclusion procedure, the two groups were not randomised separately.

Inasmuch as it found no significant difference between TAU and MST outcomes, this study conflicts with the results achieved with roughly the same target group and the same follow-up time in the USA (Borduin *et al*, 1995; Henggeler *et al*, 2006; Henggeler *et al*, 1997; Henggeler *et al*, 1999; Timmons-Mitchell *et al*, 2006) and in Norway (Ogden & Halliday-Boykins, 2004), but are similar to results obtained in Canada (Cunningham, 2002) and in a recent meta-analytic review that included six studies from the USA, one from Canada and one from Norway (Littell *et al*, 2005).

The economic outcomes of this study are also contrary to results of US studies, where MST has been shown to have favourable economic outcomes when compared to TAU. These savings come from a reduction in the extent to which substance abusing juvenile offenders are imprisoned or placed in residential treatment (Schoenwald *et al*, 1996). MST was also shown to be cost-effective in the USA by reducing the short-term costs associated with hospitalisation following psychiatric crisis among young people presenting with psychiatric emergencies (Sheidow *et al*, 2004).

MST is not the only evidence-based prevention programme that has failed to produce superior outcomes when compared to TAU in Sweden. A recent randomised controlled trial of a school-based life skills programme called Unplugged was not more effective than the control condition in the short-term in reducing tobacco, alcohol or drug use among Swedish school students, but did successfully reduce substance use in Belgium, Greece, Italy, Spain, Germany and Austria (Lindahl & Galanti, 2006). In other cases, however, programmes transported from North America to Sweden have been shown to be superior compared to TAU for delinquent young people (functional family therapy, Hansson *et al*, 2000), and attention control (classroom management training; Forster *et al*, in press) and to be better than providing no service for disruptive and aggressive children (parent management training, Kling *et al*, 2006).

Since this study evaluated MST in the context of normally occurring Swedish social work, it was not legally possible to include an untreated control group so it was impossible to disentangle the effects of MST versus TAU from those of common factors (eg. therapeutic allegiance). However, the comparison of CBCL scores from the Swedish, Norwegian and two USA MST evaluation studies indicate that the Swedish average decrease in CBCL total scores for the MST group was comparable to that of the Norwegian (Terje Ogden, personal communication, 29 August, 2006) and similar to or higher than those of a USA study that investigated two versions of MST (Henggeler *et al*, 2006). The same was true when comparing CBCL scores on internalising and externalising behaviour. In Sweden, the average decrease for the MST group was similar or higher than that of a USA study (Rowland *et al*, 2005). The decrease for the TAU group was higher in Sweden than in the other studies, and especially the USA studies. Thus, in general, both the MST and the TAU groups in Sweden and Norway decreased their CBCL symptoms considerably more in the short-term than did the groups in the USA studies. One interpretation of this result is that the Swedish MST group performed equally well as in other studies, but that the Swedish TAU group outperformed their counterparts in the USA (see *figure 2*).

This result focuses our attention on the importance of contextual factors when transporting an evidence-based method from one context to another. For instance, if the quality of TAU is relatively high, the favourable effects of an evidence-based method might disappear. One potentially important difference between Sweden and the USA is in the traditional approach to young offenders. In Sweden, there is an emphasis on therapeutic interventions. This makes in-home services quite frequent (Sundell *et al*, 2007) and not exclusive to MST as may be the case in the USA. In the USA, young offenders are dealt with within the juvenile justice system. One possible effect of this is that residential care and imprisonment, interventions with well-known

Figure 2: CBCL Change T-score in four evaluations of MST

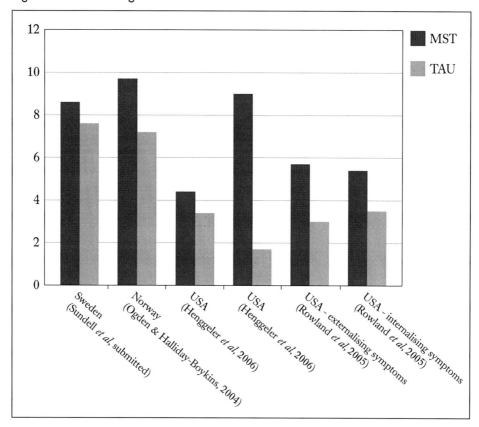

[1] Change score is the difference in the outcome of interest from pre to post test. A T-score is a standardised score with a mean of 50 and a standard deviation of 10.

risks of producing unintended adverse effects (for example, Dodge *et al*, 2006), is more frequent in the USA than in Sweden. In Sweden, 0.5% of adolescents aged 13 to 20 receive residential care annually (Socialstyrelsen, 2006b). In comparison, in 1997 4% of juveniles were in custody in the USA (Snyder & Sickmund, 1999). Furthermore, the juvenile justice system in itself may be a risk factor. In one meta-analysis, Lipsey (1999) showed that care by juvenile justice providers, as compared to other service providers, decreases the rehabilitation rate of juvenile delinquents.

In addition, the family service orientation, coupled with the broad spectrum of services that have become available to young people during the past decade in Sweden, may have played an important role in the relatively large improvements made by young people in the TAU group. The young people in this study received a relatively wide range of services, as well as multiple interventions during the period under review. This was not the case for the young people in the comparison groups in the USA studies where young people received little or no intervention at all. The young people in the USA studies received, for example, drug or family court appearance, probation, or outpatient treatment.

Another contextual consideration that might account for the differences between the results found in the USA and Swedish studies, is the socio-demographic context. Some potentially important differences are socio-economic status, teenage pregnancy rates, crime rates, and substance abuse rates. For example, in 1997 16% of all families with children in the USA were living in poverty (Snyder & Sickmund, 1999), a rare phenomenon in Sweden and Norway (Vogel, 2002). The samples from the two USA evaluations mentioned earlier (Henggeler *et al*, 2006; Rowland *et al*, 2005) confirm that those families were, in general, economically deprived. Furthermore, in 1996 the teenage birth rate in the USA was 5%, but only 0.65% in Sweden (Vinnerljung *et al*, in press). Levels of crime and substance use among juveniles are also lower in Sweden than in the USA. In 2002, for instance, lifetime cannabis use among Swedish 15-year-olds was 7% (girls) and 8% (boys) while the corresponding figures for the USA were 42% and 31% (ter Bogt *et al*, 2006). In a comparative context, both homicide and suicide rates in the USA are consistently higher than those for other industrialised countries, including Sweden. These contextual differences may provide an explanation for the differences in treatment effectiveness found in the USA and Sweden and warrant further investigation.

A third fact that might be important is that Swedes tend to have a stronger belief in the legitimacy of state interventions in families, compared to other countries (Gould, 1988; Weightman & Weightman, 1995), thus possibly making them more accepting of interventions by authorities than in other countries such as the USA. In addition, Sweden has a much more collectivist culture and the government plays a much larger role in providing social services than in the USA. These issues have been identified as important considerations when transferring behavioural interventions (Epping-Jordan, 2004). Unfortunately, very little work has been done in the area of international dissemination of behavioural interventions. This is an area of research that will be important to the field as the transfer of evidence-based practices across cultural settings becomes more commonplace.

The issue of contextual factors is complex. For example, MST has been successfully transported to Norway both in a short (Ogden & Halliday-Boykins, 2004) and long-term perspective (Ogden & Hagen, 2006). Norway is a society that is very similar to Sweden. There are some possible explanations for this contradictory result, although these are purely speculative. The first is that the implementation of MST in Norway was guided by the Ministry of Child and Family Welfare, implemented nationally and sponsored by a research unit to support and evaluate the quality of the implementation. In contrast, the Swedish implementation was guided by local initiatives without a national supporting framework. This difference might explain the somewhat lower CBCL total change scores for the MST group. A second difference that favours the Swedish TAU (if we assume that residential care has adverse effects) is that fewer young people received residential care in the Swedish (18%) than in the Norwegian (50%) study. This difference may explain why MST effects were better than TAU in Norway but not in Sweden.

The results presented here suggest the value of well-developed, mainstream services for young people and the importance of social context on the prospects for importing methods from other countries. It is important that new methods are evaluated in order to establish their effectiveness and place in an already functioning system of services. MST may be an important alternative in the Swedish setting as it has been shown to have positive effects in treating youth problem behaviour, even if these effects are not better than the more traditional services offered through the public social service system.

Acknowledgements

Support for this research was provided by the Institute for Evidence-based Social Work Practice (IMS), National Board of Health and Welfare in Sweden, and National Drug Policy Co-ordinator, Ministry of Health and Social Affairs, Sweden. We would like to acknowledge the contributions of Cecilia Andrée Löfholm and Lars-Henry Gustle, to the project from which this report originates.

References

Achenbach TM (1991a) *Manual for the Child Behavior Checklist and 1991 Profile*. Burlington: University of Vermont, Department of Psychiatry.

Achenbach TM (1991b) *Manual for the Youth Self-report and 1991 Profile*. Burlington: University of Vermont, Department of Psychiatry.

American Psychiatric Association (2000) *Diagnostic and Statistical Manual of Mental Disorders* (4th ed – text revision). Washington, DC: American Psychiatric Association.

Antonovsky A (1987) *Unraveling the Mystery of Health. How people manage stress and stay well.* San Francisco, CA: Jossey-Bass.

Babor RF, de la Fuente J, Saunders J & Grant M (1992) *AUDIT. The Alcohol Use Disorders Identification Test. Guidelines for use in primary health care.* World Health Organisation.

Berman AH, Bergman H, Palmstierna T & Schlyter F (2005) Evaluation of the Drug Use Disorder Identification Test (DUDIT) in criminal justice and detoxication settings in a Swedish population sample. *European Addiction Research* **11** 22–31.

Borduin CM, Mann BJ, Cone LT, Henggeler SW, Fucci BR, Blaske DM, & Williams RA (1995) Multisystemic treatment of serious juvenile offenders: long-term prevention of criminality and violence. *Journal of Consulting and Clinical Psychology* **63** 569–578.

Cederblad M (2005) *Källan till en Chans: Nationell Handlingsplan för den Sociala Barn- och Ungdomsvården. [Source for a Chance: National action plan for social child and youth welfare]* Statens Offentligautredningar. SOU 2005:81.

Central Intelligence Agency (2006) *CIA World Fact Book*. Washington, DC: CIA.

Cunningham A (2002). *Lessons Learned from a Randomized Study of Multisystemic Therapy in Canada* [online]. Available at: http://www.lfcc.on.ca/onestep.html (accessed November 2007).

Derogatis LR & Cleary P (1997) Confirmation of the dimensional structure of the SCL-90: a study in construct validation. *Journal of Clinical Psychology* **33** 981–989.

Dodge KA, Dishion TJ & Lansford JE (2006) *Deviant Peer Influences in Programs for Youth. Problems and Solutions.* New York: The Guilford Press.

Elliot DS, Ageton SS, Huizinga D, Konowles BA & Canter RJ (1983) *The Prevalence and Incidence of Delinquent Behavior 1976–80. Report of the National Youth Survey, project # 26.* Boulder, CO: Behavioral Research Institute.

Epping-Jordan JE (2004) Research to practice: international dissemination of evidence-based medicine. *International Behavioral Medicine* **28** 81–87.

Forster M, Sundell K, Melin L, Morris RJ & Karlberg M (in press) *A Randomized Controlled Trial of a Manualized Behavior Management Intervention Targeting Students with Behavior Problems.*

Gilbert N (Ed) (1997) *Combating Child Abuse. International perspectives and trends.* Oxford: Oxford University Press.

Gould A (1988) *Conflict and Control in Welfare Policy. The Swedish experience.* London: Longman House.

Hansson K, Cederblad M & Höök B (2000) *Funktionell Familjeterapi. En behandlingsmetod vid ungdomskriminalitet.* Socialvetenskaplig Tidskrift.

Henggeler SW (2004) Decreasing effect sizes for effectiveness studies – implications for the transport of evidence-based treatments: comments on Curtis, Ronan and Borduin (2004). *Journal of Family Psychology* **18** 420–423.

Henggeler SW, Halliday-Boykins CA, Cunningham PB, Randall J, Shapiro SB & Chapman JE (2006) Juvenile drug court: enhancing outcomes by integrating evidence-based treatments. *Journal of Consulting and Clinical Psychology* **74** 42–54.

Henggeler SW, Melton GB, Brondino MJ, Scherer DG & Hanley JH (1997) Multisystemic therapy with violent and chronic juvenile offenders and their families: the role of treatment fidelity in successful dissemination. *Journal of Consulting and Clinical Psychology* **65** 821–833.

Henggeler SW, Pickrel SG & Brondino MJ (1999) Multisystemic treatment of substance-abusing and dependent delinquents: outcomes, treatment fidelity, and transportability. *Mental Health Services Research* **1** 171–184.

Howell DC (2002) *Statistical Methods for Psychology* (5th ed). Belmont, California: Thomson Wadsworth.

Keenan K, Loeber R, Zhang Q, Stouthamer-Lober M & van Kammen WB (1995) The influence of deviant peers on the development of boys' disruptive and delinquent behaviour: a temporal analysis. *Developmental Psychopathology* **7** 715–726.

Kling Å, Sundell K, Melin L & Forster M (2006) *Komet för Föräldrar. En randomiserad effektutvärdering av ett föräldraprogram för barns beteendeproblem [Komet for Parents – A randomised controlled trial of a parent management training program]* [online]. Available at: http://www.stockholm.se/pages/378278/2006-14%20KOMET%20feb%20slugiltig.pdf (accessed Novmber 2007).

Levin C (1998) *Uppfostringsanstalten. Om tvång i föräldrars ställe [The Borstal Home].* (Lund studies in social welfare XX). Lund: Arkiv Förlag.

Lindahl A-M & Galanti MR (2006) *Unplugged! Utvärdering av ett europeiskt ANT-program i Sverige [Unplugged! An evaluation of a European ANT programme].* Stockholms läns landsting: Centrum för Folkhälsa.

Lipsey MW (1999) Can intervention rehabilitate serious delinquents? *The Annals of the American Academy of Political and Social Science* **564** 142–166.

Littell J, Popa M & Forsythe B (2005) *Multisystemic Therapy for Social, Emotional and Behavioural Problems in Youth Aged 10–17.* Chichester: John Wiley & Sons Ltd.

Official Statistics of Sweden [online] (2006) Available at: www.scb.se (accessed January 2008).

Ogden T & Hagen KA (2006) Multisystemic treatment of serious behaviour problems in youth: sustainability of treatment effectiveness two years after intake. *Child and Adolescent Mental Health* **11** 142–149.

Ogden T & Halliday-Boykins CA (2004). Multisystemic treatment of adolescents in Norway: replication of clinical outcomes outside the US. *Journal of Child and Adolescent Mental Health* **9** 77–83.

Rowland MR, Halliday-Boykins CA, Henggeler SW, Cunningham PB, Lee TG, Kruesi MJP & Shapiro SB (2005) A randomized trial of multisystemic therapy with Hawaii's Felix Class youths. *Journal of Emotional and Behavioral Disorders* **13** 13–23.

Schoenwald SK, Ward DM, Henggeler SW, Pickrel SG & Patel H (1996) Multisystemic therapy treatment of substance abusing or dependent adolescent offenders: costs of reducing incarceration, inpatient, and residential placement. *Journal of Child and Family Studies* **5** 431–444.

Sheidow AJ, Bradford WD, Henggeler SW, Rowland MD, Halliday-Boykins C, Schoenwald SK & Ward DM (2004) Treatment costs of youths receiving multisystemic therapy or hospitalization after a psychiatric crisis. *Psychiatric Services* **55** 548–554.

Snyder HN & Sickmund M (1999) *Juvenile Offenders and Victims: 1999 national report* [online]. Washington, DC: Office of Juvenile Justice and Delinquency Prevention. Available at: http://www.ncjrs.gov/html/ojjdp/nationalreport99/toc.html (accessed November 2007).

Socialstyrelsen (2006a) *Öppenvårdens Former: En nationell kartläggning av öppna insatser I socialtjänstens barn-och ungdomsvård. [National Board of Health and Welfare: A national review of non-placement services within the social services' child and family services]* [online]. Artikelnr 2006-123-29. Available at: www.socialstyrelsen.se (accessed November 2007).

Socialstyrelsen (2006b) *Barn och Unga – Insatser år 2005 [National Board of Health and Welfare, Services for Children and Youth 2005]*. Stockholm: Socialstyrelsen.

Stattin H (unpublished) *Family Relations Scale*. Örebro University.

Sundell K, Hansson K, Andrée-Löfholm C, Olsson T, Gustle L-H & Kadesjö C (submitted) *The Transportability of MST to Sweden: Short-term results from a randomized trial with conduct disorder youth*. Stockholm: Institute for Evidence-based Social Work Practice, The National Board of Health and Welfare.

Sundell K, Vinnerljung B, Andrée-Löfholm C & Humlesjö E (2007) Child protection in Stockholm. A local cohort study of childhood prevalence. *Children and Youth Services Review* **29** 180–192.

ter Bogt T, Schmid H, Gabhainn SN, Fotiou A & Vollebergh W (2006) Exonomic and cultural correlates of cannabis use among mid-adolescents in 31 countries. *Addiction* **101** 241–251.

Timmons-Mitchell J, Bender MB, Kishna MA & Mitchell CC (2006) An independent effectiveness trial of multisystemic therapy with juvenile justice youth. *Journal of Clinical Child & Adolescent Psychology* **35** 227–236.

United Nations Office on Drugs and Crime (2006) *Sweden's National Drug Policy: A review of the evidence.* Vienna: United Nations Office on Drugs and Crime.

Vinnerljung B, Franzen E & Danielsson M (in press) Teenage parenthood among child welfare clients: a Swedish national cohort study of prevalence and odds. *Journal of Adolescence.*

Vogel J (2002) Welfare production, poverty and wealth: a comparitive and longitudinal perspective. In: W Glazer (Ed) *Rich and Poor. Disparities, perceptions, concomitants.* Dordrecht, Netherlands: Kluwer Academic Publishers, pp235–270.

Weightman K & Weightman A (1995) 'Never right, never wrong': child welfare and social work in England and Sweden. *Scandinavian Journal of Social Welfare* **4** 75–84.

CHAPTER 3
Heroin-assisted treatment in Europe: a safe and effective approach

Ambros Uchtenhagen

INTRODUCTION

Prescribing pharmaceutical opiates as a substitute for street heroin started in the USA between 1914 and 1919, and was abolished on the basis of prohibitionist legislation (Musto, 1999). A new approach to maintain opiate addicts on substitution therapy was initiated in the USA in 1963, with the prescription of methadone (Dole & Nyswander, 1965). This approach found, although slowly, increasing acceptance by professionals and policy, and nowadays it is considered to be a cornerstone in the management of opiate dependence (WHO, 1998; UNODC, 2002) and for the prevention and management of HIV/Aids (WHO/UNODC/ UNAIDS, 2004). An important step was to include methadone on the WHO list of essential medicines (Uchtenhagen *et al*, 2004).

The idea of prescribing diamorphine (heroin) survived in the UK, and it continued to be practised by registered doctors, legitimated by the Dangerous Drugs Act of 1920 and the recommendations of the Rolleston Committee of 1926. During the 1960s, the number and characteristics of opiate dependent persons changed considerably, with increasing numbers of young and marginalised patients. Accordingly, regulations were adapted and specialised clinics established in 1968 (15 clinics in London and a few elsewhere). Prescriptions were handed out to patients, and prescribed heroin appeared on the illegal market. Since the late 1970s, heroin was increasingly replaced by methadone as a maintenance drug, following a rapid increase in heroin use (Strang & Gossop, 1996; Strang & Sheridan, 1997; Stimson & Metrebian, 2003). By 1995, heroin prescriptions constituted only 1.7% of all prescriptions of opioids issued to heroin addicts, while 96% of prescriptions were for methadone (Strang & Sheridan, 1997).

During the 1980s, the HIV epidemic led to a reconsideration of maintenance therapies as a public health tool, in order to reduce the number of new infections through contaminated syringes and needles. In the UK, treatment provision moved from a small number of specialists to establishing community-based drug treatment services, with a priority of harm reduction (Raistrick, 1994). Prescribing smokable heroin ('reefers') started in the UK (Marks & Palombella, 1990), and feasibility studies on heroin prescribing were initiated in Australia (Bammer *et al*, 1992;

Bammer, 1993; Bammer, 1995). Throughout Europe, the idea of maintaining heroin addicts on opioids became increasingly acceptable, instead of restricting treatment to 'abstinence-only' approaches. In 2003, there were an estimated 1.6 million opiate dependent persons in the EU member states, including 462,412 patients in substitution treatment (EMCDDA, 2005). The number of countries providing methadone maintenance increased from seven in 1980 to 28 by 2005, and the number of countries providing buprenorphine maintenance rose within a few years to 21. However, the availability of treatment varies considerably between countries (EMCDDA, 2006).

Inevitably, the number of patients who continued heroin injecting while being on methadone, increased as well, and the idea of providing those patients with the 'original drug' invited new experimentation with heroin prescribing. Research projects started in Switzerland in 1994, the Netherlands in 1995, Germany and Spain in 2002, and Canada in 2005. The UK started reconsidering the former practice and set up a similarly controlled and psychosocially assisted type of heroin prescribing as in continental Europe. In all these projects, the target population were heroin addicts for whom other treatments had previously failed. See ***table 1*** for criteria for entry to heroin-assisted treatment (HAT) studies.

PRESENT STATE OF PROVISION

So far, the research projects and their results have led to establishing heroin-assisted maintenance treatment as a routine treatment in Switzerland and in the Netherlands. In the UK, the traditional practice continues for the time being, alongside the new trials of HAT. Below is a summary of the present situation regarding HAT in Europe. The descriptions are based on published documents. The scientific results of the research projects are outlined in the following section.

United Kingdom

By 2002 there were 42 clinics prescribing heroin. They are part of the network of services provided by the National Health Service.

Heroin is prescribed as powder in ampoules for injection, as heroin linctus, heroin tablets and heroin reefers (tobacco cigarettes injected with heroin). The patients receive the ampoules at the pharmacies and inject only initially under visual control. Syringes, needles and containers for used injection material are available from a range of agencies. A minority of patients receive heroin powder (for smoking), linctus or tablets. The daily dose varies between five and 1,500 mg. The average duration of treatment is six years.

A survey in 2001 showed that among 70 doctors who have a licence for prescribing heroin, only 47 used it in practice. The licence is available through the Home Office and only for specialised psychiatrists working in public clinics. It is valid for three years. The obligation to record patients receiving heroin to a central registry was suspended in 1997. Existing guidelines for heroin maintenance are not very detailed. For example, there are no defined indication criteria for the treatment. However, as a rule, patients have tried other treatments before and have an extended career of heroin dependence (Metrebian *et al*, 2002; Stimson & Metrebian, 2003).

A study of patient satisfaction with maintenance treatment on injectable methadone and heroin (n = 104 from one large clinic, 25% on heroin, 75% on methadone) found satisfaction in half of the subjects, but many wanted to change to heroin maintenance or to increase their doses (Sell & Zador, 2004).

In view of an increased need for non-injectable diamorphine for maintenance purposes, a pilot study was made with an intranasal spray, resulting in a slower onset of effects, but effects that were at least as positive as injectable heroin. The patients gave favourable appraisals (Mitchell *et al*, 2006).

Switzerland

Twenty-three clinics are authorised by the Federal Office of Public Health to practise HAT, with a total of 1,389 treatment slots. By the end of 2005, 1,296 patients were enrolled, which represents 11% of all the maintenance treatments in the country (Hosek, 2006). One of the clinics is integrated into a prison and has eight beds. It also accepts heroin dependent inmates from other prisons. All clinics have to comply with a number of obligations regarding management, indication, safety, reporting, and data collection for monitoring. A detailed handbook describes the obligations and the practice rules (BAG, 2000).

After the end of the research project in 1996, the federal government decided to continue HAT as a routine option. New patients could be admitted. Health insurance became obliged to pay for the treatment, except for the ongoing collection of monitoring and research data and for a part of the psychosocial support. Data collection and continued education is paid for by the Federal Office of Public Health, and psychosocial support is partly financed by the communities. The decree to continue HAT after the end of the three-year cohort study, issued by the federal government, was supported in a national referendum in 1999. In 2007, parliament confirmed a revision of the narcotic law, which provides the legal basis for HAT as a routine treatment.

The legal basis for HAT is a parliamentary approved federal decree, valid until 2009. A revision of the narcotic law, as a permanent legal basis, is under way. Diamorphine is registered as a medication for maintenance treatment of opiate dependence.

HAT is conceived as a comprehensive, assessment-based therapy covering all individual social and health problems of patients, and it is not time limited (BAG, 2000). The majority of patients receive injectable heroin, and all injections are made under visual supervision in the clinics. Take-out of injectables is prohibited. Injectable heroin may be combined with oral methadone or also with oral heroin

Table 1: Criteria for entry to HAT studies in four countries

Entry criteria	Switzerland	Netherlands	Germany	Spain
Minimum age (years)	18	25	25	18
Minimum duration of opiate dependence (years)	2	5	5	-
Diagnosis	ICD-10	DSM-IV	ICD-10	ICD-10
Previous treatments	2	Methadone	Any	Any
Health problems and/or social/legal problems	+	+	+	+
Minimum duration of ongoing methadone maintenance	-	12 months (> 30–50 visits last month)	-	-
Minimum dosage in ongoing methadone maintenance	-	> 50–60 mg > 4 weeks	-	-
(Nearly) daily use of heroin	+	+	+	+ (iv)
Minimum duration of registration in the area	-	3 years	12 months	-
Informed consent	+	+	+	+
Consent to be randomised	-	+	+	+
Out of treatment for > six months	-	-	+	-

(retarded and non-retarded tablets). Such combinations are frequently practised, as they allow for a reduction of the daily visits at the clinic so the patients can engage in daytime activities (education, day programmes, jobs). Patients on stable dosages and in a stabilised psychosocial situation may be allowed take-out of oral medications.

Quality assurance has been an important issue from the beginning. An expert committee received all data on side effects and unexpected events, and an electronic exchange on problems and experiences of how to cope with problems among the clinic teams guarantees a rapid and joint reaction. At present, quality management includes:

- a comprehensive handbook on HAT
- a monitoring centre for side effects and unexpected events
- a safety assurance expert group
- continued education for the clinic teams on the basis of observed problems and new research knowledge
- permanent information exchange among teams via email groups.

The Netherlands

A first project was set up in Amsterdam in 1983 with the prescription of injectable morphine to 37 high-risk heroin addicts, resulting in an improvement in mental health, smaller improvements in somatic health, and a reduction of polydrug use. Improvements in housing, employment and criminal involvement were considered to be unsatisfactory. No negative impact on other treatment approaches was observed (Derks & Daansen, 1986).

A randomised controlled study co-prescribing injectable or inhalable heroin in addition to oral methadone, in comparison to oral methadone alone, started in 1995. The inhalable application had to be considered because the majority of Dutch heroin users prefer it over injecting.

The positive outcome of the study led to a parliamentary decision in 2004 to increase the number of treatment slots to 1,000, to be located in 11–15 cities. However, only 300 treatment slots in six cities were realised, mainly due to financial problems. Now there are eight specialist clinics prescribing heroin to about 350 patients. The centres have 25–70 treatment slots each. A further increase is intended, with mainly smaller centres with 25–30 slots. By 2007 the number of patients receiving heroin prescription may have increased to 500–600.

Injectable and inhalable heroin were registered as a substitution drug in the treatment of heroin dependence in December 2006 by the Dutch Registration Authority. HAT is authorised for chronic, treatment-resistant heroin addicts who could not be stabilised satisfactorily in a methadone maintenance programme.

New patients can be admitted. The indication criteria are practically unchanged: DSM-IV diagnosis of heroin dependence, continued heroin use during methadone maintenance treatment and severe social and health deficits. However, as during the trial, the period for receiving heroin was restricted to 12 months. Very recently (2007) HAT became acknowledged as a regular treatment under special conditions.

Germany

For many years, German authorities (and many professionals) were sceptical towards maintenance treatments, and methadone maintenance suffered from restrictive regulations. A change in government allowed for a change in drug policy, preparing the ground for an expansion and diversification of maintenance treatments.

The randomised study on HAT started in 2002 and ended in 2005. The target populations were heroin addicts who had not been in treatment for at least 12 months, and others who continued to use heroin regularly during methadone maintenance treatment. Clinics were set up in seven cities and a total of 1,032 patients were enrolled in the programme.

The present situation is a problematic one. The Registration Authority (Bundesinstitut für Arzneimittel und Medizinprodukte BfArM) is in favour of a continuation of HAT on a routine basis, but parliament could not agree on providing the necessary new legal basis for a continuation. An initiative to create such a legal basis was refused by the ruling coalition in November 2006 (Bundesministerium für Gesundheit, 2006). However, it was agreed that the treatment programme established for the trial could continue until the end of June 2007. It remained unknown if patients enrolled at the clinics will receive HAT after that date. This difficult situation led to a new initiative to adapt the law by experts and representatives of the states (Bundesländer).

Finally, a decision to continue the programme was announced by Volker Kauder (the leader of the Christian Democratic Union parliamentary group), in February 2007 (FAZ, 2007, *Der Spiegel*, 2007). The patients who are enrolled in the HAT in seven cities are allowed to continue their treatment, but for the time being diamorphine will not be registered as a medicine for maintenance treatment, and a revision of narcotic law is not supported. It seems that new patients may be admitted in the future (*Der Spiegel*, 2007).

Spain

Initiatives to set up trials with diamorphine were taken in two of the autonomous regions: in Andalusia and in Catalonia. During 2000–2001, these initiatives were discussed in the Central Agency for Drug Addiction (Plan Nacional sobre Drogas). The authorities concluded to allow the trials with the expectation to generate new scientific insight and to get the approval of the Drug and Pharmaceutical Control Office for a registration of diamorphine. A clinical trial on heroin maintenance therapy was authorised in 2001 (Bosch, 2001).

A randomised controlled trial started in Granada in 2003 and was completed in 2004. The Council of Andalusia requested continued compassionate use for the 36 patients who participated in their clinical trial. The Spanish Agency for Medicine (an organisation under the Ministry of Health) gave its consent and authorised these patients to receive heroin for life. Theoretically, every Spanish doctor could request compassionate use on the basis of the Granada research, but none had done so until 2006 (Mendez & De Benito, 2006).

The autonomous governments of the Basque country and Andalusia (among others) openly support the heroin prescription. They do not wish to evaluate their efficacy and feasibility again (which are widely proven), but their effectiveness (ie.

pilot programmes that allow development of knowledge on how, for whom and in what conditions the heroin should be prescribed). However, the Spanish Ministry of Health refuses all type of studies that are not a randomised controlled trial (Oviedo-Joekes, 2006).

Recently, the Council of Andalusia has requested the extension of heroin-assisted treatment for patients who need it for compassionate use on a case-by-case basis. The Council has developed a protocol which, beginning in February 2007, makes it possible to treat long-term addicts who have tried getting off drugs with methadone and failed, and have infectious diseases, such as Aids or viral hepatitis, and psychiatric problems. The Council will begin with addicts in Granada, where they have the infrastructure in place, and expect to enrol about 50 heroin addicts. The Ministry's decision is pending at the time of writing (Mendez & De Benito, 2006).

RESEARCH RESULTS

Much research has been carried out on HAT since 1994. A review of the former 'historical' experiments with heroin and morphine prescribing was published by Annie Mino (Mino, 1990) and the specific British experience has been described by Stimson and Oppenheimer (1982). This section will focus on the more recent research.

The Swiss studies

The design of the Swiss project, the first in this series, was a prospective observational cohort study. It enabled testing of the feasibility, safety and effects of the treatment programme as a whole, but was not able to identify the role of diamorphine in producing these effects, because there was no control group. An international expert group examined the protocol, implementation and results of the Swiss study on behalf of World Health Organisation. It confirmed the findings, but recommended that further studies should follow a randomisation design in order to determine the value of prescribing diamorphine in comparison to other substances (Ali *et al*, 1998).

In addition, it was advisable to look at the possible consequences of HAT on the treatment system as a whole, and to examine the value and costs of such an approach for reducing opiate-related problems.

A first comprehensive report on the findings from the study period 1994–1996 was published as a volume (Uchtenhagen *et al*, 1999), and the economic analysis in a second volume (Gutzwiller & Steffen, 2000). A series of journal articles followed.

The cohort study included 1,035 outpatients with complete admission data, out of 1,151 admissions (the difference is due to missing data), and 16 inpatients in a prison-based unit. For criminological analysis, the police record of 604 patients and conviction records of 561 patients was used.

The overall design was a prospective observational cohort study. Sub-studies included:

- a randomised controlled trial of HAT versus any other treatment while staying on a waiting list for the heroin programme (Perneger *et al*, 1998)
- a double-blind randomised trial with crossover design using injectable heroin versus injectable morphine (Hämmig, 1997)
- a randomised trial testing injectable heroin versus injectable methadone and injectable morphine (Ladewig *et al*, 1997)
- a study on injectable methadone (Uehlinger *et al*, 1996)
- pharmacological studies: pharmacodynamics and –kinetics of diacetylmorphine, including various application forms (injectable, smokable, inhalable, oral slow-release, suppositories) (Brenneisen *et al*, 1997)
- toxicology of diacetylmorphine including side effects (Hämmig, 1997; Ladewig *et al*, 1997; Schmied, 1997; Uehlinger *et al*, 1996)
- studies on the criminal involvement of patients in HAT (Rabasa & Killias, 1996; Killias *et al*, 1999)
- economic study on costs and cost benefit of HAT (Rossier-Affolter *et al*, Frei *et al*, in Gutzwiller & Steffen, 2000).

The main substance-related results were:

- frequent histaminic-like reactions from intravenous morphine (morphine correctly identified in double-blind study on the basis of side effects with low acceptance by patients and a high dropout rate (Hämmig 1997)
- frequent local pain at injection site from intravenous methadone, low acceptance by patients and high dropout rates (Uehlinger *et al*, 1996; Ladewig *et al*, 1997)
- inter-individual differences in the pharmacodynamics and –kinetics of diacetylmorphine, including distribution volume and clearance, in sweat and hair concentrations (independent of dosage); low bio-availability of heroin cigarettes; rush and high effects with oral preparations (slow-release tablets and capsules) and suppositories, although no heroin or its metabolite was found in the bloodstream (Brenneisen *et al*, 1997)
- mean daily dose of heroin was 491.7 mg (from 498,073 days of consumption), stable doses reached after a maximum of six months, slight decrease in dosage over 18 months in treatment (Uchtenhagen *et al*, 1999).

The main patient-related results (described in Uchtenhagen *et al*, 1999) were:

- retention rates were 89% over six months; 69% over 18 months
- somatic health increased significantly, especially in regard to general health, nutritional status and injection-related skin diseases
- new infections (HIV, hepatitis) occurred in a few cases, mainly during the first few months (Steffen *et al*, 2001a)
- pregnancies (n = 12) and birth-giving during HAT went without complications, no indications of developmental defects in the babies (Geistlich, 1996)

- psychiatric conditions (depression, anxiety disorders, delusional disorders) improved significantly
- significant reduction of illicit heroin use (daily use from 81% to 6% after six and 18 months), cocaine use (daily use from 29% to 3% at six months and 2% at 18 months), benzodiazepine use (daily use from 19% to 2% at six and 18 months); no reduction of cannabis and alcohol use (self-report and urine controls except for illicit heroin) (Blättler *et al*, 2002)
- significant improvements in social status (housing situation, employment status, financial situation)
- significant reduction of contacts with drug users and the drug scene, significant reduction in needle sharing (Steffen *et al*, 2001b)
- significant reduction of illegal income and criminal activities according to self-report (Rabasa & Killias, 1996) and police records (Killias *et al*, 1999).

The main service-related results were (Uchtenhagen *et al*, 1999):

- feasibility: 23 clinics were established (two in polyvalent clinics that also provided methadone maintenance treatment, one located in a prison)
- acceptance: after initial neighbourhood problems, clinics were well tolerated by police forces and the general population
- safety: no diversion of prescribed diamorphine to the illegal market, no overdose deaths from prescribed substances, no major aggression towards staff
- staff: competent and dedicated staff were recruited, organising their own mail groups for rapid exchange of experience.

The main economic results were (Rossier-Affolter, 2000; Frei *et al*, 2000):

- lower costs compared to imprisonment, higher costs compared to methadone maintenance treatment (due to higher cost for staffing clinics daily, including weekends and holidays)
- calculated daily benefits were almost double the daily costs (SFr. 95.50 compared to 51.17 per patient per day).

A sub-study with randomised design was carried out with an experimental group (n = 27) and a waiting list control group (who received conventional treatment, mostly methadone maintenance, n = 21). It showed significant differences after six months in daily illicit heroin consumption, mental health, social functioning, illegal income and delinquency in favour of the experimental group. There were no benefits in terms of somatic health, housing, work and use of other drugs. Unexpectedly, only nine control subjects entered the heroin maintenance programme at follow-up (Perneger *et al*, 1998).

A special study on the utilisation of the heroin clinics and on the characteristics of all admissions and discharges between 1994 and 2001 (n = 2,199) came to the following conclusions (Gschwend *et al*, 2003):

- the number enrolled in HAT increased almost constantly over the period of the study
- 10% of patients entered treatment more than once
- the average age of new admissions increased from 30 to 35 years, while the rate of female patients decreased from 33% to 25%
- patients remained in HAT on average for 3.7 years (median 2.8 years)
- 1,233 patients were discharged at least once during these years (24% within the first four months, 46% remained between four months and two years, and 30% longer than three years); early discharges decreased significantly over time.

All patients admitted to HAT between January 1994 and December 2000 (n = 2,166 cases, corresponding to1,969 patients) were followed up (Rehm *et al*, 2001):

- by December 2000, a total of 1,071 patients was discharged; 90 patients twice and seven three times
- among those who were discharged, there was a higher rate of HIV sero-positivity (21% versus 13%)
- retention was found to be relatively high (86% for three months, 70% for 12 months, 50% for two to five years and 34% for five years and longer)
- 59% of discharged patients started another treatment after discharge (22% started drug free treatment, 37% methadone maintenance)
- the proportion of those switching to drug free treatment increased with the length of stay in a heroin-assisted programme (29% of discharges after three years)
- discharge due to lack of compliance happened in 15% of discharges, mostly during the first months after entering treatment.

Analysis of three data sets showed a reduction in delinquency during the first six months in treatment. Self-report data from a subgroup of patients entering HAT after 1 April 1995, of which the first follow-up interviews six months after entry were done before 31 May 1996, were analysed for involvement in criminal activities (n = 248, Rabasa & Killias, 1996). They showed significant reductions in thefts, robbery, burglary and drug trafficking in the first six months after entering treatment (all $p < 0.0001$). An analysis of police records (n = 604) also showed a significant reduction in the mean incidence of robbery during the first six months after treatment entry (from 1.92 to 0.16 events) and mean victimisation rates for robbery during the first six months in treatment were reduced from 0.273 to 0.086 events (Killias *et al*, 1999).

The complete cohort entering heroin-assisted treatment between 1 January 1994, and 1 March 1995 (n = 366) was followed up for six years (Güttinger *et al*, 2003; Gschwend *et al*, 2003):

- 43 patients (11.7%) had died during the six years; five during treatment, the rest after leaving treatment
- 148 of the survivors were still in HAT (n = 132 available for interviews), 175 had left treatment without re-entering (n = 112 available for interviews)

- the average age was around 36 years in both groups (still in treatment and out of treatment), and in both genders
- there was a significant reduction in illegal incomes since entry to treatment in both groups, and a significant increase in dependence on welfare and other sources in the treatment group, not in the group out-of-treatment (see **table 2**)
- daily use of non-prescribed heroin, of cocaine and of benzodiazepines had decreased significantly in both groups (see **table 3**, overleaf). However, the rate of daily illicit heroin use at follow-up was lower in the treatment group than in the out-of-treatment group (3.8% versus 18.9%)
- the rate of integration into the labour market remained unsatisfactory (34% unemployment in both groups), as well as the building up of social contacts outside the drug using community (21.2% and 26.1% respectively have no close friends at all, 24.8% and 18.7% have numerous weekly contacts with currently addicted friends).

Table 2: Comparing social status of patients in HAT (n = 132) and ex-patients (n = 112), at entry and after six years (from Güttinger *et al*, 2003)

Variable	A Patients at entry	B Patients at six years	C Ex-patients at entry	D Ex-patients at six years	Significant B-D md = 0
Homelessness	9.8%	1.5%	8.0%	0.9%	ns*
Unemployed	31.1%	34.1%	29.5%	33.9%	ns**
Illegal income	53.0%	9.8%	42.2%	11.6%	ns***
Social welfare	19.1%	39.7%	23.4%	31.5%	ns****

md = missing data   *Fisher's exact test   **$\chi^2 = 0.0$ ***$\chi^2 = 0.2$ ****$\chi^2 = 1.8$

Table 3: Comparing daily use of drugs by patients in HAT (n = 132) and ex-patients (n = 112), at entry and after six years (from Güttinger *et al*, 2003)

Substance	A Patients at entry	B Patients at six years	C Ex-patients at entry	D Ex-patients at six years	Significant B-D md = 2
Illicit heroin	8.7%	3.8%	76.1%	18.9%	<0.001*
Cocaine	27.5%	5.3%	30.8%	9.8%	ns
Benzodiazepine	18.8%	4.5%	16.3%	3.6%	ns
Cannabis	30.5%	34.4%	33.3%	35.7%	ns

md = missing data   *$\chi^2 = 14.3$, degrees of freedom = 2

An analysis of mortality in HAT over a seven-year period from 1994 to 2000 found 49 fatalities during treatment and within one month from discharge (a period which constituted a total of 4,600 person-years). The crude number of deaths per year varies from 0.0273 (1995) to 0.0063 deaths per person-years in treatment (2000). The standard mortality rate between 1994 and 2000 is 9.7 (95% CI 7.3–12.8), which is low compared to death rates of heroin users out of treatment estimated to be 2.5–3%. The main causes of death (according to death certificates and coded according to ICD-10) were HIV-related (34.7% of deaths), accidents (18.4%) and suicide (16.3%). Prescribed heroin was not causally implicated in any of the deaths (Rehm *et al*, 2005).

Side effects of prescribed diamorphine were documented routinely in the HeGeBe Monitor, and a special study focused on patients' complaints in a random sample of programme participants (n = 127 out of 1,061). The most frequently named immediate symptoms after injection concerned skin itching (66.9%), profuse sweating (64.2%), and reddening of skin at injection site (62.8%); among the less frequent complaints were nausea (29.3%), headache (22.0%), and vomiting (18.5%). During the last seven days, potentially more serious symptoms are memory problems (45.6%), problems with urinating (37.1%), pain in the cardiac region (21.0%), numbness in arms or legs (20.7%), and epileptic seizures (5.9%) (Dürsteler-McFarland *et al*, 2005). Two problems became obvious during the trial: the high rate of psychiatric co-morbidity, necessitating an improved assessment and care for these patients, and the presence of a group who were unable to reduce their cocaine use during HAT.

Screening of 85 consecutive new admissions to 17 clinics with the SKID (the German version of structured clinical interview for DSM-IV) showed that 86% had a lifetime prevalence of at least one axis-I or axis-II disorder (personality disorders 58%, affective disorders 55%, anxiety disorders 26% [Frei & Rehm, 2002a]). These rates of co-morbidity were higher than those found in 16 other studies on the prevalence of co-occurring psychiatric disorders in opiate dependent persons (Frei & Rehm, 2002b). This may indicate that co-morbid patients fail more frequently in other treatments, are overrepresented in those applying for HAT, and respond better to HAT.

In view of the cocaine problem, a review of the international literature on treatment approaches for cocaine dependence was carried out and published on the internet (Stohler *et al*, 2006). Also, a randomised controlled study of methylphenidate versus placebo, with or without cognitive behavioural therapy in both groups, in addition to regular psychosocial care, was carried out. This did not find outcome differences between methylphenidate and placebo, nor between CBT and regular psychosocial care (Dürsteler-McFarland *et al*, 2006).

Studies on treatment quality included a detailed comparison of results from the 23 clinics, and also studies on patient satisfaction and quality of life. The type of treatment termination for all new admissions from January 2001 to February 2004 (n = 948) was examined. The findings included (Frick *et al*, 2006a):

- treatment centres showed remarkable differences in the ratio of unwanted terminations
- the differences were not due to patient characteristics
- an important factor was the difference in therapeutic strategies between centres
- overall, the outcomes were similar to those in the original cohort study of 1994–1996; the study found no reduction in positive findings when moving from the original scientific study to routine practice.

A study on patient satisfaction compared the subjective opinions of patients on injectable heroin with patients on oral heroin (immediate release and slow release tablets) and included all patients on injectable diamorphine in 2003 (n = 1,200) and all patients on oral diamorphine in 2004–2005 (n = 365). The findings show (Frick *et al*, 2006b):

- good satisfaction on average, with the exception of a desire for a more personal care, and dissatisfaction with bureaucracy, job opportunities and sex life
- only marginal differences between treatment groups, excepting slightly better satisfaction with the oral preparations
- the satisfaction profile is stable over time (almost identical at entry, at six and 12 months).

The Dutch trials

In contrast to, and building upon the results of the Swiss cohort study, experimentation with HAT in the Netherlands used a randomisation design with two experimental groups (intravenous heroin and inhalable heroin as an adjunct to oral methadone) and two control groups (both on oral methadone alone). The main objective was to test if supervised medical prescription of heroin can successfully treat addicts who do not sufficiently benefit from methadone maintenance treatment.

For the inhalation group, who used the 'chasing the dragon' technique, a special preparation had to be developed and manufactured, to increase the bio-availability. The sachets contain a mixture (3:1) of diacetylmorphine base and caffeine (Hendriks *et al*, 2001; Klous *et al*, 2004).

Trial participants were recruited from existing methadone maintenance programmes, including those who were attending their programme regularly and receiving at least 50 mg (inhaling trial) or 60 mg (injecting trial) of methadone per day. Recruitment of patients was easier for the inhaler group; out of 517 addicts screened for eligibility, the group resulted in 375 patients. The injector group recruited 174 patients out of 254 screened for eligibility. The overall number of participants in the trials was 549, 117 receiving inhalable heroin, 76 receiving injectable heroin, 237 randomised into the control groups and 119 into a comparison group starting out with oral methadone and transferred to inhalable heroin after 12 months. Demographic, health and drug use variables showed no significant differences among groups, except a tendency towards a higher rate of previous overdose and suicide events in the injector group (van den Brink *et al*, 2003).

The co-prescription of heroin in the two experimental groups lasted for 12 months. The maximum dose of heroin was 1,000 mg per day, of oral methadone in the experimental groups, and in the control group 150 mg per day. After termination of the co-prescription of heroin, all patients received oral methadone only. All groups were provided with ancillary standard psychosocial treatment (van den Brink *et al*, 2003; Blanken *et al*, 2005).

Every two months, the patients were assessed medically and interviewed by independent research assistants using the European Addiction Severity Index, the Health Symptoms Scale of the Maudsley Addiction Profile and the Symptom Checklist SCL-90. At baseline and after 12 months, psychiatric diagnosis was assessed using the Composite International Diagnostic Interview. Self-reported substance use data were validated against urinalysis and police registers and showed good agreement between these records (van den Brink *et al*, 2003).

Outcome was measured with a pre specified dichotomous, multi-domain index. Treatment response was defined as (Blanken *et al*, 2005):

- a health improvement of at least 40% after 12 months in treatment, in at least one health domain (somatic health, mental health, social health)
- no serious deterioration of 40% or over, in any of the other outcome domains
- no substantial increase (> 6 days per month) in cocaine or amphetamine use.

Completion rates were high in all the groups, with 93–94% of 12-month follow-up data from randomised patients. Seven per cent of addicts randomised into the experimental groups never started treatment, and 6% were discharged from heroin treatment due to repeated violation of house rules (van den Brink *et al*, 2003). Treatment response was significantly (p = 0.0001) higher in the experimental groups – 51.8% of them showed a positive response to treatment (95% confidence interval 44.7–58.9%) compared to 28.7% of the control group (95% confidence interval 22.9–34.5%). The intention-to-treat analysis showed a higher response rate in the injector group (56%) compared to the inhaler group (50%). Results from those who completed the study were similar to those from the intention-to-treat analysis (see ***table 4***). Treatment responders showed clinically relevant improvements in all outcome domains (van den Brink *et al*, 2003). The only patient characteristic predicting outcome, according to a multiple logistic regression analysis, was past abstinence-oriented treatment (Blanken *et al*, 2005).

Table 4: Comparing treatment response rates in heroin groups and control groups (based on data from van den Brink *et al*, 2003)

Treatment response rate	Inhalers		Injectors	
	Methadone plus heroin (n = 117)	Methadone only (n = 139)	Methadone plus heroin (n = 76)	Methadone only (n = 98)
Intention-to-treat	50%	27%	56%	31%
Completers only	51%	28%	58%	39%
Sustained response	22%	4%	25%	12%

Eighty-two per cent of the responders in the experimental groups deteriorated substantially during the two months following cessation of heroin co-prescription, and the mean outcome scores returned to those before entering the programme (van den Brink *et al*, 2003). No serious adverse events were related to the discontinuation of co-prescribing heroin in the injectable or inhalable application (CCBH, 2002).

Serious adverse events were recorded in almost 10% of the intent-to-treat population in all groups. Three events were probably related to the study medication: one overdose death, one non-fatal overdose and one non-fatal accident under the influence of heroin and cocaine (van den Brink *et al*, 2003). Serious adverse events were comparable in the heroin and control groups (CCBH, 2002).

There were some methodological limitations of the trials, including the absence of a double-blind design, using only self-report data (however in line with police data and urinalysis regarding cocaine use) and a difference in settings between the treatment groups (van den Brink *et al*, 2003).

A cost utility study found that co-prescription of heroin was associated with 0.058 more quality adjusted life years (QALYs) per patient per year (95% confidence interval 0.016 to 0.099), and a saving of €12,793 per patient per year. The higher programme costs for the co-prescription of heroin were compensated by lower costs of law enforcement and damage to victims of crime. Completion of treatment was found to be essential for cost-effectiveness (Dijkgraaf *et al*, 2005).

The conclusions of the trials were (CCBH, 2002):

■ the study was conducted and analysed successfully
■ supervised co-prescription of heroin to chronic, treatment-resistant heroin dependent and methadone treated patients is more effective than continuation of methadone alone
■ supervised co-prescription of heroin to chronic, treatment-resistant heroin dependent and methadone treated patients yield clinically relevant health benefits

- the beneficial effects of supervised co-prescription of heroin are linked to the continuation of treatment
- supervised co-prescription of heroin is practicable with no excess of serious medical adverse events and with a limited number of controllable public order problems
- the costs of the prescription of heroin are dependent on the type of treatment implementation.

The researchers concluded that, *'supervised co-prescription of heroin is feasible, more effective and probably as safe as methadone alone in reducing the many physical, mental and social problems of treatment resistant heroin addicts'* (van den Brink *et al*, 2003).

After four years, by February 2007, about 60% of those who received heroin had left the programme, 10–20% switching to methadone maintenance with higher dosages, or to drug-free treatment. Almost 90% of those remaining in the programme show very good functioning in all domains (van den Brink, 2007).

The German trials
The German trials had three main tasks:

- a clinical pharmacological trial to test the efficacy of HAT in comparison to methadone maintenance treatment
- an examination of potential indication criteria for HAT (which groups profit most?)
- an investigation of feasibility and efficacy of the various medical and psychosocial treatment elements.

The design was a randomised multi-centre study with two target groups: methadone patients who continue to inject heroin, and heroin addicts who had been out of treatment for at least 12 months. For each target group, comparisons were made between heroin and methadone and between psycho-education and case management with motivational interviewing.

The study was divided into two phases:

- **phase 1:** in the first 12 months, a stratified 4 x 2 randomised controlled trial in order to examine the effects of heroin prescribing as compared to methadone prescribing under similar setting conditions
- **phase 2:** follow-up study over 12 months in order to investigate the long-term effects in the experimental group; a randomly selected group of control patients receives heroin prescription, the rest leave the study and are offered regular treatment.

Special studies addressed criminological aspects, economical aspects, neuropsychological issues, psychosocial interventions, acceptability and implementation of the project.

Phase 1

There were 1,032 heroin addicts recruited into the study and randomised into the heroin group and methadone group. All received an intensive psychosocial care programme. Average daily dose was 442 mg, after the induction phase dosage was stable.

Outcome criteria were:

- an improvement in somatic or mental health of at least 20%
- a major reduction of street heroin use and no increase in cocaine consumption.

Retention during 12 months was 67% in the heroin group, 39% in the methadone group (this low retention may be because many potential patients did not agree to be randomised into the methadone group).

The findings showed better results for the heroin group in regard to both outcome criteria: 80% of patients in the heroin group had health improvements, compared to 74% of patients in the methadone group. The reduction of street heroin use was found in 69.1% of patients in the heroin group and in 55.2% of the methadone group. Patients responding positively on both criteria were 57.3% in the heroin group and 44.8% in the methadone group. The differences were statistically significant. The improvements from HAT were equal for both target groups (non-compliant methadone patients, people out of treatment) and for both types of psychosocial intervention (psycho-education, case management) (Naber & Haasen, 2006).

Phase 2

The second phase of the study recruited 434 patients, 344 from the phase 1 heroin group and 90 from the phase 1 methadone group. All patients were prescribed injectable heroin. The average daily dose was 452 mg.

Of all patients initially randomised into the heroin group (n = 515), the retention rate over 24 months was 55%. The mortality rate was 1%, no fatalities occurred from prescribed substances.

The patients of the crossover group, who switched from the methadone to heroin showed similar improvements to patients who received HAT in phase 1. No significant differences could be found at the end of phase 2 between the crossover group and the original heroin group (see **table 5**).

Table 5: Comparing mean days of substance use in heroin group and in the group switching from methadone to heroin after phase 1 (based on self-report data from Naber & Haasen, 2006)

Substance use (days per last 30 days)	At entry	At six months	At 12 months	At 18 months	At 24 months
Heroin group: illicit heroin	23	1	1	1	1
Heroin group: cocaine	9	5	4	4	3
Switcher group: illicit heroin	22	8	9	2	1
Switcher group: cocaine	8	7	6	3	2

Stabilisation and/or improvements were documented in the health status and also in the social status of patients. The overall employment rate increased by 11% and reached 27% (those who were considered to be fit for work reached an employment rate of 43%). Employment rates differed substantially between cities: after two years of HAT, the highest rates are documented from Karlsruhe (73.3%) and Munich (47.6%), while the lowest are from Hanover (16.2%) and Bonn (20.0%). However, employment was the main source of income in only 12.4%, while unemployment benefit was the main source in 44.8%.

Case management had a slightly better acceptance in comparison to psycho-education, but psycho-education was associated with better outcomes (Haasen, 2006).

Special studies on the delinquency of study participants produced the following results:

- a quantitative study was based on self-report data (n = 1,015) and police data (n = 825); crime involvement before entering the project was high, self-report data indicating an even higher involvement than police data

- reduction of criminal involvement was significantly higher in the heroin group (from 55% before entry to 39% after 12 months) than in the methadone group (from 58% to 55%); in the heroin group, violent crime was reduced by 67%, shoplifting by 40%; the crime reduction was strongest during phase 1, but continued during phase 2, indicating a stabilisation process regarding delinquency (Löbmann, 2006)

- a qualitative study was based on face-to-face interviews; the findings highlighted, among other issues, that most of the patients stopped their former participation in small-scale drug dealing; crime reductions also occurred in patients with especially heavy former crime involvement; the main reasons for the reductions were due to the lower need to purchase heroin, having less contact with active users and the fear of probationers of a revocation of suspended prison sentences (Kreutzer & Köllisch, 2006).

An economic study calculated the costs and the tangible benefits and conducted a cost utility analysis, based on data of the complete cohort n = 1,015 (Graf von der Schulenburg & Claes, 2006). This produced the data presented in ***table 6*** below.

Table 6: Cost utility analysis

Cost category	Heroin	Methadone
Average cost/patient/year (euro)	18,060	6,147
Psychosocial care costs	1,928	1,928
Change in health costs	-3,777	-1,134
Change in law enforcement costs	-3,251	+752
Change in prison costs	-1,209	-826
Change in court costs	+2,342	+3,519
Benefit from employment	163	187
Change in total costs/patient/year	+5,966	-2,069
Cost per additional QALY	154.907	170.835

A neuro-psychological study was based on a range of cognitive tests that are used in performance psychology and examinations of driving ability. The results were (Heinemann, 2006):

- patients in both groups (heroin and methadone) showed performance deficits in comparison to population studies; 84% of persons from the same age population would show a better performance
- deficits concerned mostly concentration, attention span and consolidating learned contents into long-term memory
- no significant differences in cognitive functioning between the heroin and the methadone group
- the ability to drive a motor vehicle is not excluded, but depends on a range of factors (including use of non-prescribed substances, stable dosage, waiting at least one hour after injection)
- reduced ability to cope with situations where a balance has to be kept and head positions are frequently changed.

A special study compared the two types of psychosocial care (type 1 = drug counselling with psycho-education, type 2 = case management with motivational interviewing), with the following results (Kuhn *et al*, 2006):

- good satisfaction of professional staff providing psychosocial care with both types, with the manuals and the training (client–staff ratio = 25:1)
- 23% of randomised patients did not accept type 1, 20% did not accept type 2
- overall retention in psychosocial care was 43% over 12 months

- case management took more staff time, due to contacts with other institutions, relatives etc
- no differences between types 1 and 2 in regard to outcome criteria and goal attainment
- type 1 had especially good outcomes in dual diagnosis patients
- type 2 has best outcomes when it was applied completely and was well structured
- in both types, continuous care and intensive contact allow for a good outcome.

The implementation study came to the following conclusions (Buhk *et al*, 2006):

- the reduced incidence of heroin dependence does not (yet) reduce the need for treatment
- HAT is well accepted, the indication criteria are feasible and addicts can be recruited (an estimated 3–4% of heroin addicts, which amounts to 3,600–9,500 potential patients for HAT)
- public acceptance of the project has increased, as well as networking with other medical and social services
- the positive effects of HAT are likely to be continued if it is implemented as a routine treatment
- no negative impact on other treatment approaches
- consensus among staff, patients and external experts to establish HAT as a routine treatment.

The Spanish trial

The Spanish trial is a comparative, randomised and open study on the difference between a diversified prescription use of opioid agonist backed by intravenous diacetylmorphine and the prescription of oral methadone – both treatments administered as individualised procedures following appropriate protocols and with medical and psychosocial support – through a nine-month period for the treatment of opiate dependent patients who have failed under previous treatments. This is an experimental drug prescription programme in Andalusia (PEPSA).

The main objective is to show that the individualised, diversified and protocolised prescription of opioid agonist backed by intravenous diacetylmorphine is more efficient than the prescription of oral methadone – both done with appropriate medical and psychosocial support – in improving the mental and physical health and the social integration of opiate addicts who take drugs by intravenous injection, when the addicts are, according to criteria of the CIE-10, users of multiple drugs who have serious psychological, medical, sanitary problems, with economic needs who are socially excluded and who have previously failed in at least two available standard treatments (Fernandez *et al*, 2001).

The project started in 2003 and lasted for nine months. It took place in the city of Granada. The experimental group was provided:

- oral methadone: individual dosage between 20 and 60mg/day
- intravenous diacetylmorphine: individual dosage between 100 and 500 mg/day
- medical programme of medical-psychosocial support.

The control group was provided:

- oral methadone: individual dosage between 50 and 150mg/day
- medical programme of medical-psychosocial support.

Recruitment did not meet the planned number of patients (120 in each group). The project recruited 62 heroin addicts responding to the entry criteria, 31 into each group. Eighteen patients left the treatment during the trial period. Fifty patients were included in the final analysis (March *et al*, 2006).

The experimental group received injectable heroin twice a day, plus oral methadone, for nine months. The control group received oral methadone once a day. The two groups received an equivalent opioid dosage. The average heroin dose was 274.5mg/day (range 15–600mg) and an average methadone dose in the experimental group was 42.7mg/day (range 18–124mg). The average methadone dose in the control group was 105mg/day (range 40–180mg). Comprehensive clinical, psychological, social, and legal support was given to both groups (March *et al*, 2006).

The results showed significantly better improvements in the heroin group than in the methadone group:

- physical health improvements were 2.5 times higher in the heroin group
- reduction of risk behaviour for blood-borne infectious diseases was 1.6 times higher in the heroin group
- reduction of days with drug-related problems was 2.1 times higher in the heroin group
- reduction in crime involvement was 3.2 times higher in the heroin group.

No differences between the groups were found in other psychosocial variables. Severe adverse events were observed in both groups, seven in each, mainly due to overdose through polydrug use. One death in the control group was due to an injected overdose of heroin and cocaine.

It was concluded that prescription of injectable heroin provides a viable alternative treatment for patients who have not improved with other approaches (March *et al*, 2006). By 2006, 25 out of 36 patients of the heroin group continued to receive heroin on the basis of compassionate use (Mendez & De Benito, 2006). In order to improve care for the non-injecting heroin addicts, a new study was designed in 2006 testing the applicability of an administration of diamorphine tablets (González, 2006).

A SUMMARY OF RESULTS

Based on the findings of these studies, the following conclusions can be made on the state of European research on HAT:

Feasibility

HAT can be implemented with good acceptance by patients, by law enforcement authorities and, in the case of referenda, by the general public.

Safety

HAT can be implemented without undue risks for patients, staff and public order. Under the conditions of the studies discussed in this chapter, no diversion of prescribed substances to the illicit market and no fatal overdose from prescribed heroin could be found. Adverse effects occur, as in other substitution treatments, but can be well managed.

Treatment effects

All treatment effects indicate an improvement in physical and mental health, a reduction of risk-taking behaviour, a reduction of crime involvement and some improvement in social integration (although the stigma of heroin dependence is a major obstacle). Significant positive effects are documented from all studies, at different time points (see *table 7*, opposite).

Patient satisfaction

Satisfaction is generally high. Complaints tend to concern organisational details, not the treatment or the substance itself.

Impact on other treatment approaches

No negative effects on other treatment approaches were observed. Where data are available, they show an overall increase in treatment availability, utilisation and quality for heroin addicts during the implementation of HAT. Other treatment approaches benefit from this additional therapeutic option for especially chronic and problematic heroin users.

Impact on prevention

A major concern was that more experimentation with heroin use could be incited as the substance gains the image of a prescribable medication. The Swiss experience shows the opposite effects. The incidence rates for starting heroin use have decreased continuously since HAT was implemented (Nordt & Stohler, 2006). The image of heroin and especially of the heroin user has become less attractive (von Aarburg & Stauffacher, 2005) and indirect indicators suggest a decrease in both opiate overdose deaths (BAG, 2005) and in drug-related crime (BAP, 2002) since 1991 of 50%.

Table 7: Comparing selected outcomes over time across studies (significant improvements)

Domain	6 months	9 months	12 months	18 months	24 months	6 years (patients still in treatment)	6 years (ex-patients)
Health improvements	CH	E	CH, BRD, NL	CH	BRD		
Reduction in illicit heroin use	CH, BRD	E	CH, BRD, NL	CH	BRD	CH	CH
Increased employment	CH		CH, BRD	CH	BRD		
Reduction in crime	CH, BRD	E	CH, BRD, NL	CH	BRD	CH	CH

Key: CH = Switzerland, BRD = Germany, E = Spain, NL = the Netherlands

Impact on public health and public order

HAT reduces the need for medical care in patients. It reduces the risk for blood-borne infectious disease and their transmission to others. It reduces the role of heroin addicts in recruiting new addicts by reducing their involvement in drug trafficking. It reduces the crime involvement of patients under HAT, and the nuisance caused to the public in general.

PERSPECTIVES FOR THE FUTURE

The scientific basis for an assessment of HAT is increasing and goes beyond the Cochrane review of 2006 (Ferri *et al*, 2003). The basis includes large randomised controlled studies as well as large observational cohort studies. The common characteristics of these programmes are:

- a restriction to treating heroin addicts for whom other treatments have failed
- restrictive controls over the production, storage, prescribing and intake of heroin
- availability of well-trained, professional staff
- a well-developed and diversified treatment system
- additional resources (not diverted from other treatment approaches).

The political acceptance of HAT depends largely on the willingness to take the scientific evidence into consideration. Opposition against substitution treatment for opioid dependence in general and against HAT specifically is mostly based on an 'abstinence-only' ideology, which has failed to provide adequate coverage of treatment needs. Without good coverage of treatment, the impact on public health and public order levels cannot become effective.

HAT is not supposed to replace other treatment approaches, especially because risks and costs are higher in comparison to other replacement therapies. Its contribution to the adequate coverage of treatment needs is not a quantitative one (the estimated coverage rates are between 0.3% in Germany and 4.3% in Switzerland, and it constitutes between about 0.5% in Germany and 6.4% in Switzerland of all heroin addicts in treatment). It is rather a qualitative one – to take care of a high-risk group of chronic, medically and socially problematic heroin addicts who were insufficiently served by other treatments.

A need for HAT is likely where heroin dependence is a major problem, where other treatment approaches have been well implemented and where a fraction of treatment-resistant patients becomes visible. A well-organised and wealthy society is a condition for success. Also, a monitoring system documenting the treatment population and the treatment effects will always be needed in order to safeguard the quality of programmes and to prevent dysfunctional developments.

References

Ali R, Auriacombe M, Casas M, Cottler L, Farrell M & Kleiber D (1998) *Report of the External Panel on the Evaluation of the Swiss Scientific Studies of Medically Prescribed Narcotics to Drug Addicts.* Genf: World Health Organisation.

BAG (2000) *Handbuch HeGeBe* [online]. Bern: Bundesamt für Gesundheit. Available at: www.suchtundAids.bag.admin.ch/imperia/md/content/drogen/hegebe/31.pdf (accessed December 2007).

BAG (2005) *Bundesamt für Gesundheit.* Bern: Bundesamt für Gesundheit.

Bammer G (1993) Should the controlled provision of heroin be a treatment option? Australian feasibility considerations. *Addiction* **88** 467–475.

Bammer G (1995) *Feasibility Research into the Controlled Availability of Opioids: Stage 2 (Report and recommendations).* Canberra: NCEPH.

Bammer G, Dance P, Hartland N & McDonald D (1992) Australian reports into drug use and the possibility of heroin maintenance. *Drug and Alcohol Review* **11** 175–182.

BAP (2002) *Bundesamt für Polizei.* Bern: Bundesamt für Polizei.

Blanken P, Hendriks VM, Koeter MW, van Ree JM & van den Brink W (2005) Matching of treatment resistant heroin-dependent patients to medical prescription of heroin or oral methadone treatment: results from two randomised controlled trials. *Addiction* **100** 89–95.

Blättler R, Dobler-Mikola A, Steffen T & Uchtenhagen A (2002) Decreasing intravenous cocaine use in opiate users treated with prescribed heroin. *Sozial- und Präventivmedizin* **47** 24–32.

Bosch X (2001) Spain authorizes clinical trial of heroin maintenance. *The Lancet* **357** 1347.

Brenneisen R, Bourquin D, Bundeli P, Gugger D, Gyr E, Lehmann T, Speich A, Stalder A & Vonlanthen D (1997) *Analytik, Pharmakokinetik und Galenik von Diacetylmorphin (Heroin). In-vitro und in-vivo Versuche mit verschiedenen Applikationsformen.* Bern: Pharmaceutical Institute, Bern University.

Buhk H, Zeikau T & Koch U (2006) *Versorgungsforschung: Implementierung und Transfer des Behandlungsangebots* [online]. Available at: http://www.heroinstudie.de/Versorgungsfo_ Heroin_Kurzf.pdf (accessed December 2007).

Bundesministerium für Gesundheit (2006) *Entscheidung zum Fortgang der diamorphingestützten Behandlung.* Pressemitteilung 27 November [online]. Available at: http://www.agsv.nrw.de/ Aktuelles/InfoBMG/Info27112006.html (accessed December 2007).

CCBH (2002) *Medical Co-prescription of Heroin. Two randomised controlled trials.* Utrecht: Central Committee on the Treatment of Heroin Addicts.

Derks J & Daansen PJ (1986) Injizierbare opiatverabreichung zur behandlung chronischer opiatabhängiger – das Amsterdamer morphiumexperiment. *Kriminologisches Journal* **18** 39–49.

Der Spiegel (2007) Union beendet streit über heroin-ambulanzen. *Der Spiegel,* 17 February.

Dijkgraaf MGW, van der Zanden BP, de Borgie AJM, Blanken P, van Ree JM & van den Brink W (2005) Cost utility analysis of co-prescribed heroin compared with methadone maintenance treatment in heroin addicts in two randomised trials. *British Medical Journal* **330** 1297–1303.

Dole VP & Nyswander M (1965) A medical treatment for diacetylmorphine (heroin) addiction. A clinical trial with methadone hydrochloride. *Journal of The American Medical Association* **193** (8) 80–84.

Dürsteler-McFarland K, Stohler R, Moldovanyi A, Rey S, Basdekis R, Gschwend P, Eschmann S & Rehm J (2005) Complaints of heroin-maintained patients: a survey of symptoms ascribed to diamorphine. *Drug and Alcohol Dependence* **81** 231–239.

Dürsteler-McFarland K, Stohler R, Moldovanyi A, Rey S, Basdekis R, Gschwend P, Eschmann S & Rehm J (2006) Complaints of heroin-maintained patients: a survey of symptoms ascribed to diamorphine. *Drug and Alcohol Dependence* **81** 231–239.

EMCDDA (2005) *Annual Report 2005.* Luxemburg: Office for Official Publications of the European Union.

EMCDDA (2006) *Annual Report 2006.* Luxemburg: Office for Official Publications of the European Union.

FAZ (2007) The dispute is resolved. Heroin treatment will continue. *Frankfurter Allgemeine Zeitung,* 20 February.

Fernandez MM, Alonso AH, Limón FC, López EP, Gómez RB, Hernández CA, Ramírez E S-C, Crespo FM, Pérez IR, Cerda JCM, Giner F, Rinken S & Zunzunegui V (2001) *Protocol PEPSA 2001* [online]. Available at: http://www.easp.es/pepsa/inicio/ensayo_english.htm (accessed December 2007).

Ferri M, Davoli M & Perucci CA (2003) Heroin maintenance for chronic heroin dependents. *Cochrane Database Systematic Review* **4** CD0034100.

Frei A, Greiner RA, Mehnert A & Dinkel R (2000) Socioeconomic evaluation of heroin maintenance treatment. In: F Gutzwiller & T Steffen (Eds) *Cost-benefit Analysis of Heroin Maintenance Treatment.* Basel: Karger, pp37–130.

Frei A & Rehm J (2002a) Komorbidität: Psychische Störungen bei Opiatabhängigen zu Beginn einer heroingestützten Behandlung. *Psychiatrische Praxis* **29** 251–257.

Frei A & Rehm J (2002b) Die Prävalenz psychischer Komorbidität unter Opiatabhängigen. Eine Metaanalyse bisheriger Studien. *Psychiatrische Praxis* **29** 258–262.

Frick U, Ammann J, Kovacic S, Bürki C, Mohler M, Käser R, Gerlich M, Güttinger F, Gschwend P & Rehm J (2006a) Qualitätssicherung in der Heroin-gestützten Behandlung (HeGeBe) in der Schweiz seit 2001. *Gesundheitsökonomie und Qualitätsmanagement* **11** 155–161.

Frick U, Rehm J, Kovacic S, Ammann J & Uchtenhagen A (2006b) A prospective cohort study on orally administered heroin substitution for severely addicted opioid users. *Addiction* **101** 1631–1639.

Geistlich S (1996) *Schwangerschaftsverlauf und Entzugssymptome Neugeborener von Methadonpatientinnen und von Patientinnen unter Morphinsubstitution.* Med.Diss. Zurich: University of Zurich.

González A (2006) El PEPSA suministrará heroina en pastillas a toxicómanos que la fuman. *Granada Hoy*, 26 March.

Graf von der Schulenburg JM & Claes C (2006) *Gesundheitsökonomische Begleitforschung.* Hanover: Liebnitz University.

Gschwend P, Rehm J, Eschmann S & Uchtenhagen A (2003) Heroingestützte Behandlung für Opioidabhängige in der Schweiz von 1994 bis 2001 – Inanspruchnahme und Charakteristik der Ein- und Austretenden. *Gesundheitswesen* **65** 75–80.

Güttinger F, Gschwend P, Schulte B, Rehm J, Gutzwiller F & Uchtenhagen A (2003) Evaluating long-term effects of heroin-assisted treatment – the results of a six-year follow up. *European Addiction Research* **9** (2) 73–79.

Gutzwiller F & Steffen T (Eds) (2000) *Cost-benefit Analysis of Heroin Maintenance Treatment.* Basel: Karger.

Haasen C (2006) *Das Bundesdeutsche Modellprojekt zur Heroingestützten Behandlung Opiatabhängiger. Klinischer Studienbericht zum Abschluss der 2 Studienphase* [online]. Available at: http://www.heroinstudie.de/Zusammenfassung_H-P2.pdf (accessed December 2007).

Hämmig RB (1997) *Hochdosiertes Intravenöses Heroin Versus Intravenöses Morphin bei Drogenabhängigen. Eine randomisierte Kontrollierte Doppelblindstudie mit Crossover.* Bern: Federal Office of Health.

Heinemann A (2006) *Kognitives, Psychophysisches und Optisch-vestibuläres Funktionsniveau bei Patienten in Heroingestützter Behandlung* [online]. Available at: www.heroinstudie.de (accessed December 2007).

Hendriks VM, van den Brink W, Blanken P, Bisman IJ & van Ree JM (2001) Heroin-self adminstration by means of 'chasing the dragon': pharmacodynamics and bioavailability of inhaled heroin. *European Neuropsychopharmacology* **11** 241–252.

Hosek M (2006) Substitutionsbehandlungen in der Schweiz: Fortsetzung einer Erfolggeschichte. *Suchtmagazin* **1** (6) 3–9.

Killias M, Aebi MF, Ribeaud D & Rabasa J (1999) *Schlussbericht zu den Auswirkungen der Verschreibung von Betäubungsmitteln auf die Delinquenz von Drogenabhangingen* (2nd ed). Lausanne: Université de Lausanne.

Klous MG, Nuijen B, van den Brink W, van Ree JM & Beijnen H (2004) Process characterisation, optimisation and validation of production of diacetylmorphine/caffeine sachets: a design of experiments approach. *International Journal of Pharmacology* **285** 65–75.

Kreutzer A & Köllisch T (2006) *Qualitative Kriminologische Untersuchung* [online]. Available at: http://www.heroinstudie.de/Kriminologie_qualitativ_Kurzf_abg.pdf (accessed December 2007).

Kuhn S, Farnbacher G, Verthein U, Haasen CH, Schu M, Schlanstedt G, Vogt I, Simmedinger R & Schmid M (2006) *Binnenevaluation der Psychosozialen Begleitung* [online]. Available at: http://www.heroinstudie.de/Binnenevaluation_Kurzfassung.pdf (accessed December 2007).

Ladewig D, Battegay I, Stohler R, Erb P, Rohr HP, Uchtenhagen A & Gyr K (1997) *A Randomised Trial with Methadone, Morphine and Heroin in the Treatment of Opioid Dependence.* Bern: Federal Office of Public Health.

Löbmann R (2006) *Der Einfluss Heroingestützter Behandlung auf die Delinquenz Drogenabhängiger* [online]. Available at: http://www.kfn.de/Forschungsbereiche_und_Projekte/Abgeschlossene_Projekte/Der_Einfluss_heroingestuctzter_Therapie_auf_die_Delinquenz_Drogenabhaengiger.htm (accessed December 2007).

March JC, Oviedo-Joekes E, Perea-Milla E, Carrasco F & PEPSA team (2006) Controlled trial of prescribed heroin in the treatment of opioid addiction. *Journal of Substance Abuse Treatment* **31** 203–211.

Marks J & Palombella A (1990) Prescribing smokable drugs. *The Lancet* **335** 864.

Mendez R & De Benito E (2006) Andalucia to provide prescription heroin to long term addicts. *El Pais,* 29 December.

Metrebian N, Carnwath T, Stimson GV & Storz T (2002) Survey of doctors prescribing diamorphine (heroin) to opiate dependent drug users in the United Kingdom. *Addiction* **97** 1155–1161.

Mino A (1990) *Analyse Scientifique de la Littérature sur la Remise Controlée d'Héroine ou de Morphine. Expertise rédigée à la commande de l'Office Fédéral de la Santé Publique, Berne.* Berne: Federal Office of Public Health.

Mitchell TB, Lintzeris N, Bond A & Strang J (2006) Feasibility and acceptability of an intranasal diamorphine spray as an alternative to injectable diamorphine for maintenance treatment. *European Addiction Research* **12** 91–95.

Musto DF (1999) *The American Disease. Origins of narcotic control* (3rd ed). New York: Oxford University Press.

Naber D & Haasen C (2006) *Das Bundesdeutsche Modellprojekt zur Heroingestützten Behandlung Opiatabhängiger. Abschlussbericht zur klinischen Vergleichsstudie zur Heroin- und Methadonbehandlung* [online]. Available at: http://www.heroinstudie.de/ZIS_HBericht_P1_DLR.pdf (accessed December 2007).

Nordt O & Stohler R (2006) Incidence of heroin use in Zurich, Switzerland: a treatment case register analysis. *The Lancet* **367** 1830–1834.

Oviedo-Joekes E (2006) Policy makers ignoring science not only in Canada: current state of heroin-assisted treatment for opiate addicts in Spain. *Harm Reduction Journal* **3** 16.

Perneger TV, Giner F, del Rio M, Mino A (1998) Randomised trial of heroin maintenance programme for addicts who fail in conventional treatments. *British Medical Journal* **317** 13–18.

Rabasa J & Killias M (1996) Evaluation de l'impact des essays suisses avec prescription médicale de stupéfiants sur la criminalité des sujets traits: resultants à court terme. *Kriminologisches Bulletin* **22** 63–78.

Raistrick D (1994) Report of the Advisory Council on the Misuse of Drugs: AIDS and drug misuse update. *Addiction* **89** 1211–1213.

Rehm J, Frick U, Hartwig C, Gutzwiller F, Gschwend P, Uchtenhagen A (2005) Mortality in heroin-assisted treatment in Switzerland 1994–2000. *Drug and Alcohol Dependence* **79** 137–143.

Rehm J, Gschwend P, Steffen T, Gutzwiller F, Dobler-Mikola A, Uchtenhagen A (2001) Feasibility, safety and efficacy of injectable heroin prescription for refractory opioid addicts: a follow-up study. *The Lancet* **358** 1417–1420.

Rossier-Affolter R (2000) Cost analysis of the medical prescription of narcotics. In: F Gutzwiller & T Steffen (Eds) *Cost-benefit Analysis of Heroin Maintenance Treatment.* Basel: Karger 9–36.

Schmied M (1997) *Wirkungen und Nebenwirkungen des Morphins bei Substitution von Abhängigen.* Thesis. Faculty of Medicine, Zurich University.

Sell L & Zador D (2004) Patients prescribed injectable heroin or methadone – their opinions and experiences of treatment. *Addiction* **99** 442–449.

Steffen T, Blättler R, Gutzwiller F & Zwahlen M (2001a) HIV and hepatitis virus infections among injecting drug users in a medically controlled heroin prescription programme. *European Journal of Public Health* **11** 425–430.

Steffen T, Christen S, Blättler R & Gutzwiller F (2001b) Infectious diseases and public health: risk-taking behaviour during participation in the Swiss program for a medical prescription of narcotics (PROVE). *Substance Use & Misuse* **36** 71–89.

Stimson G & Metrebian N (2003) *Prescribing Heroin. What is the evidence?* [online]. York: Joseph Rowntree Foundation Available at: http://www.jrf.org.uk/knowledge/findings/socialpolicy/943.asp (accessed December 2007).

Stimson G & Oppenheimer E (1982) *Heroin Addiction. Treatment and control in Britain.* London: Tavistock.

Stohler R, Berthel T, Herzig M, Burkhard P, Meyer T, Olgiati M, Meili D, Sprenger B & Schaub M (2006) *Glossar Kokainbehandlungen. Überblick über den Stand der Behandlungen von kokainbedingten Störungen* [online]. Available at: http://www.kokainbehandlung.ch/de/content/glossar/Glossar2007.pdf (accessed December 2007).

Strang J & Gossop M (1996) Heroin-prescribing in the British system: historical review. *European Addiction Research* **2** 185–193.

Strang J & Sheridan J (1997) Heroin prescribing in the 'British system'. *Drug and Alcohol Review* **16** 7–16.

Uchtenhagen A, Ali R, Berglund M, Eap C, Farrell M, Mattick R, McLellan T, Rehm J & Simpson S (2004) *Methadone as a Medicine for the Management of Opioid Dependence and HIV/Aids prevention.* Geneva: World Health Organisation.

Uchtenhagen A, Dobler-Mikola A, Steffen T, Gutzwiller F, Blättler R & Pfeifer S (1999) *Prescription of Narcotics to Heroin Addicts. Main results of the Swiss National Cohort Study.* Basel: Karger.

Uehlinger C, Veinny A & Oeuvray K (1996) *Projet Fribourgeois de Méthadone Injectable PROMI. Rapport final pour l'Office Féderale de Santé Publique.* Berne: Office Féderale de Santé Publique.

UNODC (2002) *Contemporary Drug Abuse Treatment. A review of the evidence base.* Vienna: United Nations Office on Drugs and Crime.

van den Brink W (2007) Personal communication.

van den Brink W, Hendriks VM, Blanken P, Koeter MW, van Zwieten BJ & van Ree JM (2003) Medical prescription of heroin to treatment resistant heroin addicts: two randomised controlled trials. *British Medical Journal* **327** 310–312.

von Aarburg HP, Stauffacher M (2005) Bedeutungswandel schweizerischen Heroinkonsums in zeit- und lebensgeschichtlicher Perspektive. *Suchttherapie* **5** 1–6.

WHO (1998) *WHO Expert Committee on Drug Dependence. 30th report.* Geneva: World Health Organisation.

WHO/UNODC/UNAIDS (2004) *Position Paper: Substitution maintenance therapy in the management of opioid dependence and HIV/Aids prevention.* Geneva: World Health Organisation, United Nations Office on Crime and Drugs, Joint United Nations Programme on HIV/Aids.

CHAPTER 4
Drug consumption rooms: between evidence and opinion

Neil Hunt and Charlie Lloyd

INTRODUCTION

Drug consumption rooms (DCRs) are a response to problem drug use that aims to improve the health and well-being of drug users while simultaneously reducing public nuisance. Despite the fact that they have existed in their present form for over 20 years and now operate in at least eight countries, they remain controversial. The evidence base surrounding their effectiveness is still developing, their legal basis is to some extent contested, and their very operation offends the sensibilities of some who favour prohibitionary approaches to drug control. Nevertheless, the evidence increasingly suggests that, in carefully targeted settings, they may make some useful contribution to the reduction of drug related harm and that more and more cities in an expanding number of countries identify DCRs as a worthwhile component of a pragmatic, integrated response to problem drug use. Using the UK as a case study, this chapter summarises the evaluation research regarding the potential impact of DCRs and locates this within the interplay between the roles of the media, government and public opinion. This is considered as part of a process of achieving pilot evaluations that will allow the role of DCRs to be appraised within an evidence-based approach to drug policy.

This chapter draws extensively on work to which the authors contributed substantively and which was undertaken over 20 months by an Independent Working Group (IWG), supported by the Joseph Rowntree Foundation (JRF). The IWG reviewed the available evidence and, where there were gaps, research was commissioned in order to assess whether there was a case for the introduction of DCRs in the UK. Within this process, a review by the European Monitoring Centre on Drugs and Drug Addiction was used extensively because of its comprehensiveness, recency and the fact that it was able to incorporate literature from languages other than English, which are often otherwise excluded from English language reviews due to translation costs (Hedrich, 2004). The IWG's final report was published in 2006 (Independent Working Group, 2006). With updates from new evidence, where applicable, this provides the basis here for an account of the background to DCRs, the evidence of the effectiveness of DCRs, an appraisal of the level of identified need within the UK, legal issues, and the conclusions of the IWG. We then present a commentary on the subsequent responses to the report from the government and the media, and end with a consideration of the factors that are likely to determine whether pilot DCRs are introduced in the UK in the future.

BACKGROUND

Drug Consumption Rooms (DCRs) have been defined as,

'*...protected places for the hygienic consumption of preobtained drugs in a non-judgemental environment and under the supervision of trained staff*' (Akzept Bundesverband & Carl von Ossietzky University of Oldenburg, 2000).

They have been set up in response to a range of concerns and needs. Broadly these can be regarded as *public* harms, which affect communities (eg. open drug scenes, public injecting and discarded syringes, and drug litter) and *private* harms, which affect the drug user directly (eg. overdose and blood-borne infections).

The public nuisance caused to residents and businesses close to drug markets has been a crucial factor leading to the introduction of DCRs in Switzerland, Germany and the Netherlands (Hedrich, 2004). The story of Platzspitz or 'Needle Park' in Zurich, Switzerland, is an example of how public concern led to a sequence of events culminating, in, among other things, the establishment of a DCR (MacCoun & Reuter, 2001). Large numbers of drug users began to use this park in the centre of Zurich during the 1980s. The increasing numbers of drug users and amount of drug-related litter in this public park eventually led to its closure, the relocation of users to the local train station and, finally, the setting up of a DCR. Similarly, the focus on public nuisance is prominent in the Netherlands, where local concerns about drug taking in public places underpin a highly targeted approach that is limited to the most visible drug users (Hedrich, 2004).

The private harms associated with drug use, especially overdose, have been an important driving factor in Norway, Spain and Canada and were also influential in Switzerland (Hedrich, 2004; Skretting 2006). However, differences in the goals of services are typically a matter of emphasis rather than being absolute, with most services addressing both public and private harms.

To date, services have been established in Germany, Switzerland, the Netherlands, Spain, Norway, Luxembourg, Australia and Canada. While there is some history of earlier, unofficial injecting rooms for drug users, the first official DCR was opened in June 1986 in Berne, Switzerland with services following shortly after in Germany and the Netherlands (Hedrich, 2004). In 2004, Hedrich identified 64 operational services in 37 cities, most of which are located in Switzerland, Germany and the Netherlands. The first Spanish DCR was set up somewhat later during 2000. DCRs have since been established as part of scientific trials in Sydney, Australia and Vancouver, Canada and these studies have added considerably to the literature on their effectiveness. Services in Norway and Luxembourg were set up more recently still and seem likely to add further to the evidence base in future.

EVIDENCE OF EFFECTIVENESS

Debates about new developments in the treatment of drug problems should be informed by the extent to which they reduce the harms that are the target of drug policy. It is therefore essential to ask in what ways and to what extent are DCRs effective? Hedrich's (2004) review for the European Monitoring Centre for Drugs and Drug Addiction (EMCDDA) remains a relevant and comprehensive review of the evidence, however, more recent research – much of which comes from the trial in Vancouver – has further improved our understanding.

As we have noted, DCRs have been developed in response to private and public harms. Within these broad spheres there are a number of outcomes and aspects of process that have been examined and the strength of the evidence across these is variable. When appraising the literature, the IWG examined the following questions: who attends DCRs; what is their impact on health; what is their impact on local communities; what can be said about the cost-effectiveness of DCRs? This section provides an overview of the evidence across these four areas.

REACHING THE TARGET GROUP

The EMCDDA review states that the target populations of DCRs are,

'typically defined as high-risk problem drug users, especially regular or long-term users of heroin and cocaine, drug injectors, drug-using sex workers, street users and other marginalised, often not in treatment, groups' (Hedrich, 2004).

This review identified 15 'key studies' and concluded that the typical DCR user is a male over 30 years of age, who is a frequent user of heroin and/or cocaine and has been injecting for at least 10 years. A substantial proportion of a typical DCR's users will have been injecting in public places prior to using the DCR (for example, 39% of the Sydney Medically Supervised Injecting Centre [MSIC] users had injected in a public place within the last month). A similar profile has since been reported for users of the Vancouver service (British Columbia Centre for Excellence in HIV/Aids, 2004).

The homeless are often an explicit target group of services. The proportion of attenders who are homeless varies according to the emphasis on this objective. Sixty per cent of the users in a DCR in Barcelona were defined as homeless, reflecting this DCR's targeting of marginalised users. By comparison, a recent survey of all German consumption rooms found that 5% lived *de facto* in the street (Hedrich, 2004). Twenty-two per cent of the Vancouver sample were defined as of no fixed abode or living in the street (British Columbia Centre for Excellence in HIV/Aids, 2004).

The extent to which DCRs provide a point of contact that might be used to engage people in treatment has also been examined and Hedrich reports that between 15% and 50% of attenders have never been in treatment before (Hedrich, 2004).

Heroin and cocaine are the main drugs used, sometimes in combination, and the main mode of use in most services is injecting. However, in the Netherlands, where heroin and cocaine are more often smoked than injected, some services have separate areas for those who inhale and those who inject. DCRs with facilities for the inhalation of drugs have also been established in Switzerland and Germany in order to address these modes of drug use.

DCRs vary enormously in the extent of their use, depending on the number of spaces for users, the size of the local user population and the eligibility criteria. In one small service, a weekly average of 50 supervised consumptions has been reported; at the other of the scale, the Vancouver project reported a weekly average of over 3,000 (Hedrich, 2004; British Columbia Centre for Excellence in HIV/Aids, 2004). Studies in Germany and Switzerland show that many people use services on an average of five times a week. In the Netherlands, where projects usually focus on comparatively small groups of homeless users, average usage rates per person can be as high as six days per week (Hedrich, 2004). The Vancouver project was used by 3,036 individuals in a six month period, during which 79,962 injections took place. The average individual usage rate was 11 visits per month (British Columbia Centre for Excellence in HIV/Aids, 2004).

IMPACT ON HEALTH

The evidence of who attends DCRs begins to suggest their potential impact. It shows that it is possible to transfer large numbers of injections into a supervised and hygienic environment, and that DCRs can provide many opportunities for intervention with large numbers of the most marginalised drug users – notably the homeless. We now examine more detailed aspects of process and outcome, which point towards the impact that DCRs may actually have on health.

Moving 'street injecting' to a managed environment is likely to promote the largest gain in injecting hygiene and, since their inception, millions of injections have been transferred into the safer environment of a DCR (Independent Working Group, 2006). Evaluation of the Sydney Medically Supervised Injecting centre found that among 3,782 clients, 42% reported that their next injection would have been in a public place (MSIC Evaluation Committee, 2003). Furthermore, Taylor *et al*'s (2004) video-based research on 48 injecting events suggests that, although injecting indoors is associated with fewer risks than injecting outdoors, there are still numerous ways in which risks can be introduced when people inject indoors.

A managed environment also creates opportunities for advice-giving on injecting hygiene and technique. Again, evidence from Australia suggests that in nearly 14% of the visits to the MSIC, advice on injecting and/or vein care appears to have been given to the user: a total of 7,732 occasions over an 18-month period (MSIC Evaluation Committee, 2003).

Most DCRs have doctors on-site either part-time or full-time and where they do not, most have nursing staff on-site. Some services also provide food and drink, showers and laundry services. A small number of DCRs form part of integrated services, which include hostel accommodation on the same site. Medical consultation, wound care services and counselling are provided in between 5% and 10% of visits to DCRs (Hedrich, 2004). The Sydney MSIC provided a total of 13,696 services (in addition to supervision of injection) to 2,186 users over an 18-month period. After injecting and vein care advice, the most common service provided was 'general counselling', but there followed a long list of the provision of other information, medical and social services (MSIC Evaluation Committee, 2003).

With regard to referrals to other services, rates vary significantly across DCRs, from 9% to 54% (although direct comparison is difficult – Hedrich, 2004). The Sydney MSIC referred 15% of its users to other agencies, many on more than one occasion. Fifty-five per cent of the 1,385 referrals were verbal, and 45% written. Forty-three per cent of all referrals were for drug treatment, 32% health care, and 25% social welfare. Of course, the act of referring a person to another agency does not mean that that person will show up and receive help. 'Referral cards' were sent out with the written referrals and more than one in five of these were returned as confirmation of the MSIC client's attendance. With regard to treatment, 49 of the 300 written referrals (16%) resulted in a user attending the agency to which they were referred (MSIC Evaluation Committee, 2003). DCRs have also provided a pathway into treatment in Canada, with the Vancouver project making 262 referrals to addiction counselling services over a six-month period and 78 referrals to withdrawal management programmes (British Columbia Centre for Excellence in HIV/AIDS, 2004). Furthermore, more regular use of the Vancouver service plus contact with the facility's counsellor has been found to be associated with more rapid entry into detoxification services (Wood *et al*, 2006).

Overdose
Concern about drug-related deaths has been a factor in the development of DCRs in most of the countries hosting them. By providing safety-related rules, supervision of the injecting process, medically trained staff and emergency facilities, overdose deaths can be prevented. DCRs provide the potential to intervene at an early stage in the overdose process, reduce harm and also avert the need for emergency services and hospitalisation – with its corresponding economic costs.

The large majority of reported emergencies within DCRs are overdoses relating to heroin, but there are also small numbers of cocaine overdoses and epileptic seizures (Hedrich, 2004). DCRs can prevent death from respiratory arrest by enabling the early provision of respiratory first aid and, if required, administration of the opioid antagonist naloxone. Should more intensive intervention be needed, DCRs also enable emergency services to be summoned earlier.

There is a considerable amount of evidence on the incidence of emergencies within DCRs. The rate of emergencies seems to vary very widely: from 0.5 to seven emergencies per 1,000 supervised injections (Hedrich, 2004). Reasons for this wide variation are likely to include differences in the nature of the target group and different definitions of what constitutes an emergency requiring intervention. However, it is clear that dangerous situations that require intervention arise frequently in DCRs (as they do in any drug-injecting context). The Sydney MSIC had the highest rate of emergencies (seven per 1,000 injections) and 329 heroin-related overdoses were managed by the staff over the 18-month evaluation period.

The proportion of emergencies dealt with by DCR staff will depend on the extent to which medically trained staff and the necessary equipment are present (Hedrich, 2004). Ninety-eight per cent of the emergencies at the Sydney MSIC, which has a doctor or nurse present at all times, were dealt with by the staff. DCRs that do not have a doctor present have much higher ambulance attendance levels: up to 70% of emergencies (Hedrich, 2004).

Despite the large number of overdose events that have occurred within DCRs, there has only been one reported death in a DCR since the first service was introduced in 1986: in December 2002 a drug user died from anaphylaxis (a severe, whole-body allergic reaction) in a German consumption room (Hedrich, 2004). Given that injecting is such a risk-laden, dangerous activity, and that millions of injections have taken place within DCRs since their inception, this statistic offers powerful evidence of the safety of DCRs.

While it is therefore clear that DCRs largely prevent overdoses occurring while clients are injecting within them, a more testing question is whether a DCR can be shown to have an impact at a community level. However, the impact of a DCR in this respect will always be limited by the following factors (MSIC Evaluation Committee, 2003):

- a DCR can only prevent deaths during its hours of operation
- a proportion of the local users will not use the DCR
- those that do use the DCR will inject elsewhere some of the time.

Nevertheless, such analyses have been attempted in Sydney and Germany. The evaluation of the Sydney MSIC included a sophisticated set of analyses of the impact of the DCR on drug-related deaths. However, the community-level measurement of impact was undermined by the rapid decrease in the availability of heroin, which occurred shortly before the MSIC opened (Bush *et al*, 2004). This was associated with a rapid decrease in overdose deaths and made the measurement of the impact of the MSIC at community level impossible. Nevertheless, using the proportion of overdose ambulance call outs in New South Wales that end in the death of the user, and applying this figure to the 81 more serious overdose cases in the DCR (which were treated with naloxone), a conservative estimate was made of four lives saved per annum.

Evidence of community level impact is provided by a 'time series' analysis of the impact of DCRs on overdose death rates in four German cities (Poschadel *et al*,

2003). This research concluded that DCRs were *statistically significantly related to the reduction of drug-related deaths.* Another analysis of German data, which applied estimated overdose mortality rates to the number of supervised consumptions, found that 10 deaths per year were prevented by the German DCRs (Hedrich, 2004).

Transmission of blood-borne viruses

The problems involved in establishing whether or not a project has had an impact on the transmission of viruses are considerable. The low incidence of blood-borne viruses means that it is very difficult to measure impact (MSIC Evaluation Committee, 2003). As Hedrich concludes, *'it is likely that the direct and personalised safer use education in the setting of supervised consumption rooms contributes to a reduced risk of transmission of infectious diseases even outside the room',* but this is very hard to show beyond doubt.

Bearing in mind such shortcomings, what does the evaluation evidence show? Earlier studies have indicated an increased knowledge and awareness of risk and a decrease in self-reported needle and syringe sharing among DCR clients (Hedrich, 2004). The methodological problems associated with these evaluations have precluded a stronger conclusion. However, the evaluation of the Vancouver project has employed a more sophisticated approach, drawing on previous epidemiological surveys of intravenous drug users (IDUs), which has shown that the introduction of the DCR was associated with reduced reported syringe sharing among those attending the project (Kerr *et al*, 2005; Wood *et al*, 2005).

Other physical health problems

DCRs frequently offer medical services on-site and also refer users to off-site medical services. Given the large number of visits to DCRs, this can mean large numbers of treatments. The three Zurich consumption rooms delivered an annual average of 3,122 wound care services; for the Sydney MSIC, this figure was 847, and the DCR in Madrid provided medical services on an average of 3,902 occasions per year. The Sydney MSIC also referred clients to off-site health care services on 439 occasions over an 18-month period and health care referrals had the highest uptake rate. Given that many people who use DCRs are highly marginalised, and have poor access to health care services, this evidence strongly suggests that DCRs can fulfil an important function in providing primary health care interventions to a very needy population.

IMPACT ON DRUG USE

As has been shown, DCRs provide psychosocial counselling on-site and refer users to a range of agencies including treatment services. It could, therefore, be anticipated that DCRs could have a beneficial impact on drug use, both through referral to treatment, but also through impacting on some of the multiple social problems experienced by socially excluded users. Alternatively, it might be thought that the presence of a safe place to inject drugs is enabling and acts to increase drug use. A number of studies of attenders have examined this question and most find a minority of people (up to 16%) who report increased frequency of drug use since using the DCR and others who report decreased use (up to 22%) (Hunt, 2006a). A recent study of drug users in Vancouver found that the opening of the DCR was not associated with any measurable negative changes in injecting drug use. The only significant change was a reduction in the initiation of binge drug use following the introduction of the DCR (Kerr *et al*, 2006).

IMPACT ON LOCAL COMMUNITIES
Reduction in public injecting
A range of evidence points to DCRs resulting in a decrease in injecting in public places (Hedrich, 2004). Interviews with DCR users in Rotterdam and Hamburg have shown that users report reduced rates of public drug use as a result of their attendance at the DCR. However, while DCR users may reduce their rate of public injecting, some residual public use continues. Clearly these outcomes are partly determined by the accessibility and coverage of services. Research in Hamburg, which found that 37% of respondents had used in public during the past 24 hours, identified withdrawal symptoms, in conjunction with long waiting times for access to the injecting room, distance from place of purchase and limited opening hours as the main reasons for doing so.

More convincing evidence of impact comes from Switzerland, where users of low-threshold drug services have been regularly surveyed in order to evaluate the Swiss Aids prevention strategy (Hedrich, 2004). Survey data were collected from users in Biel and Geneva, before and after the introduction of DCRs. Before introduction, 21% and 18% of users in Biel and Geneva respectively, reported using mainly in public places. After the introduction of DCRs, these figures had fallen to a single individual in Biel and 10% of users in Geneva. Forty-nine per cent of the users in Biel and 29% of the users in Geneva referred to DCRs as their most frequent location for drug use.

The strongest evidence comes from the evaluation of the Vancouver project, which involved an array of observational measures, including people seen injecting in public places. Comparing the six-week period before the establishment of the DCR with the 12-month period afterwards, there was a statistically significant reduction in the number of users seen injecting in public places, from a daily average of 4.4 to a daily average of 2.4. This relationship held true when rainfall (which was expected to be associated with lower rates of outdoor drug use) and police presence were taken into account (Wood *et al*, 2004).

Reduction in discarded syringes and drug-related litter
Until recently, research on discarded syringes and needles has been largely equivocal. While, following the introduction of the DCR, a drop in discarded syringes was recorded in the area around the Sydney MSIC, it was unclear whether this could be attributed to the DCR or the decline in heroin availability.

A slight increase in discarded syringes was recorded following the setting up of the DCR in Biel, despite a high return rate for needles and syringes given out. Researchers suggested that this might be due to an increase in cocaine use (and the associated increase in the frequency of injecting). Surveys of residents living near the Dutch DCR in Venlo showed a reduction in discarded syringes following implementation (Hedrich, 2004).

Again, the strongest test of the impact of DCRs on drug-related litter comes from the Vancouver study (Wood *et al*, 2004). Whereas a daily average of 11.5 discarded syringes were found before the opening of the DCR, this average figure dropped to 5.3 after its opening. Injection-related litter (syringe wrappers, syringe caps, sterile water containers and 'cookers') showed a drop in the average daily count from 601.7 to 305.3. Both these differences were statistically significant and independent of law enforcement activity and rainfall patterns.

Public nuisance: 'honey-pot' effects, crime and dealing

One of the main concerns surrounding the setting up of a DCR is that it will attract even more users to the area – a 'honey-pot' effect. Research has been conducted on the proportion of service users who live locally and has found that between 63% and 93% report living in the local area, however defined (Hedrich, 2004). The numbers of people that are attracted to a DCR from outside the immediate area is likely to depend on a number of factors, including the DCR's policy, the local policing policy, the number of other DCRs in the locality, the location and nature of drug markets, and the availability of needle-exchange, treatment and hostel facilities for users.

DCRs have generally been introduced where there are well-established drug markets and/or open drug scenes. A number of studies have now shown that DCRs located any distance from drug markets attract very few users (Hedrich, 2004). Once people have obtained their drugs there is often a degree of urgency about using them and Hunt *et al*, (2007) have found that public injecting becomes more likely among people who live further from the place of purchase. Thus, there appears little reason to assume that a DCR will act as a magnet for users, drawing them in from other areas, so long as drug dealing is excluded from the premises and the immediate surrounding area.

Some of these issues are borne out by the history of the first DCR in Hanover (Hedrich, 2004). This DCR was set up in 1997, one km from the city centre drug market and 'open drug scene'. Three months into its operation the weekly number of injections had reached 300 but this figure fell sharply to 130 in the fifth month. Among the users' explanations for this fall was the distance from the drug market and police interventions on the route to the service. Changes in police practice were agreed (as well as some amendments to procedures in the DCR) and this was followed by a return to the earlier levels of usage. At this point, there was no dealing occurring outside the facility and very little trouble between users and residents or the police. However, in subsequent years the police put increasing pressure on the local drug market, with the result that the area in front of the DCR became a new meeting place for users. By 2001, average weekly use had reached 800 and the relocated drug scene led to much more nuisance for people living in the local area.

There has been a strong focus on general drug-related nuisance in the Netherlands, where DCRs have been set up largely in response to such community concerns. Research has shown a positive impact, with the five studies comparing nuisance levels before and after implementation finding lower levels of reported nuisance after the DCRs were set up (Hedrich, 2004).

A study of all the consumption rooms operating in Germany found that the level of reported nuisance problems was related to the quality of co-operation between the police and drug services: where there was agreement about the need for DCRs and a shared understanding of their public health and public order functions, fewer public order problems occurred. In others such as Hanover, where this did not appear to be the case, problems did arise.

Recent evidence on the overall impact of a DCR on the local community comes from the evaluation of the Sydney MSIC, which included surveys of local public opinion. A recently published paper has compared the views of local people and businesses seven months before the DCR opened with those reported 17 months after it had opened. Results show that support for the MSIC increased significantly over this period and that residents' perceptions that DCRs attract drug users or make law enforcement difficult decreased significantly (Thein *et al*, 2005).

On the specific issues of crime and drug dealing, various studies have drawn on local police data to assess whether there is any impact of DCRs on acquisitive crime, including robbery. No impact on crime levels (in either direction) has been found. As DCRs do not seek to replace illicit drugs with prescribed drugs, this approach does not break the need for dependent drug users to commit crime in order to finance their drug use. However, 'integrated' DCRs, which directly or indirectly provide access to a range of other services such as treatment, housing and employment may lead to a reduction in the need for illicit drugs and associated crime in individual cases.

A number of studies have reported some dealing in the immediate vicinity of DCRs. Due to the proximity of most DCRs to drug markets, it is hard to differentiate between dealing that would have occurred in the area in any case and dealing specifically associated with DCR users. Such problems can be addressed through DCR policies that prohibit dealing and 'loitering' near the premises and police action and surveillance to prevent users gathering in the immediate areas surrounding drug consumption rooms (Hedrich, 2004).

COSTS

DCRs have been established in highly divergent ways. These different operational models are likely to incur very different costs. Stand-alone demonstration projects seem most likely to be the most expensive models, whereas services integrated with other components of drug treatment seem likely to be cheaper.

The Sydney MSIC operating cost for one year was the equivalent of approximately £850,000 (MSIC Evaluation Committee, 2003). The annual cost of the Canadian SIS trial was the equivalent of approximately £1,200,000, although this also includes the evaluation expenses (City of Vancouver Four Pillars Drug Strategy, 2003). However, these represent the very top end of the scale, being large, stand-alone demonstration projects. Cost data on European services, some of which operate on an integrated model, are not readily available. Nevertheless, the marginal cost of extending a service to include a supervised consumption facility must inevitably be much less than those arising from a specialised project such as the MSIC and SIS.

While it is evident that DCRs have an impact on a range of process and outcome measures, the size of this impact is variable according to the setting, objectives and operational model for the service. Consequently, it is impossible to say anything definitive about cost-effectiveness. However, noting the high cost of stand-alone services, DCRs integrated with other treatment services – for which marginal costs are therefore likely to be smaller – and that provide a service to large numbers of injecting drug users appear most likely to offer the best 'value for money'.

EVIDENCE OF NEED

Within debates about new treatment responses it is necessary to appraise the likely need. 'Need' is conventionally taken to mean that there is some 'capacity to benefit'. It is distinguished from 'want', as people may want services that are ineffective. It is also distinct from 'supply', as services may sometimes be provided that do not work. However, with any new treatments/innovative services there is an inescapable phase where the evidence gap means there is ambiguity as to the capacity to benefit. This can only be determined accurately by research. Within the UK, need can only be determined in a provisional sense because there have been no evaluations of DCRs and their effectiveness in the UK is therefore uncertain. The evidence reviewed from other countries points to indicators of likely need by highlighting areas where DCRs appear likely to confer some benefit; however, some residual uncertainty necessarily exists when interventions are transferred from one cultural context to another. The IWG examined a range of these indicators in order to assess the extent to which need in the UK may exist. In most respects, evidence was derived from published research; where this was absent original research was commissioned. A detailed account of need within the UK is provided by Hunt (2006b). Key elements of this are now summarised with reference to problem drug use, infections, overdose, drug litter, public injecting and its social impact.

PROBLEMATIC DRUG USE

DCRs largely target injecting drug users/users of heroin and crack cocaine – a population that broadly equates to 'problem drug users' as they are defined by the EMCDDA. Estimates of problematic drug use suggest that England has in the order of 327,000 problematic drug users (Hay *et al*, 2006 p4). The 2005 report from the EMCDDA shows the prevalence of problematic drug use in the UK to be higher than for any of the other countries represented within the European Union (EMCDDA, 2005). Furthermore, despite the increases in treatment spending of recent years it nevertheless appears that as many as three out of four IDUs are still not in treatment (Hickman *et al*, 2004).

Problematic drug use is relatively high in the UK and DCRs may contribute to the engagement of those people who are currently outside of treatment.

Overdose

Since 1996 the UK has consistently reported the highest number of drug-related deaths in Europe (EMCDDA, 2005), although the rate has recently declined a little, meaning that those in a small number of other countries (Denmark, Luxembourg, Malta and Norway) surpassed those of the UK in the last reported year (EMCDDA, 2006). In much of Europe problem drug users have an annual risk of mortality of over 1%, which is around 15 times higher than the risk for the general population of young adults (aged 15–44), potentially contributing over 10% of young adult mortality (Hickman *et al*, 2003; Bargagli *et al*, 2005).

Fatal and non-fatal overdoses are relatively common occurrences among heroin injectors. There were 1,608 deaths related to 'drug misuse' in England and Wales during 2005 (Office for National Statistics, 2007). Non-fatal overdose is more common, with somewhere in the region of 20% to 40% of injecting heroin users reporting 'ever' having such an experience (Gossop *et al*, 1996; Powis *et al*, 1999).

Given the high rates of fatal and non-fatal overdose in the UK, DCRs may have a useful role to fulfil in their reduction.

Viral and bacterial infection

Compared to most industrialised countries, HIV infection among IDUs in the UK is low but has recently been rising after a prolonged period of stability (Judd *et al*, 2005; Health Protection Agency, 2006). Since 1997, sharing rates for injecting equipment have been high and appear to provide the conditions for epidemic spread of blood-borne infections (Health Protection Agency, 2006). Unlike HIV, hepatitis C is widespread and its incidence among new injectors has increased from 12% in 1998 to 20% in 2004. (Health Protection Agency, 2005). It is also becoming evident that IDUs in the UK experience high rates of bacterial infection. Three-fifths of all injectors reported a possible infection at an injecting site within the past year and a third of those surveyed had either an abscess, sore or open wound; only half of the latter group had sought any medical attention (Health Protection Agency, 2005).

The prevalence of blood-borne and other infections is widespread, as are the corresponding risk behaviours. DCRs provide an opportunity to prevent infections by shifting injecting into a hygienic environment in which sharing of equipment is not possible. They also provide opportunities for early access to viral testing and treatment with viral/bacterial infections.

Drug litter, public injecting and its social impact

Public injecting is both a source of nuisance within communities and a cause of increased risk to the drug user. It is associated with drug litter and can affect people's sense of safety. At the same time, injecting in public often means that hygiene and safety is compromised for the drug user.

One of the most visible indicators of public drug injecting is discarded drug litter – notably used syringes. Although it cannot be assumed that all discarded injecting equipment arises from public injecting, it is nevertheless likely that a substantial proportion does. Research by Environmental Campaigns (ENCAMS) carried out in 1998, 2001 and 2004 (ENCAMS, 2005) showed a rapid increase in the annual number of publicly discarded needles collected in England over this period: from 3,570 in 1998/9 to 147,345 in 2003/4. While caution needs to be exercised in interpreting these statistics, they conclude that *the quantity of needles found is increasing dramatically year on year*' (ENCAMS, 2005 p34). It is clear from this report that the problem is an increasingly widespread one, with growing numbers of rural and seaside authorities reporting finds. The sites reported by most local authorities were parks/playing fields, public toilets, residential areas, car parks and footpaths. Over the three-year period up to 2004 there had been 169 recorded needlestick injuries, the majority of those injured being local authority employees (ENCAMS, 2005).

The IWG found that direct data on public injecting and its impact were disappointingly rare. Consequently, two studies were commissioned – a survey of public injecting by people attending needle and syringe programmes (NSPs), and a study of the social impact of public injecting.

Within the NSP study, 301 IDUs were surveyed using a brief questionnaire across five services in London and Leeds between April and June 2005. Injection in a public place in the past week was reported by 55% of the sample and associated with insecure housing, unsafe needle and syringe disposal in the past month and willingness to use a DCR. When asked about their willingness to use DCRs, 84% of all respondents reported willingness to use such services if they were available (Hunt *et al*, 2007).

Regarding the social impact of public drug-taking, Taylor *et al*, (2006) investigated four sites around the UK known to be associated with public use of drugs ie. the type of locations in which services are typically situated. They interviewed a purposive sample of local people, including council cleaners, toilet attendants, park keepers, local business employees and local residents. Interviews were carried out with 100 people, 61 of whom took the researchers on 'walkabout tours' of the local area, pointing out sites where they had seen people using drugs or found evidence of public drug use. Drug-using locations were identified in alleyways, car parks, derelict open spaces, neglected property, cafés, toilets, gardens and stairwells. Half of the participants reported drug dealing, over a third had seen people injecting and nearly four-fifths had seen at least one used syringe. Twelve of the 100 participants had witnessed drug users who had collapsed and/or overdosed. Participants were annoyed by the drug litter and visible drug use – particularly if it occurred close to their own homes or where it could be observed by children. They were also intimidated by groups of users 'hanging about' and referred to finding vomit and excrement that they associated with drug users, some of whom were sleeping rough. Respondents generally reacted to these issues with anger, disgust and fear. The relentlessness of these problems was often viewed as part of a wider social malaise, which included the sex industry, homelessness, begging and drug-related crime. The authors conclude that public drug use and related litter are associated with significant levels of community concern, reflected in feelings of reduced safety, public amenity and quality of life.

Regarding need and public harms, public injecting therefore appears to be commonplace in the UK and there is widespread evidence of the drug litter that DCRs may help reduce. Recent evidence also improves our understanding of the intensity of the nuisance by members of communities where public drug use occurs.

LEGAL ISSUES

Debates about DCRs frequently include questions about their legal basis with reference to the UN Conventions (1961, 1971, 1988). Signatories to the conventions have translated these into domestic legislation in a variety of ways and other domestic laws may also be relevant. The IWG commissioned two legal reviews to appraise these issues (Fortson, 2006a; 2006b) and the conclusions derived from these are now briefly summarised.

Within the conventions, the legality and status of DCRs is open to interpretation and there is disagreement between the UN's own legal experts and the International Narcotics Control Board (INCB). However, the introduction of DCRs elsewhere has often been preceded by a legal appraisal, and it is evident that the eight countries in which they have been introduced so far have not found the conventions to be an impediment to their introduction.

Domestic legislation within the UK has some bearing on how DCRs should operate if they are to be within the law. Key legislation includes The Misuse of Drugs Act (1971), The Offences Against the Person Act (1861), the law relating to manslaughter and, potentially, the Anti-social Behaviour Act (2003). The main implications that arise from these concern supply and administration of drugs by one person to another. DCRs in the UK would need to have clear rules preventing these activities.

From a legal standpoint, DCRs would, ideally, be set up with the approval and support of the government and within a framework enshrined within primary legislation, secondary legislation or some combination of the two. However, this was not judged essential by the IWG. Pilot DCRs could be set up with clear and stringent rules and procedures that were shared with – and agreed by – the local police (and crime and disorder partnerships), the Crown Prosecution Service (CPS), the Strategic Health Authority and the local authority. An 'accord' might be established that action would not be taken against the DCR, its staff and, in normal circumstances, its users. The local police and CPS would need to agree that they would not charge users for possession offences within the DCR or on their way to the DCR. Of course, they would arrest users suspected of other offences in the usual way. Such local agreements have allowed DCRs to be set up in Frankfurt.

CONCLUSIONS AND RECOMMENDATIONS OF THE INDEPENDENT WORKING GROUP

The IWG concluded that DCRs are effective in providing safe and clean injecting environments, advice on safer injecting and on-site medical and counselling interventions. They have a significant impact on preventing the escalation of overdose incidents and there is convincing evidence that they can prevent overdose deaths. They also contribute to the better health of users, provide opportunities to link with structured treatment and may well prevent the spread of blood-borne viruses. The evidence shows that they clearly can reduce injecting in public places, discarded syringes and drug-related litter.

Based on the assessed need within the UK, the problems addressed by DCRs are widespread and DCRs would almost certainly have a beneficial impact. The frequency of overdose, the prevalence of blood-borne viruses and other injection-related infections, the amount of public injecting and the damage caused to communities in the UK would all be addressed, at least to some degree, by DCRs. Although other, existing services also address some of these needs, it is clear that DCRs offer the unique potential to ensure safer, on-site injecting and thereby directly prevent health problems, overdose and drug-related nuisance.

The IWG considered that DCRs have a particular potential to impact on the serious health and social problems associated with two overlapping groups in the UK: homeless drug users and those that inject in public. The potential dividends in terms of reduced damage to communities, improved health and saved lives seem much greater for these groups.

In conclusion, the IWG recommended that pilot DCRs are set up in the UK, and that the focus should be on injecting rather than other routes of administration such as smoking. Within the UK, well-run needle and syringe programmes were thought to offer an especially promising location for them, as allowing users to inject safely on the premises is a natural progression from giving them clean injecting equipment but expecting them to inject elsewhere.

At present, it is clear that it would be premature to roll out DCRs on more than a pilot basis. Despite the encouraging international literature, their potential impact within the UK requires assessment. Sound drug policy should be closely referenced to evidence and the IWG therefore recommended that any pilots are rigorously evaluated.

POLITICAL RESPONSES

The publication of the IWG report was not the first time that a body had recommended the setting up of injecting rooms to the UK government. In 2002, the Home Affairs Select Committee (HASC) recommended that,

'...an evaluated pilot programme of safe injecting houses for (illicit) heroin users is established without delay and that if, as we expect, this is successful, the programme is extended across the country'.

The Home Office's evidence to the HASC had already made clear the government's opposition to DCRs on a number of grounds (Home Affairs Select Committee, 2002).

- International legal position means that the rooms could be (but have not been) open to legal challenge.
- The government could be accused by the media and others of opening 'drug dens'.
- There is no guarantee that public or political tolerance will be the same as in Switzerland.
- It will directly increase health service costs as they would be a new service provision requiring additional capital and revenue costs.
- It still leaves the possibility of unsafe injecting during the hours they are closed.
- There may be problems in some areas on occasion with drug dealers congregating near to venues, leading to reduced local tolerance for the presence of injecting rooms in their neighbourhood.
- It is likely to raise the issue of policing low level dealing in the vicinity of injecting rooms.

The Home Office statement went on to explain that, *'the current government position is that injecting rooms for illicit drugs should not be introduced in this country while we have no evaluations of those developed in other European countries'.*

Consistent with this position, the government's response to the Home Affairs Select Committee's recommendation to set up pilot injecting rooms was rejected.

Problems in the Home Office

The IWG's recommendations came out against this particular historical backdrop. However, governmental responses to sensitive issues are not just dictated by the priorities in that particular area of social policy. They are also dictated by the political well-being of individual politicians, government departments and, indeed, the government as a whole. The IWG was unfortunate in this respect, as its report came out when the UK department for home affairs, the Home Office, was reeling from one high-profile crisis to the next and a time of debate about whether its functions could be properly overseen by any one minister – not an ideal time for endorsing new initiatives that are likely to produce controversy.

John Reid, the Home Secretary at the time (the government minister in charge of the Home Office), had taken up his post less than three weeks before the IWG report came out – describing some parts of the Home Office as *'not fit for purpose'*. He replaced the former Home Secretary, Charles Clarke, who had been ousted in the radical ministerial reshuffle that had followed the Labour party's heavy losses in the local government elections. Clarke had only been in post as Home Secretary for less than 17 months, during which his position had been greatly weakened by the public scandal surrounding the failure of the authorities to deport foreign national prisoners on release from prison. The Home Office's inability to trace some of the most serious offenders caused considerable embarrassment. Moreover, Charles Clarke had himself only taken over the job of Home Secretary following widely-publicised problems in David Blunkett's personal life, which culminated in his resignation in December 2004, following the fast-tracking of a visa application for his ex-lover's nanny.

In the specific area of drug policy, a further problem affecting the Home Office over this period was the classification of cannabis. Cannabis had been moved from Class B to Class C in January 2004 by David Blunkett, a move that was loudly criticised in some sections of the media. Following a wave of panic surrounding the links between cannabis (in particular 'skunk') and schizophrenia over 2004–2005, the following Home Secretary came under increasing pressure to move cannabis back to Class B (despite a lack of evidence that this would make any difference to the consumption of cannabis – or even the policing of cannabis). Clarke referred the issue to the Advisory Council on the Misuse of Drugs (ACMD) and eventually accepted its recommendation that cannabis should remain a Class C drug in early 2006. Again, the media included much critical coverage, painting the government as 'going soft' on drugs. So, it had been a time of great turmoil at the Home Office – hardly an environment that was likely to foster an open-minded and evidence-based response to a highly sensitive drug policy issue.

Considerable effort had nevertheless been made to prepare the way for a positive response from the UK government. A year beforehand, a letter had been written to the then Home Secretary (Charles Clarke), informing him of the work of the IWG. The response indicated the Home Secretary's intention to ask the ACMD to consider the report's findings and advise him accordingly.

A month prior to the report's publication, the IWGs chair, Dame Ruth Runciman, had meetings with officials in the Home Office and Department of Health to brief them on the content of the report and discuss the possible political responses. Again, it was thought that the likely course of action would be for the report to be referred to the ACMD.

When the report was actually launched, the government's response was confused but negative. Initially, the response put out by the Home Office press department was that the Home Office would consider the report. However, later the same day (23 May), the Parliamentary Under Secretary at the Home Office, Vernon Coaker, appeared on television stateing that, *'drug consumption rooms do not form any part of our strategy'* and that, *'The reasons for rejecting it in 2002 are as valid today – the risk of an increase in localised dealing, antisocial behaviour and acquisitive crime'.*

A further indication that the Home Office was in some disarray stems from the fact that the last of these reasons, acquisitive crime, did not appear among the arguments against the idea put forward by the government in 2002 (Home Affairs Select Committee, 2002 p226–227).

As a sign of the political times in the UK, it was the leader of the Conservative party, David Cameron, who gave a more positive reaction. Asked whether he backed the IWG recommendation to pilot DCRs, he responded thus, *'I certainly would not rule them out because anything that helps get users off the streets and in touch with agencies that can provide treatment is worth looking at'.* Likewise the shadow home affairs minister was reported as saying, *'We do not rule out [these] recommendations. If this is to take place in a controlled environment and is to be used as a stepping stone to actually getting people off drugs, we will look at this carefully'.*

There is an interesting backdrop to these comments. David Cameron was a member of the Home Affairs Select Committee, which recommended the piloting of injecting rooms in 2002. He appears to have been fully supportive of the idea, having voted against a proposed amendment that would have led to the dropping of this particular recommendation (Home Affairs Select Committee, 2002). In this light, his carefully positive comments are less surprising.

MEDIA RESPONSES

A press release was put out by the Joseph Rowntree Foundation on 22 May 2006 and was followed by a strong wave of interest from newspapers, television and radio. Most of the national daily newspapers covered the story on the following day. There was considerable variation in emphasis and language from, for example, the *Guardian* headline 'Heroin addicts could inject themselves at supervised centres in police-backed plans' to *The Sun* headline, referring to support for the idea from David Cameron, 'Cam up for junkie galleries'.

The fact that the IWG membership had included a senior police officer clearly brought some respectability and weight to the IWG's recommendations in the eyes of many sections of the media. The *Daily Telegraph* opened its story as follows,

'Drug addicts should be allowed to take heroin, crack cocaine and other illegal drugs in legalised rooms run by the government, says a group of experts who include one of Britain's most senior police officers.'

The *Guardian* and the *Daily Mail* also put a strong emphasis on the police backing for the proposal. The fact that Ruth Runciman had chaired the IWG also appeared to give the report 'standing'. The otherwise, largely hostile *Daily Mail* referring to IWG being *'headed by the highly influential drug reformer Dame Ruth Runciman'.*

Some of the language used in these articles was pejorative. Half of the national newspapers referred to 'shooting galleries', including the *Times*, and two (the *Mirror* and the *Daily Mail*) referred to 'junkies'.

However, the key conclusion from a more detailed analysis of the national newspaper coverage was that nearly all of these articles reported a number of the IWG's recommendations more or less accurately and included a description of the potential benefits of DCRs.

There was also a lot of coverage in local newspapers, some coverage on national television and radio, and almost blanket coverage on local radio. The story also ran in a range of specialist publications, such as the *New Statesman* and *Nursing Times*. However, one of the most influential pieces was an editorial in *The Lancet*, which went on to be quoted elsewhere. Referring to the comparatively high rate of drug-related deaths in the UK and the government's rejection of the Home Affairs Select Committee recommendation for pilot DCRs in 2002, the editorial concluded,

'After four years, and thousands of needless drug-related deaths, a thorough trial of DCRs is a requirement the government cannot afford to refuse a second time'.

As we have described, the government disagreed.

NEXT STEPS TOWARDS AN EVIDENCE-BASED APPROACH TO DCRS IN THE UK

It is premature to assume that DCRs would confer benefits in the UK, or that they would not have undesirable consequences. We do not properly understand how they might optimally be established or what value for money they might provide – all important questions for an evidence-based drug policy that is funded from the public purse. Carefully evaluated pilots are the way to answer these questions, so we conclude by considering how these might yet be achieved. In doing so, the chapter in this book by Kerr and colleagues is instructive, as a comprehensive account of factors that led to the establishment of the Vancouver safer injecting facility. Some distinctive features of the process are that it:

- took a long time – approaching 10 years
- focuses on a locality with co-existing public health crises of overdose deaths and HIV/Aids and a highly visible drug problem
- is underpinned by an accumulation of high-profile policy analyses that recommend safer injecting facilities as part of the response and which received high-profile media coverage
- was greatly assisted by effective drug user organising and direct action and a well-orchestrated media campaign, which in turn shaped public opinion positively and put pressure on politicians
- received strong electoral and political support at the municipality level through the elected city mayor, which allowed local representatives to advocate for the service at the provincial and federal level, where safer injecting facilities were opposed
- drew on research and legal analysis that highlighted the likely beneficial impact and feasibility of a DCR.

In the UK, the public debate about DCRs might best be said to have begun properly in 2002 with the publication of the HASC report, so by Canadian standards the UK might well expect the process of achieving pilots to take several more years.

There are differences in the nature and distribution of the problems experienced. The UK does not have any single locality that corresponds to Vancouver's Down Town East Side (where the DCR is located), with its exceptionally high density of problem drug use and acute public health crisis – not dissimilar to the conditions that led to the establishment of Sydney's Medically Supervised Injecting Centre. The UK has a public health crisis among drug users featuring high rates of overdose, climbing HIV incidence, endemic hepatitis C, and burgeoning crack injecting. However, the UKs problems are more geographically distributed. Nevertheless, there are a number of parts of the country where public injecting is more visible and overdose rates are higher. These are the settings in which DCRs might most readily be piloted.

There is an accumulating body of UK policy analysis that supports DCR pilots, not only the HASC report and that of the IWG, but also the recent Royal Society of Arts report (RSA, 2007) and a subsequent drug policy review by the UK Drug Policy Commission (Reuter & Stevens, 2007). By contrast, local public health reports that identify the way that DCRs may relate to problems of a particular city, town or locality are less evident. One next step may therefore be for local partnerships to appraise whether DCRs seem relevant to the needs of their populations and to introduce these questions into local policy debates. Strategically, it is of note that, based on experience in Germany, large urban regeneration programmes in areas with high rates of visible drug use have provided particular opportunities for investing in services to meet the needs of the populations they displace. It seems possible that the forthcoming 2012 Olympics will provide conditions that could favour developing services in one city – London, where a desire to 'clean up' the city is likely to precede the anticipated influx of tourists that will accompany the games.

In terms of drug user organising and direct action, the UK now has a wide range of user groups, many of which have developed with the encouragement of the National Treatment Agency for Substance Misuse. However, these largely fulfil a consultation role for service development and treatment advocacy rather than the more radical role exemplified by the Vancouver Area Network of Drug Users (VANDU), which adopted a strategy incorporating a series of high-profile direct actions. Although there have been similar attempts to self-organise among UK drug user activists – notably through the now defunct National Drugs Users Development Agency – to date these have not produced corresponding, sustainable organisations that have been able to push forward more radical programmes through effective engagement with the media and political processes. Although some current groups may have the potential to organise in the way that VANDU have done, this component currently appears to be largely missing within the UK situation. There are nevertheless some developing signs of support for the use of DCRs among English drug user representatives (NTA, 2007).

Similarly, strong political champions at the local government level have not yet emerged. Although there are exceptions such as London, Hartlepool and Middlesbrough, local government in most parts of the UK does not involve elected mayors like Vancouver's Larry Campbell, whose powerful, personal mandate proved so influential in the setting up of the DCR there. Local government is mostly more diffuse and seems likely to require strong, local agreement among a range of elected representatives, rather than being able to rely upon any single charismatic individual. Nevertheless, it became evident to the IWG that formative discussions of this sort are occurring in several parts of England and Wales and may produce the required consensus and political will at the local level. In some respects, this appears to parallel processes 20 years ago when largely health-led, local, initiatives to introduce needle and syringe programmes preceded central government support.

Finally, there are signs that a research agenda with corresponding legal analysis is being developed in the UK. The work of the IWG is the most obvious example, with studies commissioned to better understand people's experience of nuisance within local communities and to quantify rates of public injecting and drug users' propensity to use DCRs (Taylor *et al*, 2006; Hunt *et al*, 2007). There are also indications that these questions are now being investigated by other researchers seeking to understand the potential applicability of DCRs in different areas (Rhodes *et al*, 2006).

For the first time, the IWG's legal analysis (Fortson, 2006a; 2006b) has set out the issues that surround the operation of DCRs in the UK in detail and how the potential problems might be addressed. In its report, the IWG was clear that support from central government was not a *sine qua non* for the piloting of DCRs:

'Ideally, this piloting process would be supported and co-ordinated by central government. However, if the government is unable to play this role, the IWG hopes that local agencies will be able to devise local schemes where it is in the public interest to do so.'

In the absence of central government support and legal change to facilitate the piloting of DCRs, a potential way through has been identified that is predicated on developing a local 'accord' with the police and Crown Prosecution Service and the development of clear operational guidelines. Such a model accord and corresponding guidance is currently being developed with the support of the JRF.

CONCLUSION

Internationally, the accumulated evidence base is becoming clearer about the potential of DCRs to enhance drug users' health and reduce nuisance from public injecting, as one component of an integrated drug policy. The extent of problem drug use in the UK, and the severity of the public health crisis among those of its citizens who inject drugs, suggest that DCRs may confer valuable benefits that are currently denied to one of the most marginalised groups within its population. The evidence also suggests that DCRs should reduce the problems experienced by local communities with regard to public injecting and discarded needles. However, the extent to which these benefits would be realised in the UK cannot be properly appraised without well-developed pilot programmes that are rigorously evaluated. This is the logical conclusion of an evidence-based approach to drug policy. Nevertheless, although the decision whether or not to pilot DCRs is shaped in part by a discourse about evidence, it is also influenced by the interplay between the media, public opinion, national politics and local pragmatics. There are signs that some of these non-evidential factors that have paved the way for the introduction of DCRs elsewhere are coalescing in the UK but others are currently absent or poorly developed. As a result, if the goal of DCR pilots is to be realised, this will involve a sustained and determined effort, which is as sensitive to local and national politics as it is to the evidence base.

References

Akzept Bundesverband & Carl von Ossietzky Universität Oldenburg (Eds) (2000) *Guidelines for the Operation and Use of Consumption Rooms.* Lektorat: W Schneider & H Stöver, Materialien No. 4. Münster: Akzept.

Bargagli AM, Hickman M, Davoli M, Perucci CA, Schifano P, Buster M, Brugal T & Vicente J (2005) Drug related mortality and its impact on adult mortality in eight European countries. *European Journal of Public Health.* Originally published online on 12 September. Available at: http://eurpub.oxfordjournals.org/cgi/content/full/16/2/198 (accessed January 2008).

British Columbia Centre for Excellence in HIV/Aids (2004) *Evaluation of the Supervised Injection Site: Year one summary.* Vancouver: BCCE in HIV/Aids.

Bush W, Roberts M & Trace M (2004) *Upheavals in the Australian Drug Market: Heroin drought, stimulant flood. DrugScope briefing paper 4.* London: DrugScope & The Beckley Foundation.

City of Vancouver Four Pillars Drug Strategy (2003) *Supervised Injection Sites (SISs): Frequently asked questions.* Vancouver: City of Vancouver Four Pillars Drug Strategy.

EMCDDA (2005) *Annual Report 2005: The state of the drugs problem in Europe.* Lisbon: EMCDDA.

EMCDDA (2006) *Supporting Table DRD 5 Part ii* [online]. Available at: http://stats06.emcdda.europa.eu/en/elements/drdtab06b-en.html (accessed January 2008).

ENCAMS (2005) *Drugs-related Litter Survey 2005.* Wigan: ENCAMS.

Fortson R (2006a) *IWG Paper E. Harm Reduction and the Law of the United Kingdom.* York: Joseph Rowntree Foundation.

Fortson R (2006b) *IWG Paper F. Setting up a Drug Consumption Room: Legal issues.* York: Joseph Rowntree Foundation.

Gossop M, Griffiths P, Powis B, Williamson S & Strang J (1996) Frequency of non-fatal heroin overdose: survey of heroin users recruited in non-clinical settings. *British Medical Journal* **313** 402.

Hay G, Gannon M, MacDougall J, Millar T, Eastwood C, McKeganey N & Gordon L (2006) Local and national estimates of the prevalence of opiate use and/or crack cocaine use (2004/05). In: N Singleton, R Murray & L Tinsley (Eds) *Measuring Different Aspects of Problem Drug Use: Methodological developments.* London: Home Office.

Health Protection Agency (2005) *Shooting Up – Infections among injecting drug users in the United Kingdom 2004. An update: October 2005.* London: HPA.

Health Protection Agency (2006) *Shooting Up – Infections among injecting drug users in the United Kingdom 2005. An update: October 2006.* London: HPA.

Hedrich D (2004) *European Report on Drug Consumption Rooms.* Lisbon: EMCDDA.

Hickman M, Carnwath Z, Madden P, Farrell M, Rooney R, Ashcroft R, Judd A & Stimson G (2003) Mortality and fatal overdose risk – pilot cohort study of heroin users recruited from specialist drug treatment sites in London. *Journal of Urban Health* **90** 274–87.

Hickman M, Higgin V, Hope V & Bellis M (2004) *Estimating the Prevalence of Problem Drug Use: Multiple methods in Brighton, Liverpool and London. Home Office Online Report 36/04* [online]. Available at: http://www.homeoffice.gov.uk/rds/pdfs04/rdsolr3604.pdf (accessed January 2008).

Home Affairs Select Committee (2002) *Proceedings of the Committee Relating to the (Third) Report, 2001–2* [online]. Available at: http://www.publications.parliament.uk/pa/cm200102/cmselect/cmhaff/318/31817.htm (accessed January 2008).

Hunt N (2006a) *IWG Paper B. The Evaluation Literature on Drug Consumption Rooms.* York: Joseph Rowntree Foundation.

Hunt N (2006b) *IWG Paper A. Indicators of the Need for Drug Consumption Rooms in the UK.* York: Joseph Rowntree Foundation.

Hunt N, Lloyd C, Kimber J & Tompkins C (2007) Public injecting and willingness to use a drug consumption room among needle exchange programme attendees in the UK. *International Journal of Drug Policy* **18** 62–65.

Independent Working Group (2006) *Report of the Independent Working Group on Drug Consumption Rooms.* York: Joseph Rowntree Foundation.

Judd A, Hickman M, Jones S, McDonald T, Parry JV, Stimson GV & Hall AJ (2005) Incidence of hepatitis C virus and HIV among new injecting drug users in London: prospective cohort study. *British Medical Journal* **330** 24–25.

Kerr T, Stoltz J, Tyndall M, Li K, Zhang R, Montaner J & Wood E (2006) Impact of a medically supervised safer injection facility on community drug use patterns: a before and after study. *British Medical Journal* **332** 220–222.

Kerr T, Tyndall M, Li K, Montaner J & Wood E (2005) Safer injection facility use and syringe sharing in injection drug users. *The Lancet* **366** (9482) 316–318.

MacCoun RJ & Reuter P (2001) *Drug War Heresies: Learning from other vices, times and places.* Cambridge: Cambridge University Press.

MSIC Evaluation Committee (2003) *Final Report of the Evaluation of the Sydney Medically Supervised Injecting Centre.* Sydney: MSIC Evaluation Committee.

National Treatment Agency for Substance Misuse (2007) *'Nothing about us, without us': The English user representatives' report from the 2007 International Harm Reduction Conference.* London: NTA.

Office for National Statistics (2007) Deaths related to drug poisoning: England and Wales, 1993–2005. *Health Statistics Quarterly* **33** 82–88.

Poschadel S, Höger R, Schnitzler J & Schreckenberger J (2003) *Evaluation der Arbeit der Drogenkonsumräume in der Bundesrepublik Deutschland: Endbericht im Auftrag des Bundesministeriums für Gesundheit. Das Bundesministerium für Gesundheit und Soziale Sicherung (Schriftenreihe Bd 149).* Baden-Baden: Nomos-Verlags-Gesellschaft.

Powis B, Strang J, Griffiths P, Taylor C, Williamson S, Fountain J & Gossop M (1999) Self-reported overdose among injecting drug users in London: extent and nature of the problem. *Addiction* **94** (4) 471–8.

Reuter P & Stevens A (2007) *An Analysis of UK Drug Policy.* London: UK Drug Policy Commission.

Rhodes T, Kimber J, Small W, Fitzgerald J, Kerr T, Hickman M & Holloway G (2006) Public injecting and the need for 'safer environment interventions' in the reduction of drug-related harm. *Addiction* **101** 1384–1393.

RSA (2007) *Drugs – Facing Facts: The report of the RSA Commission on Illegal Drugs, Communities and Public Policy.* London: RSA.

Skretting A (2006) The Nordic countries and public drug-injection facilities. *Drugs: Education, Prevention and Policy* **13** (1) 5–16.

Taylor A, Cusick L, Kimber J, Rutherford J, Hickman M & Rhodes T (2006) *IWG Paper D. The Social Impact of Public Injecting.* York: Joseph Rowntree Foundation.

Taylor A, Fleming A, Rutherford J & Goldberg D (2004) *Examining the Injecting Practices of Injecting Drug Users in Scotland.* Edinburgh: Effective Interventions Unit.

Thein H, Kimber J, Maher H, MacDonald M & Kaldor JM (2005) Public opinion towards supervised injecting centres and the Sydney Medically Supervised Injecting Centre. *International Journal of Drug Policy* **16** 275–280.

Wood E, Kerr T, Small W, Li K, Marsh DC, Montaner JSG & Tyndall MW (2004) Changes in public order after the opening of a medically supervised safer injecting facility for illicit injection drug users. *Canadian Medical Association Journal* **171** (7) 1–4.

Wood E, Tyndall MW, Stoltz J, Small W, Lloyd-Smith E, Zhang R, Montaner JSG & Kerr T (2005) Factors associated with syringe sharing among users of a medically supervised safer injecting facility. *American Journal of Infectious Diseases* **1** (1) 50–4.

Wood E, Tyndall MW, Zhang R, Stoltz J-A, Math CLM, Montaner JSG & Kerr T (2006) Attendance at supervised injecting facilities and use of detoxification services. *New England Journal of Medicine* **354** (23) 2512–2514.

CHAPTER 5
Establishing North America's first safer injection facility: lessons from the Vancouver experience

Thomas Kerr, Donald MacPherson and Evan Wood

INTRODUCTION

Vancouver, Canada has long been the site of severe health and community harms resulting from illicit injection drug use. These challenges eventually led to calls for a new health-focused approach to drug addiction in the city, including the establishment of North America's first safer injection facility (SIF). Herein, we provide an insider's account of the key events, actions, and policy changes that led to the establishment of Insite, Vancouver's SIF. Due to the controversial nature of this type of public health intervention, years of community mobilisation, activism, public education, and research and policy development were required to ensure the establishment of the facility. The SIF has now been in operation for over three years and a wealth of published research studies indicate that the SIF has been successful in addressing an array of health and social harms resulting from injection drug use. The SIF still remains controversial, and its future is uncertain, suggesting the multifaceted approach that led to its creation may now also be needed to ensure its continuation.

BACKGROUND

Illicit drug use continues to be associated with severe health and social consequences throughout the world (Kerr & Wodack *et al*, 2004). In urban and rural settings, injection drug use in particular, presents major challenges. For example, in many of the regions now hardest hit by HIV, such as parts of Asia, eastern Europe and the former Soviet Union, injection drug users (IDUs) and their sexual contacts account for the majority of new infections (UNAIDS, 2004). As well, fatal overdose is a major source of premature death among IDUs, and other health challenges, such as soft-tissue infections, account for high rates of hospitalisation among this population (Darke & Hall, 2003).

Injection drug use has also been a source of community concern in many settings due to challenges arising from open and visible drug markets and drug use, as well as the presence of discarded syringes in public venues (Wood, Kerr & Small *et al*, 2004). In response, the dominant approach within cities has involved intensifying law enforcement in an effort to limit the supply and use of drugs (Drucker, 1999; Kerr & Kaplan *et al*, 2004; Wodak, 2001; Knutsson, 2000). The use of law enforcement as an isolated intervention has, however, become increasingly controversial since a rapidly growing body of research has demonstrated that these approaches often produce various physical, social, and behavioural impacts that result in the exacerbation of health related harms (Kerr, Small & Wood, 2005; Drucker, 1999). As well, experience has shown that the positive impacts of police crackdowns on visible drug activity are typically time limited, and often result in simply displacing visible drug activity to neighbouring areas (Wood & Spittal *et al*, 2004; Kerr, Small & Wood, 2005).

THE CONTEXT

For most of the last decade, the city of Vancouver has consistently ranked near the top of United Nations indices of the world's 'most livable' cities. With a mild climate by Canadian standards, clean air, mountains, and beautiful beaches, the city's economy has become dependent on a booming tourism industry and will host the 2010 Winter Olympic Games. As a gateway to the rest of Canada, and with critical links to the ports of Asia, the city also has a growing business culture centered in the city's downtown core.

Like most modern cities, Vancouver also has a concentrated lower income neighbourhood, which borders both the central business district and a bustling tourist area. This neighbourhood, known as the Downtown Eastside (DTES), is a concentration of low income single room occupancy (SRO) hotels that traditionally serviced seasonal workers who would come to Vancouver to work in the salmon canneries and other industries that sprang up along the port of Vancouver during the turn of the century.

In response, bars and taverns sprang up in the neighbourhood to service migrant workers, and the DTES has long been the epicentre of Vancouver's illicit drug and sex trade economies. In fact, the culture of the neighbourhood with its mix of ethnic minorities, low income workers, and increased rates of alcoholism and drug use is characteristic of the low income neighbourhoods that exist in most large urban areas in the western world. As was observed throughout most of North America, intravenous heroin injection was documented in the neighbourhood in the late 1960s, and in 1989 the city's first needle exchange opened to respond to the growing number of IDUs (Bardsley *et al*, 1990).

However, in the mid-1990s, a series of factors culminated in the small neighbourhood becoming a vortex of drug related harm that brought international attention. These factors have been described previously (O'Shaughnessy *et al*, 1998), and included a marked decrease in the number of low income housing units built and a major deinstitutionalisation of the city's mentally ill patients, which led to a concentration of the city's low income and mentally ill populations into the only primary low income neighbourhood in the city (Wood & Kerr, 2006). Most of these individuals remained homeless or sought refuge in the DTES's hotels, many of which had evening $10 're-entry' or 'guest' fees. These fees (which are still in place in many SRO hotels) were a lucrative income stream for hotel owners and dissuaded 'guests' from going out on the street at night, but had the deadly effect of also hindering individuals from seeking sources of sterile syringes. Not surprisingly, the unstable housing situation in the DTES has been associated with elevated HIV risk behaviour among Vancouver IDUs (Corneil *et al*, 2006).

Unfortunately, the concentration of high risk IDUs in the neighbourhood coincided with a dramatic shift in the local illicit drug supply that resulted in a major increase in powder cocaine injection (Wood & Kerr, 2006). As has been well described, the short half-life of cocaine, in comparison to heroin, is such that cocaine injectors can inject upwards of 20 times per day, whereas the long half-life of heroin is such that even heavy heroin injectors might be expected to inject only 2–4 times per day (Tyndall *et al*, 2003). The severe impacts of increased cocaine injection were also documented in Vancouver IDUs, and in 1997, Strathdee *et al* demonstrated an explosive outbreak of HIV among the city's IDUs, which culminated in an annual HIV incidence rate of 18% – the highest incidence rate ever documented among IDUs in the developed world (Strathdee *et al*, 1997).

Also linked to the emergence of the challenges experienced in the DTES are the periodic police sweeps that have characterised the neighbourhood for over a decade (Wood, Kerr & Small *et al*, 2003). Early police crackdowns had the unintended consequence of driving IDUs off the streets, deep into the recesses of the SROs where sources of sterile syringes were absent, and where syringe sharing become common place (O'Shaughnessy *et al*, 1998). Unfortunately, these efforts also displaced the drug problem to other neighbourhoods, and in some areas, reduced sterile syringe access during periods of elevated police presence (Wood, Kerr & Small *et al*, 2003).

Despite the shift towards increased cocaine injection, throughout this time, heroin injection continued to have a horrible impact on the morbidity and mortality of the local community, with as many as 200 fatal overdoses per year documented throughout the mid-1990s in Vancouver (Miller *et al*, 2001; Tyndall *et al*, 2001). As a whole, the province experienced one overdose death per day in 1996, and many of these deaths were not restricted to the local community. In fact, between 1992–2000, over 1,200 fatal overdoses were recorded in Vancouver. The drug problem was becoming a province-wide phenomenon and was not restricted to low income populations in inner city neighbourhoods, but now was beginning to have horrifying consequences for many middle class families.

The inner city of Vancouver was being overrun with a growing public drug market, while its hospitals were groaning under the strain of infectious diseases and other health related harms (Kuyper *et al*, 2004; Palepu *et al*, 1999). A city that prided itself on being one of the world's best places to live, was gaining increased notoriety for the high rates of death and disease that were occurring among its citizens. Although relevant authorities had worked to respond with an array of programmes and policies, including syringe exchange programmes and a limited amount of supportive housing, the drug problem in Vancouver was continuing unabated, and new and innovative approaches were desperately needed.

SAFER INJECTION FACILITIES: A CHANGE IN DIRECTION

Within the context of ongoing discussions regarding the drug problem in Vancouver, a new idea emerged. For the first time in North America, a major municipality began considering the role that safer injection facilities could play in addressing the ongoing drug related harms that were occurring locally (Kerr & Palepu, 2001). Safer injection facilities (SIFs), where IDUs can inject pre obtained illicit drugs under the supervision of health care staff, had been implemented in several European cities, and anecdotal reports and data derived from programme evaluations suggested that SIFs could play a role in reducing public disorder related to injection drug use, and could also help to reduce the risks associated with infectious disease transmission and overdose (Broadhead *et al*, 2002).

In September 2003 Vancouver opened North America's first SIF. This was a remarkable development, especially given the Canadian government's long-standing emphasis on enforcement of drug laws, and the proximity of Canada to the USA, where drug prohibition and enforcement have long been the dominant policy approach (Kerr & O'Briain, 2002). The establishment of the Vancouver SIF did not come easily. In fact, the SIF opened close to a decade after Chief Coroner of British Columbia, Vince Cain had called for new and innovative approaches to be implemented in response to the province-wide overdose epidemic in 1993 (Cain, 1994). The opening of North America's first SIF was, in part, the culmination of 10 years of focused advocacy, activism, public education and policy development. These efforts involved a large cast of individuals and groups, with each playing a unique and important role. The aim of this chapter is to describe some of the key processes and events that led to the establishment of Vancouver's SIF.

THE CAIN REPORT – 1994

In 1993, the Chief Coroner of British Columbia, Vince Cain, formed a special task force to look into what was becoming an epidemic of drug overdose deaths in the province. While there had only been 18 drug overdose deaths in Vancouver in 1988, by 1993 there were 200 in the city of Vancouver alone. The provincial figure had gone from 39 in 1988 to 331 in 1993 (Cain, 1994). Cain's task force travelled to all parts of British Columbia in an effort to better understand what was occurring that was contributing to all of these deaths, the vast majority of them preventable. His report to the government of British Columbia was an indictment of how the system in place at the time addressed those with addictions to illegal drugs.

Cain called for the total overhaul of the drug treatment system and the fashion in which the criminal justice system dealt with addicted individuals. He suggested that the criminalisation of heroin and cocaine contributed significantly to the harm that was occurring to drug users and the broader community. He recommended, therefore, the decriminalisation of simple possession of specific substances and that those directly affected be dealt with through a 'medical model' rather than a 'criminal model' (Cain, 1994). The conclusions of Cain's analysis were clear: the status quo was not working and urgent action was required to fix it.

Cain's report was a watershed in that it so clearly articulated the problem of drug addiction as a health and social issue rather than a criminal matter, and it further indicated that a combination of adequate health services and policy changes at provincial and federal levels would have a much more positive impact on addicted individuals and communities than the criminal justice approach that was dominant at the time. Cain's thinking significantly informed the public discussion that would come years later with regard to SIFs, although the conceptual language of 'injection sites' was not in the public discourse at the time.

Cain's recommendations were not quickly taken up by the government of the day and several more years were to pass and many more deaths were documented across the province before the authorities began to formulate a more comprehensive public health response to this situation.

IV FEED AND THE BACK ALLEY DROP-IN – 1996

A key part of the larger movement to establish a SIF in Vancouver involved the operation of illegal or unsanctioned SIFs by local drug users and community activists (Kerr, Wood & Palepu *et al*, 2003). In 1996, an organisation that included many active and former drug users formed to take action in response to the ongoing harms facing local IDUs. This group, called IV Feed, soon succeeded in raising funds to provide peer-based support to local IDUs. These funds were eventually used to open and operate an unsanctioned drug-user-run, supervised injection site in the DTES known as the Back Alley Drop-in (Kerr, Wood & Palepu *et al*, 2003). Programme records kept at the time indicate that that over 100 IDUs used the facility each night (Kerr, Wood & Palepu *et al*, 2003). Although some local IDUs reported being referred by police to the Back Alley SIF, it was the police who eventually closed the site. Still, the existence of this site sent a message that drug users were intent on fighting for the establishment of a SIF, even if they had to illegally operate one themselves.

HIV EPIDEMIC AMONG VANCOUVER IDUs – A PUBLIC HEALTH EMERGENCY IS DECLARED

Shortly after Cain's report on the overdose epidemic was released, a new public health problem was identified in Vancouver's Downtown Eastside: HIV/Aids. In 1996–1997, researchers at the British Columbia Centre for Excellence in HIV/Aids recorded the explosive growth of HIV infection among local IDUs (Strathdee *et al*,

1997), which has been described as the fastest growing HIV epidemic ever recorded in the developed world. In response to these findings, the overdose epidemic, and growing pressure from local community groups, the Vancouver Richmond Health Board declared a public health emergency in the neighbourhood (Wood & Kerr, 2006). Unfortunately, it was several years before this declaration resulted in concrete action to combat the dual epidemics of overdose and HIV that were plaguing the community. Still, the public health emergency became an important part of the local discourse that eventually prompted changes in the approach to the drug problem.

THE EMERGENCE OF THE VANCOUVER AREA NETWORK OF DRUG USERS (VANDU) – 1997–98

In 1997, in response to the emerging health crisis among local IDUs and government inaction, a group of individuals gathered in Vancouver to form a drug-user-run organisation. This group eventually became known as the Vancouver Area Network of Drug Users (VANDU) (Kerr & Small *et al*, 2006). As with other social movements, this organisation is a product of its unique environment, which was characterised by a long history of grass roots activism and severe public health problems resulting from injection drug use. Advocating for the establishment of SIFs, and operating unsanctioned SIFs were among the key activities of this organisation.

VANDU also brought considerable attention to the issues facing local IDUs by travelling to the provincial capital of British Columbia and holding various demonstrations in strategic locations, including the front steps of the BC Legislature buildings (Kerr & Small *et al*, 2006). During such events VANDU members would often produce large black coffins and placards that pleaded with the government to 'act now' to stop the continuing deaths from drug overdoses. VANDU also brought this imagery to Vancouver City Hall and interrupted Council business one day by parading into Council chambers with a coffin and staging an impromptu speech again pleading with city councillors to do whatever they could to stop the unnecessary drug related deaths that were occurring in the community.

Building on the experience of IV Feed, VANDU later went on to operate at least two unsanctioned peer-run SIFs. Among the more notable was the 327 Carrall Street SIF, which has been described in detail elsewhere (Kerr, Oleson & Wood, 2004). These SIFs, although unlike most sanctioned SIFs, served to sustain pressure on policy makers to establish a legitimate SIF locally (Kerr, Oleson & Wood, 2004).

THE KILLING FIELDS CAMPAIGN – 1998

Since government reports on the dire situation in the DTES were not leading to significant action in response to the public health emergency, community members took it upon themselves to highlight the ongoing epidemics. A local community-based housing organisation, the Portland Hotel Society, began a campaign that they dubbed the Killing Fields. In 1998 they partnered with the Vancouver Area Network of Drug Users and other community organisations to stage a public demonstration that saw 1,000 crosses planted in Oppenheimer Park, the local neighbourhood green space (Kerr & Small *et al*, 2006). This event was repeated again in 2000, this time stopping traffic at a major intersection in the inner city and burning all of the reports that had been written over the years in a public gesture that highlighted government inaction. At both of these events a large red banner with the phrase 'The Killing Fields: Federal Action Now' was displayed. The media response to these events was significant and federal politicians took notice.

PAY NOW OR PAY LATER – JOHN MILLAR, PHO – 1998

In June of 1998 British Columbia's Chief Medical Health Officer entered the discussion concerning what needed to be done about the significant level of harm that was occurring among injection drug users across British Columbia. (Millar, 1998). Millar pointed out that not only did the province have a serious drug overdose epidemic, but he also pointed out that the health care system would ultimately have to deal with concurrent epidemics of hepatitis C, hepatitis B and HIV among injection drug users as well. Millar's report to the provincial government articulated an economic argument for action. Millar argued that a relatively small investment by the provincial government and an appropriate expansion of health services for those with addictions in the short term would yield significant cost savings to the government in the long term, hence the title of his report: *HIV, Hepatitis and Injection Drug Use in British Columbia: Pay now or pay later* (Millar, 1998).

Millar argued that, *'(O)nce it is realised that injection drug users are suffering from a chronic relapsing medical condition similar to diabetes or high blood pressure, it becomes obvious that they are as deserving of compassion, respect and adequate care as anyone else. The continuation of this epidemic is a measure of the failure of our society to live up to this value'* (Millar, 1998). According to Millar, the marginalisation and general abuse that IDUs experience within society perpetuates the aforementioned epidemics within British Columbia and the general lack of political will to address the problem in North America (Millar, 1998 p4).

Millar's recommendations echoed many from Vince Cain's report four years earlier, including the expansion of addiction treatment services, increasing access to methadone across British Columbia, the adoption of a harm reduction approach to illegal drug use and a trial of heroin prescription – citing initial successful results from the Swiss heroin-assisted treatment programme that demonstrated good outcomes in treating heroin addictions in a cost-effective fashion (Wood, Kerr, Spittal & Tyndall *et al*, 2003).

Once again a major authority in British Columbia's health care system, the Provincial Health Officer, had pointed to, among other things, the criminalisation and marginalisation of IDUs as a significant cause of the ongoing and concurrent epidemics of disease and death in the province. In June of 1998 when Millar's report was released, the concept of a safe injection site as one of the possible responses to these epidemics did not yet have a large presence in the public and professional discourse. This was about to change.

INTERNATIONAL SYMPOSIUM ON CRIME PREVENTION AND DRUG TREATMENT – JUNE 1998, OUT OF HARM'S WAY – NOVEMBER 1998

In 1998 two pivotal events took place in Vancouver that moved the discussion on new and innovative approaches forward. The first event was staged by the Mayor's Coalition for Crime Prevention and Drug Treatment and brought individuals to Vancouver who were either critical of the status quo, the war on drugs approach, or who were involved in new and innovative approaches such as the Swiss heroin trials. The event was sponsored by the Mayor and the Police Chief and was the first time that drug users were invited into the Mayor's Coalition.

In November of the same year, the Portland Hotel Society staged a one-day conference in the heart of the neighbourhood where the concurrent epidemics of overdose and HIV/Aids were occurring. The Portland Hotel Society is a non-profit organisation that provides supportive housing to some of the most marginalised and difficult to house residents of the DTES. The organisation also operates various community and health services, including a life skills centre for drug users and a café. During the Out of Harm's Way event over 700 people crammed into a large circus tent in the pouring rain to listen to speakers from Europe, the USA and Canada talk about interventions that had been successful in Europe in significantly reducing harm to individuals and the community resulting from injection drug use. This conference strengthened the movement for implementing safe injection sites in Vancouver as it gave a local audience a chance to hear from health and police officials from Europe about the success of SIFs and how police and health care worked together to address the situation at the street level. The public discussion of SIFs and heroin prescription programmes was in full swing by the end of 1998.

KEEPING THE DOOR OPEN CONFERENCE AND THE HARM REDUCTION ACTION SOCIETY

In 1999, a coalition of community groups formed, built on the success of the Out of Harm's Way event, and created a conference series called Keeping the Door Open. These conferences brought together drug users and their families, service providers, academic researchers, police, policy makers and other key stakeholders, and were key to the ongoing public education efforts specific to SIFs. The meetings also generated considerable media attention. Among the more important outcomes of the conferences was the building of key coalitions. At the end of one conference in

1999, a local activist, Ann Livingston, invited all those attending to meet with her and a group of drug users from VANDU for the purpose of 'taking action to save lives'. This ultimately led to the formation of the Harm Reduction Action Society (HRAS), which included individuals from an array of backgrounds and organisations. Included were members of VANDU, individuals from Downtown Eastside community organisations, Aids service organisations, health care professionals, researchers, and parents of drug users.

HRAS quickly decided that its goal was to promote the establishment of a SIF in Vancouver. Using donations from various organisations, the group soon hired a consultant who developed the first ever detailed proposal for a pilot of a SIF in Vancouver (Kerr, 2000). This document was widely disseminated and also generated considerable media attention. HRAS went on to engage in 'insider lobbying' (ie. meeting with politicians behind closed doors), and also conducted various public education activities. Among the more successful were two 'mock' SIFs, which were set up in a Downtown Eastside church. The mock SIFs were constructed to closely resemble a real SIF, and individuals knowledgeable about public health and drug use were on hand to provide information, including written materials, to individuals interested in learning more about SIFs. Both mock SIFs attracted considerable media attention, and the second was open for public viewing for an entire week. These public education efforts were also critical in so far as they served to dispel many of the common fears associated with SIFs, including the fear that such programmes encourage drug use and exacerbate drug-related crime.

FROM GRIEF TO ACTION – 2000

Another significant development that prompted changes in public attitudes regarding SIFs was the emergence of the group From Grief to Action (FGTA). From Grief to Action was a support group of families who had relatives who were addicted to drugs. In 2000 the group became very much involved in public advocacy work calling for a comprehensive continuum of care for drug users including harm reduction services. From Grief to Action comprised parents from across the broader community and represented a more mainstream voice calling on all levels of government to implement life-saving harm reduction and treatment programmes for those with addictions. The addition of the voices of middle class professionals such as lawyers, university professors, civil servants and their children was a significant development in the movement for establishing a SIF in Vancouver. For the first time the issue was clearly defined as a societal problem that cut across class boundaries. The people who were dying from drug overdoses were the sons, daughters, sisters and brothers of everyday people – regardless of the community in Vancouver that they lived in. The notion that the tragedy that was unfolding in Vancouver was simply about marginalised individuals in one inner city neighbourhood who made bad choices – the undeserving poor – was no longer accepted, and as a result, the movement for establishing a SIF gained considerable momentum.

THE FEDERAL, PROVINCIAL, TERRITORIAL TASK FORCE ON INJECTION DRUG USE IN CANADA

At the same time a report prepared by a national task force for the federal and provincial Ministers of Health, *Reducing the Harm Associated with Injection Drug Use in Canada*, recommended a series of actions to respond to the growing problem of injection drug use across the country. One of the recommendations in this report was to *'Establish a task group, consisting of law enforcement, justice, health and social services, addiction, and community perspectives to conduct a feasibility study of establishing a scientific, medical research project regarding supervised injection sites in Canada'* (Federal, Provincial and Territorial Advisory Committee on Population Health, 2001). This report was significant in that it opened the door for the municipality of Vancouver to align its policy work with the work of the task force and push for implementation of the feasibility work around SIFs.

THE VANCOUVER AGREEMENT – 2000

The ongoing public outcry for action to address the urgent situation in the inner city resulted in the federal, provincial and Vancouver governments coming together to sign an urban development agreement that would enable better co-ordination of government actions in the areas of social, economic and community development. This created a number of opportunities to introduce to all levels of government the notion of SIFs as an important and innovative intervention that could address some of the more immediate street level impacts and function as a component of a more comprehensive system to address addictions issues in Vancouver.

VANCOUVER'S FOUR PILLAR DRUG STRATEGY – 2000–2003

In the spring of 2000 the city of Vancouver created the position of Drug Policy Co-ordinator in an effort to bring more focus to how the municipality could be engaged in addressing the public health crisis that was taking place in the inner city. The Mayor of Vancouver at the time, Philip Owen, knew that the city had to take more action to bring a focus to the public health emergency that had been declared in Vancouver's inner city. In 1997 he had established a coalition for crime prevention and drug treatment that brought people together across business, professional and community sectors to look at promising directions in crime prevention and drug treatment. The new position of Drug Policy Co-ordinator was intended to further this work and to develop a drug strategy for the city.

In the fall of 2000 the mayor released the city's draft drug strategy: *A Framework for Action: A four-pillar approach to drug problems in Vancouver* (MacPherson, 2000). The strategy called for a public health and public order approach to the deteriorating situation in Vancouver and called on all levels of government to come to the table to support a range of actions across the four pillars of prevention, treatment, enforcement and harm reduction.

The strategy gave the Mayor of Vancouver some ammunition when meeting with provincial and federal levels of governments, which had mandates to address the public health crisis. Of the 36 recommendations in the final version of the city's drug strategy, two struck a major chord with the public. The recommendation that a committee be established to study the feasibility of implementing a SIF and the recommendation for the city to support the development of a clinical trial of heroin-assisted treatment for long-term heroin addicts indicated a new and radically different approach to the problem of injection drug use. This caught the public's attention, and with the Mayor's leadership, a broad public discussion was held during the winter/spring of 2001. Mayor Owen received much kudos from all sectors for his leadership and support for new, innovative, albeit controversial initiatives to address the concurrent epidemics taking place in Vancouver's Downtown Eastside.

In May of 2001, Vancouver city council unanimously endorsed the *Framework for Action* as the City's drug strategy. The political discussion regarding facilities where injection drug users could inject themselves with illegal drugs in much safer settings than the back alleys and hotel rooms of the Vancouver's Downtown Eastside was about to move into a higher gear. At this time it was still politically dangerous to publicly support SIFs as a part of the solution. The public support for Mayor Owen was strong, but as he headed towards the 2002 election, internal party politics caused him to resign. His belief in the need for a change in Canada's drug policies to allow SIFs and heroin prescription though popular with the public was not shared by all in his political party. Owen was replaced by a candidate who was perceived by many as being lukewarm to the idea of SIFs. She ran against a popular ex-coroner Larry Campbell who fully endorsed implementing SIFs immediately in an effort to stem the death and disease that was occurring in the inner city. By the time the election came around later that year, public support for SIFs had grown considerably, and it became politically dangerous for any party leader to oppose the establishment of such a facility. Throughout the election, SIFs remained a major topic of discussion, and eventually Larry Campbell won the election with an overwhelming majority, decimating the party that had ruled Vancouver for over a decade. This in turn made SIFs a part of the mainstream public discourse on how to respond to the public health crisis among IDUs in Vancouver.

THE ROLE OF RESEARCH

As public discussion of the need for a SIF in Vancouver began to escalate, so did the efforts of researchers, who were interested in assessing the potential impacts of SIFs. Researchers from the BC Centre for Excellence in HIV/Aids conducted a series of SIF feasibility studies during the years 2001–2003 (Wood, Kerr, Spittal & Li *et al*, 2003; Kerr, Wood & Palepu *et al*, 2003; Kerr, Wood & Small *et al*, 2003). The studies consistently showed that a pilot SIF in Vancouver had potential to reach a substantial proportion of local IDUs, including those most at risk for HIV infection and drug overdose, as well as those most responsible for public disorder resulting from injection drug use. These studies, like other documents specific to SIFs, generated an immense amount of media interest, and thereby served an important public education function and also provided a body of evidence from which to initiate further discussion regarding the merits of SIFs in the Vancouver context.

THE LEGAL ISSUES

While there was growing agreement that SIFs could play an important role in the larger public health response to the problems associated with injection drug use, local and national police forces maintained that such facilities could never be allowed to operate in the Canadian context because their operations would contravene several domestic and international laws and treaties. These statements from police and some politicians had the temporary effect of stalling discussions regarding the establishment of SIFs in Vancouver and eventually sparked a series of legal analyses of SIFs from various academics, lawyers and legal research organisations. Among the more comprehensive was the report prepared by the Canadian HIV/Aids Legal Network (Canadian HIV/Aids Legal Network, 2002). The authors of this report concluded that SIFs could operate legally in Canada, and they made several recommendations for how the legal operation of a SIF in Canada could be achieved. The authors also argued that, from a human rights perspective, it could be argued that governments had a duty to pilot SIFs in Vancouver, given the many severe forms of drug-related harm that had been documented. Further, the authors argued persuasively that the operation of a SIF in Canada would not contravene international drug control treaties that were said to be outdated and irrelevant since the emergence of HIV/Aids.

THE DR PETER CENTRE

The movement to establish North America's first official SIF continued while other organisations attempted to respond to the issue of injection drug use in their own way. The drug users had already had a short run at opening a grass roots SIF in 1996. Now another organisation entered the fray. The Dr Peter Centre includes a day programme and a residential facility that provides comfort care to people living with HIV and Aids. In 2002, the Dr Peter Centre announced that as a part of their services the centre nurses would begin allowing those IDUs attending their day programme to use a small room as a supervised injection site (Wood, Zettel & Stewart, 2003). This announcement followed a series of consultations with the provincial professional nursing association, the Registered Nursing Association of British Columbia (RNABC). Representatives from RNABC informed the Dr Peter Centre nurses that, in the opinion of the association, the supervision of injections fell within the scope of acceptable nursing practice even if those injections were of illegal substances (Wood, Zettel & Stewart, 2003). The RNABC also went one step further and indicated that the supervision of injections in a setting like the Dr Peter Centre was part of the nurses' ethical obligations, given the potential harms that could arise from unsupervised injections (Wood, Zettel & Stewart, 2003). Like many other developments specific to the SIF, the supervision of injections at the Dr Peter Centre generated considerable media attention and, ironically, led to media statements from the local police force suggesting that nothing illegal was occurring at the Dr Peter Centre as a result of the supervised injecting programme.

FIX: THE STORY OF AN ADDICTED CITY

Another public education effort that played a key role in educating the general public about the suffering of local drug users and the potential benefits of SIFs was the feature-length documentary, *FIX: The Story of an Addicted City*. This film, made by Vancouver-based documentary film-maker Nettie Wild, focused on the efforts by VANDU to advocate for establishing the SIF and had a significant impact on public discussion and garnered much attention during the local municipal election of 2002. During the running of the film, public forums were held in theatres immediately following the showing of the film. A range of individuals, including mayoral candidates, public health experts, drug users, and researchers participated in these discussions with those attending the film. Through these interactive forums, the film-makers reached out to a segment of the public that was otherwise less directly involved in the ongoing discourse surrounding SIFs.

THE NEW MAYOR – NOVEMBER 2002

Within two weeks of Larry Campbell winning the 2002 civic election on a platform of addressing drug problems in the Downtown Eastside of Vancouver and opening up a SIF, he was in Canada's capital city, Ottawa, vigorously lobbying the federal government, in particular Health Canada, to approve an application for a SIF as soon as they received it. Back in Vancouver, Campbell had convened the CEO of the local health authority and the chief of police to work on a plan of action. The local police did not support SIFs because they saw them as being illegal. There was no indication that they would not support such initiatives should the federal government sanction them and remove any legal obstacles to setting one up. Several weeks later Vancouver Coastal Health, the regional health authority, submitted an application to the federal government for an exemption from Section 56 of Canada's Controlled Drugs and Substances Act, which would allow them, for the purposes of scientific research, to implement a pilot SIF for a period of three years. Ultimately, the Vancouver Police Department supported the application, and thereby allayed concerns that the police would continue to oppose such an initiative.

THE 327 CARRALL STREET SIF

In the spring of 2003 the Vancouver Police Department initiated a police crackdown on the open drug scene in the Downtown Eastside. At this time, Vancouver's SIF was in the planning stages but was months away from opening. The crackdown involved extra police officers taken from other areas of the city and being assigned to a new unit with the intention of significantly increasing the visible police presence in the area of the open drug scene (Small & Kerr *et al*, 2006). This action was one of the most vigorous enforcement efforts on the street-level drug scene that had been seen in many years and it was not without controversy. While some in the community welcomed the increased police action in the neighbourhood, the drug users' organisation VANDU and many service providers were concerned about the displacement of the drug market and the many vulnerable addicted, mentally ill and marginalised individuals that were negatively impacted by this increased enforcement. In time, consistent with a large body of research on police crackdowns (Kerr, Small & Wood, 2005), research conducted locally confirmed that this crackdown did displace drug users out of the Downtown Eastside neighbourhood, and away from important health services (Wood & Spittal *et al*, 2004). Although the crackdown did reduce the visible open drug scene locally, the crackdown was also associated with elevations in risk behaviour among local IDUs (Small & Kerr *et al*, 2006).

In response to the police crackdown and delays in the opening of the sanctioned and much promised SIF, a group of drug users and a local nurse opened up another unsanctioned SIF (Kerr, Oleson & Wood, 2004). This facility was both a response to the police crackdown by local activists and a way to put pressure on the authorities to expedite the opening of the official SIF. The '327 Carrall Street SIF' operated for 184 days. During the operation of the SIF, volunteers supervised over 3,000 injections by a high-risk injection drug-using population (Kerr & Oleson *et al*, 2005). This SIF, like many of the other unsanctioned SIFs before it, was eventually closed due to pressure from local police and policy makers following the opening of the Vancouver sanctioned SIF on 22 September 2003 (Kerr & Oleson *et al*, 2005).

DISCUSSION

The implementation of North America's first SIF was the culmination of a broad social movement across many sectors that took place over a number of years starting with Chief Coroner Vince Cain's report in 1994 that so emphatically maintained that addiction must be seen as a health issue with robust health care responses rather than an issue that the criminal justice system could adequately address. While Cain's report set a clear direction for government to act, the report was ignored by the government of the day. Whereas drug users themselves had attempted to respond one year after the Chief Coroner's report by opening up their own grass roots 'safe site', the Back Alley, it took seven more years of hard work by a cast of thousands to build the community consensus and foster the political will to open the SIF pilot project in Vancouver. As noted by others, the process leading eventually to the opening of the pilot SIF was lengthy and multifaceted, and involved a process of culture change locally (Small, Palepu & Tyndall, 2006). Included was an array of distinct approaches, ranging from grass roots activism and civil disobedience to research, legal analysis, public education, coalition building, and policy development. It may be that any of these approaches working in isolation may not have been enough to prompt the establishment of this innovative and controversial public health initiative.

Consistent with the theories of policy development espoused by Kingdon (1995) and Baumgartner and Jones (1993), the establishment of Vancouver's SIF was realised through the work of various actors and 'policy entrepreneurs' who highlighted and navigated relevant local problems, policies, and politics, and recognised 'policy windows' specific to the problem of addiction. Kingdon (1995) described three policy streams as being critical to the policy making process: the problem stream, the policy stream, and the political stream. The problem stream involves identifying and promoting the recognition of a problem through documentation of indicators and through what Kingdon (1995) calls 'focusing events'. In the case of the Vancouver SIF, local problems associated with injection drug use (for example, HIV/Aids overdoses) were forced into the policy realm by activists, lobbyists, journalists, and later on, decision makers and their aides. A number of focusing events also helped illuminate the problems of addiction and promote attention to them. For example, the attendance of local drug users at policy meetings and a series of public protests were key focusing events that helped place the problems of injection drug use and the associated harms within public discourse. The policy stream involves policy communities and 'policy entrepreneurs' who formulate potential solutions and alternatives to identified problems. During the early discussions of SIFs in Vancouver, local community groups and policy makers helped to make SIFs a potential solution by promoting their feasibility and acceptance. The political stream involves shifts in public opinion, relevant administrative changes, and interest groups who force action. Through ongoing discussion and planning a 'policy window' specific to the problems of addiction opened, and SIFs eventually became part of the agenda-setting activity of the local municipal government. Important administrative changes further moved the agenda along as organisations and policy makers developed the initial 'structural arrangements' (Baumgartner & Jones, 1993; Kindgon, 1995) needed to implement SIFs. The intentional and strategic institutionalisation of the SIF issue by the municipal government later prompted the provincial and federal governments to act and articulate policy positions specific to SIFs. This political momentum was further fuelled by an ever-evolving public opinion that favoured a new approach to the problems of addiction. The SIF finally became fully realisable as a result of the work of non-governmental organisations who articulated the legal and policy structures needed to allow for the operation of the SIF under Canadian and international laws and treaties.

Given the ongoing controversy surrounding harm reduction approaches in most settings, elaborate social and political processes often precede the establishment of harm reduction interventions. This is certainly the case when it comes to establishing SIFs, as most SIFs have been established after lengthy discussions within public and political arenas. The first three years of experience with the Vancouver SIF further suggest that additional advocacy and policy work may be needed to ensure that the SIF remains in operation.

THE FIRST THREE YEARS OF INSITE: VANCOUVER'S FIRST MEDICALLY SUPERVISED SAFER INJECTION FACILITY

As part of the federal approval to operate Insite, the SIF was subjected to a rigorous three-year scientific evaluation (Wood, Tyndall & Montaner *et al*, 2006). Given the controversial nature of the programme, it was agreed that the researchers responsible for the evaluation had to seek the highest standard of scientific scrutiny (Wood, Kerr & Lloyd-Smith *et al*, 2004). Therefore, all studies were subjected to peer-review by the top medical and public health journals in the world. Because of ethical concerns, the SIF evaluation could not be conducted as a randomised clinical trial, and instead a variety of prospective cohort studies involving IDUs were utilised to conduct observational epidemiological analyses of the impacts of the SIF (Wood, Kerr & Lloyd-Smith *et al*, 2004). The first three years of the evaluation were remarkably productive and resulted in no fewer than 22 articles published in the top journals, such as *The Lancet, New England Journal of Medicine,* the *British Medical Journal,* and the *Canadian Medical Association Journal* (Wood, Tyndall & Montaner *et al*, 2006; Wood, Tyndall & Zhang *et al*, 2006; Kerr & Tyndall *et al*, 2005; Kerr & Stolz *et al*, 2006). The studies revealed a number of health and social benefits, including evidence that the SIF and its usage were associated with reductions in public disorder, reduced syringe sharing and increases in safer injecting practices (Kerr & Tyndall *et al*, 2005; Stoltz *et al*, 2007), increased use of addiction treatment (Wood, Tyndall & Zhang *et al*, 2006), and reduced risks associated with drug related overdose (Kerr *et al*, 2007). Further, the evaluation confirmed the projections of earlier feasibility studies by showing that the SIF was attracting an exceptionally high-risk segment of the local IDU community, including those at heightened risk for HIV infection and fatal overdose, as well as those responsible for public disorder (Wood *et al*, 2005). The evaluators also took the unusual step of publishing a series of studies showing that the SIF was not associated with any of the much feared potential negative impacts, including increased crime and drug use (Wood, Tyndall & Lai *et al*, 2006; Kerr & Stolz *et al*, 2006).

During the final year of the three-year SIF pilot, there was a change in Canada's federal government. The new 'conservative' government and its leader had made a number of public statements indicating their opposition to the SIF. In the months before the conclusion of the original three-year federal SIF exemption (Wood, Tyndall & Montaner *et al*, 2006), the operators and evaluators of Insite submitted a proposal to Health Canada to extend the pilot SIF for an additional three-and-a-half years. Health Canada then reassured the evaluators that they had enlisted international experts in the areas of injection drug use and HIV/Aids to conduct a rigorous and independent scientific peer review of the proposal. The reviews indicated that the proposal was highly rated by all three reviewers. For example, one reviewer stated the following:

'Basically, I consider this proposal to be superb and of extremely high importance. The research team has, to date, produced extremely valuable research results. In summary, I am in full and enthusiastic support for this proposed research.' (Health Canada, 2006a)

Ironically, three days before the federal Health Minister announced his decision regarding the fate of Insite, the federal police force, the Royal Canadian Mounted Police, released a statement, without providing any supporting data, suggesting that the SIF experiment had failed (Wood, Tyndall & Montaner *et al*, 2006). Also ironic was the release of a statement by the Canadian Association of Police only hours before the Health Minister's announcement, which also, without providing any supporting data, suggested that the SIF had failed and called for its closure (Wood, Tyndall & Montaner *et al*, 2006). Then, late one Friday afternoon, only weeks before the expiry of the initial three-year SIF exemption, the federal Health Minister released a statement saying that the decision concerning the three-year extension of Insite had been deferred for 17 months, during which additional studies of the SIF would be undertaken. The release further indicated that during this period, the SIF would be allowed to operate. Despite the high volume of research generated by the evaluation team, the Health Minister made the following statement in his press release: *'Do safe injection sites contribute to lowering drug use and fighting addiction? Right now the only thing the research to date has proven is drug addicts need more help to get off drugs'* (Health Canada, 2006b). This statement appeared particularly odd in light of the external peer reviews conducted by Health Canada and studies indicating that the SIF was increasing the rate of referral to abstinence-based addiction treatments among local IDUs (Wood, Tyndall & Montaner *et al*, 2006). The Health Minister also took the additional step of banning the initiation of any new SIF research in Canada. These actions led to accusations of political interference in the natural development of evidence-based public health policy by the researchers involved in the evaluation. Although the federal Health Minister eventually cut all federal funding for the evaluation of Insite, there was considerable support for the SIF provincially, and evaluation funding was restored by the provincial Ministry of Health. It was later revealed that the federal conservative government had conducted a national opinion poll that elicited the opinions of Canadians on several issues specific to drug policy. The results showed that the majority of Canadians support the establishment of SIFs. In the province of British Columbia, where Insite operated, 64% of Canadians reported their support for SIFs as one part of the response to the harms associated with drug use (Woods, 2007).

In the months following the federal Health Minister's announcement that Insite's licence to operate was extended by 18 months, Canada's conservative government announced its plan to implement a new national drug strategy. Consistent with the government's neo-conservative agenda, the new drug strategy is a 'get tough' approach that focuses exclusively on prevention, treatment, and enforcement. It appears as though harm reduction will not be part of the new strategy that has been named the 'Anti-drug Strategy'. In other words, it appears that there is no place for SIFs in the policies of the new federal government.

CONCLUSION

The establishment of Vancouver's first SIF involved an array of players and a great deal of work within public and political arenas. The SIF is a direct result of sustained pressure by many sectors in the community, within government, the research sector and among politicians willing to take a strong advocacy position for changing direction in addressing injection drug use in the inner city and to reject the status quo. The establishment of the SIF has been a significant intervention and the SIF research project has clearly demonstrated that the site attracts the relevant vulnerable population of IDUs and has reduced health and community harms associated with injection drug use, while having no negative impact on the surrounding community. At the same time its future remains fragile due to the ideological position taken by many within the new federal government. The movement to establish a SIF started at the grass roots level, with IDUs and local community organisations pushing for new ways to address the death and despair within the community. The effort started with the drug users themselves and over time garnered support from all levels of the community. Although these efforts were successful in prompting the establishment of Vancouver's SIF, they may once again become essential to the fight to keep this innovative public health intervention in operation for the years to come.

References

Bardsley J, Turvey J & Blatherwick J (1990) Vancouver's needle exchange program. *Canadian Journal of Public Health* **81** (1) 39–45.

Baumgartner F & Jones B (1993) *Agendas and Instability in American Politics*. Chicago: University of Chicago Press.

Broadhead RS, Kerr T, Grund JP & Altice R (2002) Safer injection facilities in North America: their place in public policy and health initiatives. *Journal of Drug Issues* **32** (1) 329–355.

Cain JV (1994) *The Cain Report. British Columbia task force into illicit narcotic overdose deaths in British Columbia. Report of the task force into illicit narcotic deaths in British Columbia*. Victoria, BC: Ministry of Health.

Canadian HIV/Aids Legal Network (2002) *Establishing Safe Injection Facilities in Canada: Legal and ethical issues. Canadian HIV/Aids Legal Network (2002)*. Montreal: Canadian HIV/Aids Legal Network.

Corneil TA, Kuyper LM, Shoveller J, Hogg RS, Li K, Spittal PM, Schechter MT & Wood E (2006) Unstable housing, associated risk behaviour, and increased risk for HIV infection among injection drug users. *Health & Place* **12** (1) 79–85.

Darke S & Hall W (2003) Heroin overdose: research and evidence-based intervention. *Journal of Urban Health* **80** (2) 189–200.

Drucker E (1999) Drug prohibition and public health: 25 years of evidence. *Public Health Reports* **114** (1) 14–29.

Federal, Provincial and Territorial Advisory Committee on Population Health (2001) *Reducing the Harm Associated with Injection Drug Use in Canada*. Ottawa: Federal, Provincial and Territorial Advisory Committee on Population Health.

Health Canada (2006a) *Anonymous Peer Reviews of the Proposal to Evaluate Vancouver's Supervised Injection Site*. Vancouver: Office of Canada's Drug Strategy, Health Canada.

Health Canada (2006b) *No New Injection Sites for Addicts until Questions Answered Says Minister Clement*. Ottawa: Health Canada.

Kerr T (2000) *Safe Injection Facilities: Proposal for a Vancouver pilot study*. Vancouver: Harm Reduction Action Society.

Kerr T, Kaplan K, Suwannawong P, Jurgens R & Wood E (2004) The global fund to fight Aids, tuberculosis and malaria: funding for unpopular public health programmes. *The Lancet* **364** (9428) 11–12.

Kerr T & O'Briain W (2002) Drug policy in Canada – the way forward. *Canadian HIV–Aids Policy & Law Review* **7** (1) 1–32.

Kerr T, Oleson M, Tyndall MW, Montaner J & Wood E (2005) A description of a peer-run supervised injection site for injection drug users. *Journal of Urban Health* **82** (2) 267–275.

Kerr T, Oleson M & Wood E (2004) Harm-reduction activism: a case study of an unsanctioned user-run safe injection site. *Canadian HIV Aids Policy Law Review* **9** (2) 13–19.

Kerr T & Palepu A (2001) Safe injection facilities in Canada: is it time? *Canadian Medical Association Journal* **165** (4) 436–437.

Kerr T, Small W, Moore D & Wood E (2007) A micro-environmental intervention to reduce the harms associated with drug-related overdose: evidence from the evaluation of Vancouver's safer injection facility. *International Journal of Drug Policy* **18** 37–45.

Kerr T, Small W, Peeace W, Pierre A & Wood E (2006) Harm reduction by a 'user-run' organisation: a case study of the Vancouver Area Network of Drug Users. *International Journal of Drug Policy* **17** (2) 61–69.

Kerr T, Small W & Wood E (2005) The public health and social impacts of drug market enforcement: a review of the evidence. *International Journal of Drug Policy* **16** 210–220.

Kerr T, Stoltz JA, Tyndall M, Li K, Zhang R, Montaner J & Wood E (2006) Impact of a medically supervised safer injection facility on community drug use patterns: a before and after study. *British Medical Journal* **332** (7535) 220–222.

Kerr T, Tyndall M, Li K, Montaner J & Wood E (2005) Safer injection facility use and syringe sharing in injection drug users. *The Lancet* **366** (9482) 316–318.

Kerr T, Wodak A, Elliott R, Montaner JS & Wood E (2004) Opioid substitution and HIV/Aids treatment and prevention. *The Lancet* **364** (9449) 1918–1919.

Kerr T, Wood E, Palepu A, Wilson D, Schechter MT & Tyndall MW (2003) Responding to explosive HIV epidemics driven by frequent cocaine injection: Is there a role for safer injecting facilities? *Journal of Drug Issues* **33** (3) 579–608.

Kerr T, Wood E, Small D, Palepu A & Tyndall MW (2003) Potential use of safer injecting facilities among injection drug users in Vancouver's Downtown Eastside. *Canadian Medical Association Journal* **169** (8) 759–763.

Kingdon JW (1995) *Agendas, Alternatives and Public Policies* (2nd ed). Boston, Massachusetts: Addison-Wesley.

Knutsson J (2000) Swedish drug markets and drugs policy. In: M Hough & M Natarajan (Eds) *Illegal Drug Markets: From research to policy*. Monsey, New Jersey: Criminal Justice Press, 179–202.

Kuyper LM, Hogg RS, Montaner JS, Schechter MT & Wood E (2004) The cost of inaction on HIV transmission among injection drug users and the potential for effective interventions. *Journal of Urban Health* **81** (4) 655–660.

MacPherson D (2000) *A Framework for Action: A four-pillar approach to drug problems in Vancouver.* Vancouver: City of Vancouver.

Millar JS (1998) *HIV, Hepatitis, and Injection Drug Use in British Columbia: Pay now or pay later?* Vancouver: British Columbia Provincial Health Officer.

Miller CL, Chan KJ, Palepu A, Wood E, Tyndall MW, Wood E, Hogg RS & O'Shaughnessy MV (2001) Socio-demographic profile and HIV and hepatitis C prevalence among persons who died of a drug overdose. *Addiction Research and Theory* **9** (5) 459–470.

O'Shaughnessy MV, Montaner JS, Strathdee S & Schechter MT (1998) Deadly public policy. *International Conference on AIDS* **12** (982) (abstract no. 44233).

Palepu A, Strathdee SA, Hogg RS, Anis AH, Rae S, Cornelisse PG & Schechter MT (1999) The social determinants of emergency department and hospital use by injection drug users in Canada. *Journal of Urban Health* **76** (4) 409–418.

Small W, Kerr T, Charette J, Wood E, Schechter MT & Spittal PM (2006) Impact of intensified police activity upon injection drug users in Vancouver's Downtown Eastside: evidence from an ethnographic investigation. *International Journal of Drug Policy* **17** 85–95.

Small D, Palepu A & Tyndall M (2006) The establishment of North America's first state sanctioned supervised injection facility: a case study in culture change. *International Journal of Drug Policy* **17** 73–82.

Stoltz JA, Wood E, Small W, Li K, Tyndall M, Montaner J & Kerr T (2007) Changes in injecting practices associated with the use of a medically supervised safer injection facility. *Journal of Public Health* **29** (1) 35–39.

Strathdee SA, Patrick DM, Currie SL, Cornelisse PG, Rekart ML, Montaner JS, Schechter MT & O'Shaughnessy MV (1997) Needle exchange is not enough: lessons from the Vancouver injecting drug use study. *AIDS* **11** (8) F59–65.

Tyndall MW, Craib KJ, Currie S, Li K, O'Shaughnessy MV & Schechter MT (2001) Impact of HIV infection on mortality in a cohort of injection drug users. *Journal of Acquired Immune Deficiency Syndrome* **28** (4) 351–357.

Tyndall MW, Currie S, Spittal P, Li K, Wood E, O'Shaughnessy, MV & Schechter MT (2003) Intensive injection cocaine use as the primary risk factor in the Vancouver HIV-1 epidemic. *AIDS* **17** (6) 887–893.

UNAIDS (2004) 2004 *Report on the Global Aids Epidemic.* Geneva: UNAIDS.

Wodak A (2001) Drug laws. War on drugs does more harm than good. *British Medical Journal* **323** (7317) 866.

Wood E & Kerr T (2006) What do you do when you hit rock bottom: responding to drugs in the city of Vancouver. *International Journal of Drug Policy* **17** (2) 55–60.

Wood E, Kerr T, Lloyd-Smith E, Buchner C, Marsh DC, Montaner JS & Tyndall MW (2004) Methodology for evaluating Insite: Canada's first medically supervised safer injection facility for injection drug users. *Harm Reduction Journal* **1** (1) 9.

Wood E, Kerr T, Small W, Jones J, Schechter MT & Tyndall MW (2003) The impact of police presence on access to needle exchange programs. *Journal of Acquired Immune Deficiency Syndromes* **34** (1) 116–118.

Wood E, Kerr T, Small W, Li K, Marsh D, Montaner JS & Tyndall MW (2004) Changes in public order after the opening of a medically supervised safer injecting facility for illicit injection drug users. *Canadian Medical Association Journal* **171** 731–734.

Wood E, Kerr T, Spittal PM, Li K, Small W, Tyndall MW, Hogg RS, O'Shaughnessy MV & Schechter MT (2003) The potential public health and community impacts of safer injecting facilities: evidence from a cohort of injection drug users. *Journal of Acquired Immune Deficiency Syndromes* **32** (1) 2–8.

Wood E, Kerr T, Spittal PM, Tyndall MW, O'Shaughnessy MV & Schechter MT (2003) The healthcare and fiscal costs of the illicit drug use epidemic: the impact of conventional drug control strategies and the impact of a comprehensive approach. *BC Medical Journal* **45** (3) 130–136.

Wood E, Spittal PM, Small W, Kerr T, Li K, Hogg RS, Tyndall MW & Montaner JSG (2004) Displacement of Canada's largest public illicit drug market in response to a police crackdown. *Canadian Medical Association Journal* **170** 1551–1556.

Wood E, Tyndall MW, Lai C, Montaner JS & Kerr T (2006) Impact of a medically supervised safer injecting facility on drug dealing and other drug-related crime. *Substance Abuse Treatment Prevention Policy* **1** 13.

Wood E, Tyndall MW, Li K, Small W, Montaner JS & Kerr T (2005) Do supervised injecting facilities attract higher risk injection drug users? *American Journal of Preventative Medicine* **2** 126–130.

Wood E, Tyndall MW, Montaner JS & Kerr T (2006) Summary of findings from the evaluation of a pilot medically supervised safer injecting facility. *Canadian Medical Association Journal* **175** (11) 1399–1404.

Wood E, Tyndall MW, Zhang R, Stoltz JA, Lai C, Montaner JS & Kerr T (2006) Attendance at supervised injecting facilities and use of detoxification services. *New England Journal of Medicine* **354** (23) 2512–2514.

Wood RA, Zettel P & Stewart W (2003) Harm reduction nursing practice: the Dr. Peter Centre supervised injection project. *Canadian Nurse* **99** (5) 20–24.

Woods A (2007) Canada: Tories shrugged off drug poll. *Times Colonist*.

CHAPTER 6
Quasi-compulsory treatment in the Netherlands: promising theory, problems in practice

Marianne van Ooyen-Houben

INTRODUCTION: QCT AS A SOLUTION FOR A PERSISTENT PROBLEM

Ever since the end of the 1980s, the Netherlands has suffered at the hands of a group of problematic drug users who are also persistent offenders. These users form a considerable burden for the judicial authorities and society alike. For example, in a one-year period (2005), the police registered more than 9,000 offenders as 'drug users', the majority of whom had been arrested more than 10 times; one in five had more than 50 previous arrests (van Laar *et al*, 2007). This is just the tip of the iceberg: a multitude of other offences may not be included in the official record (Koeter, 2002; Meijer *et al*, 2003; van 't Land *et al*, 2005).

The individuals in question are mainly long-term users of heroin and cocaine have numerous problems in various areas. Usually their offences are minor and are followed by a (short) prison sentence. Once free, they normally revert to their old routine of drug use and crime. Therefore, in time, they clash with the law again. This vicious circle cannot be ended by incarceration alone; prison can even be a harmful environment (EMCDDA, 2003). If care is offered to addicts, this can help break this routine (Rigter *et al*, 2006).

Confronted with this persistent drug-related crime, policy makers in the 1980s and 1990s created new ways to deal with the above users. The solution was not sought in stricter judicial intervention and punishment, but in more effective care interventions (Lower House of the States General, 1988; Lower House of the States General, 1993). The criminal justice system plays an important role in this. It makes it possible to bring criminal problematic drug users into contact with care providers and treatment. When doing this, the means of exerting pressure provided by law may be used to move the above users to enter care programmes (quasi-compulsion). Nowadays, these highly criminal problematic drug users come under the head of 'very frequent offenders' (Ministry of Justice, 2004). They form 72–73% of this group in 2003 and 2004 (Tollenaar *et al*, 2006). Since 2002, the Dutch government is putting a lot of effort in attempts to reduce their criminality in the framework of the comprehensive safety programme of the Dutch government *Towards a Safer Society [Naar een Veiliger Samenleving]* (Lower House of the States General, 2002a). Quasi-compulsion is still an important approach in 2007, and it will even be strengthened in the near future (Lower House of the States General, 2002b; Miedema *et al*, 2005; Justitiële Verslavingszorg, in preparation).

THE QCT PRINCIPLES

When using quasi-compulsion, efforts are made to push persistent offenders, who find themselves once again in the criminal justice system for the latest in a long line of offences, in a certain direction. Most of them are charged for crimes other than contraventions of drug laws, especially property crimes without violence, although offences against drug laws can also be dealt with in this way. These offenders are given the choice between care and a penal sanction. This choice is influenced by use of the legal framework. In the event of the offender's participation in a treatment programme, prosecution and sentencing are suspended. However, the threat of prosecution and sentencing do remain in the background as a 'last resort': these will be enforced if a user fails to comply with the conditions set by the judicial authorities. In this way, a user is persuaded to take part in and complete a care programme, so that a change can be achieved in their drug-dependent behaviour and in their criminal recidivism.

In Dutch culture, support and treatment are closely connected to the concept of individual self-determination. In principle, a person that seeks help or undergoes treatment does this voluntarily. Their aim is to achieve a better situation for themself or to prevent further deterioration. The classical doctor–patient relationship is based on this idea, and it is supported by the law on the Medical Treatment Agreement *[Wet op de Geneeskundige Behandelovereenkomst (WGBO)]*. However, other possibilities also exist, including treatment against someone's will or without someone's permission. In these cases, someone other than the individual in question determines whether or not they should be helped or treated. Examples are the Psychiatric Hospitals (compulsory admission) Act *[Wet Bijzondere opnemingen in psychiatrische ziekenhuizen (Wet BOPZ)]*, which facilitates, on the basis of civil law, the compulsory admission to a psychiatric hospital of people who form a danger to themselves or their environment, and the measure providing for Detention under a Hospital Order with Compulsory Psychiatric Treatment *[Terbeschikkingstelling (TBS)]*, which serves to protect society against the risk that disturbed delinquents will reoffend. From 2001 until 2005, the Netherlands also had a judicial measure that made compulsory admission to the Judicial Custody Programme for Addicts possible *[Maatregel van Strafrechtelijke Opvang van Verslaafden (SOV)]*. These cases involve compulsion. The person in question has no choice and their permission is not required. Others will decide for them. Intervention occurs not only in order to ensure the welfare of the person in question, but also with a view to the prevention of (further) damage to other individuals and to society. In these cases, there are two reasons for care. On the one hand, the person in question receives help and their situation is improved. On the other, the negative consequences of their behaviour are reduced, for other people and for society. A notable difference between the BOPZ and Detention under a Hospital Order compared to SOV that with the first two measures, *danger* is the criterion that forms the basis for the application of quasi-compulsion, while *criminal nuisance caused to society* is at issue in SOV. It should be noted, however, that SOV and Detention under a Hospital Order only aim at compulsory admission, not at compulsory treatment. Addicts in the SOV stayed there for a maximum of two years and were continuously stimulated to participate in the rehabilitation programme. If they did not want to participate, they stayed in a so-called 'unit 4' with a basic prison regime with the normal sports and recreative activities but without treatment.

Quasi-compulsion occupies the middle ground between voluntary and compulsory care. The twofold objective also applies here. The aim is both for a user to improve their situation and that they cause less criminal nuisance. However, where quasi-compulsion is the case, the choice between a care programme and a penal sanction is one ultimately taken by the user in question. Although their decision is influenced, they will not be *forced* to enter a care programme, as is the case with compulsory placement.

The quasi-compulsory approach encroaches upon individual self-determination less than the compulsory approach does. Quasi-compulsion is more appropriate to the concepts on which the provision of care and treatment are based in the Netherlands than compulsion is because it leaves the autonomy of the drug user intact. It is less controversial. On the other hand, quasi-compulsion occupies a complicated position between voluntary and enforced care and, what is more, where two systems intersect, between the criminal justice system and the care system. Quasi-compulsion is a hybrid in which care and criminal law converge.

Quasi-compulsion has now been used for problematic drug users for more than 18 years in the Netherlands and its future looks promising. But how does it work, and does it work? Which mechanisms ought to be at work in this approach and how can it be used to achieve a lower level of criminal recidivism? We will seek answers to the following questions.

1. What is the QCT system in the Netherlands: for which users, in which judicial framework and in which care context is QCT used?
2. Which mechanisms are assumed to work in QCT and which outcomes should it bring?
3. To what extent has it been applied to date and what is known about outcomes?

Finally, we ask ourselves: what lessons can be learned?

The answers given in this chapter are based on policy and other documents (for example those of Parliament and of the Health Council) and all available research reports of the period 1988–2007.

THE QCT SYSTEM IN THE NETHERLANDS

QCT for problematic drug users in the Netherlands is mainly targeted at long-term users with long criminal records. The vast majority of these users are male. Their lives have been heavily affected by addiction. There are usually also many other problems in the field of finances, accommodation, work and social relationships. Many of these long-term users are also suffering from psychiatric problems. So QCT aims at highly problematic, highly criminal users.

QCT is used in the case of users who have been arrested and detained in a detention centre *[Huis van Bewaring]* or a penal institution. A wide range of legal possibilities exists to achieve entry into a care programme through the judicial system, as an alternative for prosecution or sentencing. The law offers possibilities for conditional release from remand to custody and conditional custodial sentence. *Table 1*, opposite, provides an overview. It should be noted that these legal options are not exclusively used for addicts; they can be applied for every person that comes into the judicial system. Quasi-compulsion is used in the framework of conditional penalties or conditional release from prosecution or detention. In the case of addicts it is normally used under conditional suspension of pre trial detention and, to a lesser extent, via special conditions stipulated as part of the sentence. At the start and the end of the process, no legal pressure is possible. However, the police phase can be used to actively approach users and steer them in the direction of a care programme. Addiction rehabilitation services have a formal activity in this framework, which is called 'vroeghulp' (early help).

Addiction rehabilitation – in the form of pre trial assistance intervention during the earlier stages of the judicial process – fulfils a key role. It picks up addicts during the judicial process, it ascertains whether care can be offered, it reports to and advises the Public Prosecutions Department and the Court and leads users into care programmes. It forms the bridge between the judicial authorities and the care programme. Decisions about diversion to care are taken by the Public Prosecutor, the Judge or the director of the penitentiary institution. Municipalities play a central role in the aftercare-trajectory.

There are three recent changes in the system, which create new possibilities for QCT. The first is an important recent measure, called the Placement in a Penitentiary Facility for Frequent Offenders *[Maatregel tot plaatsing in een Inrichting voor Stelselmatige Daders (ISD)]*. This has been implemented since the beginning of 2005 (Stb, 2004). Under this measure, imprisonment for a maximum of two years is possible. Prisoners under this measure are screened and assessed. This can lead to a referral for participation in a programme, which can be inside prison or outside prison in a treatment facility. If they do not participate in a programme, they will stay in a basic regime in the penitentiary facility. The selection criteria for the programmes include motivation, the problem situation and the availability of an appropriate programme. Participation in a programme has priority over pure incarceration – as insisted on by the Dutch parliament (Lower House of the States General, 2003). The original

Table 1: Options for quasi-compulsory referral to treatment and care programmes from the criminal justice system, February 2007

Phase in judicial process	Options under criminal law
During remand in custody and police custody without extension (police phase)	No legal pressure possible
During pre trial detention	• (Conditional) decision not to prosecute by the Public Prosecutions Department (Article 167 of the Code of Criminal Procedure [*Wetboek van Strafvordering*]). • Suspension of pre trial detention under certain conditions (Article 80 of the Code of Criminal Procedure).
During court hearings	• Stay court hearing/postpone judgement delivery (Article 281 of the Code of Criminal Procedure and Article 346 of the Code of Criminal Procedure). • Imposition of (partially) suspended sentence, subject to completion of a care programme proposed during the court hearing (Articles 14a and 14c of the Criminal Code [*Wetboek van Strafrecht*]).
During detention	• Participation in a care programme, where necessary outside the penal institution in institutions intended for this purpose (non-custodial treatment) (Article 43 of the Prisons Act [*Penitentiaire beginselenwet*]). • Participation is an extramural care programme, when conditions for improvement are present (Article 38m-u of the Criminal Code [*Maatregel tot Plaatsing in een Inrichting voor Stelselmatige Daders*]). • Participation in a penitentiary programme (Article 4 of the Prisons Act).
After detention	• In preparation: conditional release.

ISD concept was aimed primarily at incapacitation by incarceration. Almost all persons in ISD are problematic drug users (Biesma *et al*, 2006). By introducing ISD, selection for programmes is more systematic and the period of a quasi-compulsory placement is extended, because the measure can have a duration of two years. Before ISD, the available prison sentences were short (a few months), which made the quasi-compulsory options more short-term.

The second recent change concerns the end of the judicial process and is a new law for conditional release, which is in preparation (Commissie Vrijheidsbeperking, 2003). Third, policy makers are also looking to expand the available range of conditional penalties (Lower House of the States General, 2006). A recent study showed that the use of conditional penalties is certainly possible and it pointed at concrete improvements in this direction (Jacobs *et al*, 2006). This broadening of conditional penalties will be implemented in the near future. The use of QCT as a condition for postponing a penalty has much support from policy makers (Justitiële Verslavingszorg, in preparation).

Users can enter any type of treatment under quasi-compulsion. The treatment centres used are usually facilities where clients are also treated on a voluntary basis. The facilities generally used for clients subject to quasi-compulsion are described in **Table 2**, opposite. Clients subject to quasi-compulsion can be found in clinical addiction care programmes (35% in 2005): addiction clinics, intramural motivation centres *[Intramurale Motivatie Centra]*, long-term, phased programmes or the forensic addiction clinic *[Forensische Verslavingskliniek]*. To a slightly greater extent, they can be found in outpatient and part-time programmes (37% in 2005). Other facilities are much less frequent.

Penitentiary institutions have addict guidance departments *[Verslaafden Begeleidings Afdelingen (VBA)]*. These are drug-free units that offer a programme for detained addicts. They are intended for addicts who are motivated to stop their drug use and who are, as such, eligible for a programme preparing them for treatment outside of detention. Thus, preparatory programmes are concerned here. They offer a broader regime with more freedom and opportunity for activities and visits. There are 15 of them. In 2005, 284 detainees participated, but not all of them are addicts (van Laar *et al*, 2007).

Two common trajectories of care in the framework of quasi-compulsion, found in the literature, are: pre trial assistance intervention → IMC → phased care programme → sheltered accommodation with a learning/working pathway. Or, from the detention context: VBA → phased care programme or addiction clinic.

Sometimes the object of care is to achieve the stabilisation of living conditions together with regulation of substance use and, sometimes, an addiction-free existence. Programmes always comprise a combination of interventions, varying from individual sessions, group sessions and skill training.

Table 2: Normal facilities for clients subject to quasi-compulsion in the Netherlands

Facility	Description according to objective
Addiction clinic	Geared towards abstinence and stability in terms of psychological and social performance. Therapeutic, also crisis intervention.
Intramural motivation centre	Low-threshold facility, geared towards motivating and preparing clients for entry in a follow-up care programmes or towards the improvement of their welfare and well-being. Not geared towards abstinence and therapy. Programme duration 3–4 months.
Long-term, phased programmes	Geared towards reintegration (work/training, leisure time, accommodation, finances, social relationships), abstinence and a reduction in the nuisance and crime committed by participants. Phased structure: closed-half open-open phase. Duration 16–18 months.
Forensic addiction clinic	Clinic with a national function. Phased structure. Strict security during the first, closed phase. Geared towards abstinence, social stability and improved functioning. Therapeutic and used only for the judicial target group in the last phase of detention. Duration 6–18 months.
Sheltered accommodation and long-stay facilities	Small-scale facilities in which clients are trained and coached in aspects relating to accommodation, learning and working. If possible, addicts are prepared for life in independent accommodation. Often in combination with learning/working pathways. Long-stay facilities aim at addicts with serious mental problems who will not profit from treatment any more.
Ambulant and part-time addiction care programme	Geared towards the improvement or stabilisation of a client's situation by means of (various forms) guidance and counselling.

THE THEORY OF QCT

For a thorough description of QCT, it is necessary to lay bare the underlying assumptions on how quasi-compulsion ought to work. This involves breaking it down into its basic components: the context, the assumed active mechanisms and the assumed outcomes (Pawson & Tilley, 1997; Pawson, 2002; Leeuw, 2003). In studying QCT in the Dutch context, we used all kinds of literature on the subject (policy documents, project plans and project evaluations, research reports and articles) and interviewed experts. This enables description of the theoretical assumptions, the 'programme-theory' of QCT. **Table 3**, opposite, shows this theory. The basic assumption underlying the programme theory would appear to be that dependent drug use results in criminal behaviour and that care programmes have an effect on drug use and, so, on criminal behaviour. The programme theory is roughly as follows. If users find themselves in the criminal justice system, they are not only 'locatable', it also becomes possible to exert legal means of pressure on them. A combination of positive and negative external incentives are intended to push users to enter care programmes. Together with growing intrinsic motivation, the incentives lead to retention (ie. users remain in and complete care programmes). Retention is assumed to be a requisite for improvement. In this way, users achieve a stable, improved social situation with less drug use and less criminal behaviour.

When looking closely at QCT, three steps can be distinguished where the quasi-compulsory approach is applied. The first step is when a user is moved out of the criminal justice system towards a care programme. The second step is when a user is to remain in the care programme. The third step is when a user returns to society in a better situation and is expected to remain stable. External pressure (quasi-compulsion) plays a dominant role in the first step. External pressure also plays a role in the second step, but intrinsic motivation must be encouraged in order to achieve change. This motivation is encouraged by well-chosen interventions. In this way, improvements are achieved that are well suited to the user. In this way, their intrinsic motivation becomes the motor for change, which enables him to progress to the third step without external pressure, possibly with the aid of voluntary care. The role played by external incentives decreases during the process, while the role played by intrinsic motivation increases.

It is clear from this explanation of the programme theory that the concept of 'instrinsic motivation' is a crucial issue in QCT. QCT builds upon the idea that motivation is mutable and can be deliberately changed.

It is also clear that there is no direct causal relationship between the application of quasi-compulsion during the judicial process and the assumed ultimate outcome – a reduction in criminal recidivism. There are a number of interim steps. In each of these steps, different mechanisms need to be activated. Quasi-compulsion consists of a series of consecutive processes involving different actors. It is a complicated process.

During the process, two types of outcome are expected. At the first step, the assumed outcome is entry into care. At the second, it is retention in treatment. The ultimate, overall outcome is an improved and stable social situation for the user, one with less drug use and, as such, less criminal behaviour. This outcome is assumed in the third and final step.

Table 3: The programme theory underlying QCT

Context	Assumed mechanisms	Assumed outcomes
Step 1: from the criminal justice system to care programme		
Problematic drug users in criminal justice system who continually cause criminal nuisance and return time and time again.	Users are able to choose between a care programme and a penal sanction and are 'seduced' into entering a care programme by external positive and negative incentives.	→ Entry into a care programme
Step 2: remaining in the care programme		
Problematic drug users in care programmes who often drop out before completion.	External positive and negative incentives are used to push users to stay. In addition, the care provided offers effective interventions and intrinsic motivation is promoted. Switch from external pressure to intrinsic motivation.	→ Retention in care programme
Step 3: back into society, having achieved an improved social position		
Drug users who achieve insufficient change or relapse after completion of the care programme.	Care programmes offer interventions that reflect the broad issue and tackle problems. Improvement has an intrinsically motivating effect; user wants to maintain improved situation.	→ Improved social situation, less drug use → Less criminal behaviour → Less criminal nuisance in society. → Stable in the longer term.

QCT IN PRACTICE IN THE NETHERLANDS

To what extent do the assumed active mechanisms actually operate? Are the outcomes achieved? To answer these questions, we can follow the steps of the programme theory. In addition, we can use existing Dutch studies on quasi-compulsion. A literature search resulted in 19 studies in which any form or aspect of quasi-compulsion is evaluated. These focus on various judicial frameworks and care programmes. Measurement tools and follow-up periods vary between studies. Most studies report comprehensive data from registration systems maintained by care providers and the police, often in combination with file data. Much information is qualitative and obtained from interviews. The samples taken from direct quantitative measurements are usually not large, which limits the representative validity of the study in question. Four studies include pre measurements and post measurements in experimental and similar control conditions (Jongerius & Koeter, 1997; van den Hurk, 1998; Koeter, 2002; Bieleman *et al*, 2002). Four studies include pre measurements and post measurements without similar control conditions (van Ooyen *et al*, 1993; Oosterhoff & Vermeulen, 1995; de Koning, 1998; Vermeulen *et al*, 2000). Three studies comprise measurements taken at one particular time, with registration data being used to observe the initial situation (Drouven *et al*, 2001; van Gestel, 1999; Schutte & Bleker, 2001). Two studies have a more qualitative approach (Bieleman & Kroes, 1991; Korf *et al*, 2000) whereas three other studies combine statistics with interview data on the functioning of facilities (Miedema *et al*, 2005; Snippe & Ogier, 2006; Snippe & Stoep van der, 2006; Biesma *et al*, 2006). Finally, two studies give an overview, bringing together the results of a number of different projects (Broër & Noyon, 1999; Koeter & van Maastricht, 2006). We also used the results of the process evaluation of the compulsory measure SOV, because the same agencies are involved there and the same processes play a role. Moreover, QCT functions as a control group for SOV (van 't Land *et al*, 2005). We included results from a study on local initiatives on young offenders because these initiatives are being broadened out for repeat offenders, among whom are drug dependent repeat offenders (Terpstra & Bakker, 2002).

Most studies do not permit any conclusions on effects; only four studies prove to have sufficient validity to be able to draw conclusions on the effects resulting from the quasi-compulsory approach (Farrington & Welsh, 2001; Farrington *et al*, 2002). However, all the studies do contain information on the programme theory, on the application of assumed active mechanisms or on the conditions in which these mechanisms are more or less effective. That is why all of the studies were included in our analysis (see Pawson, 2002).

Conclusions are drawn on the basis of the knowledge gathered in this manner. The variability and quality of the studies warrant caution. The conclusions arrived at are not definitive, but give cause for further study.

QCT in reality – step one: from the criminal justice system to a care programme

It is presumed that criminal problematic drug users are presented with a choice between entry into a treatment programme and prosecution/penal sanction. External positive and negative incentives are designed to push them in the direction of a treatment programme. This mechanism, however, is not applied consistently in practice. Some problematic drug users who are eligible for QCT are not approached or given the choice between a treatment programme and further prosecution and sentencing (Broër & Noyon, 1999; Korf *et al*, 2000). Nor is a treatment programme always actually available for those that decide to enter one. At this stage, 10% of eligible clients fall by the wayside. In many cases, the threat of punishment is limited, since the offence committed is too minor to warrant a serious punishment (Broër & Noyon, 1999; Korf *et al*, 2000). This situation has changed since 2005, when the measure of Placement in an Institution for Frequent Offenders started being implemented. The threat of punishment rose considerably to two years. We do not know yet whether this makes a difference for the rate of entry into treatment.

Given the situation in the evaluation period, it is not surprising that the percentage of users from the target group who enter a treatment programme from the criminal justice system is low (Miedema *et al*, 2005). It varies from 7% (after pre trial assistance; Koeter, 2002) to 37% (in the Forensic Addiction Clinic; Schutte & Bleker, 2001). Of those that receive a QCT offer, half do not opt to enter a treatment programme. Approximately 90% of those individuals that do opt for care actually receive an offer. Ultimately, only some of them actually enter a treatment programme (Korf *et al*, 2000). A filter would seem to apply to entry, with just a minority of individuals from the initial target group actually taking part in a care programme (Koeter & van Maastricht, 2006). Several studies explicitly state that entry is problematic. The majority of entrants are already known to the treatment system because they have been there before, implying that QCT is not reaching new, untreated drug users (van Ooyen *et al*, 1993; van Gestel, 1999; Drouven *et al*, 2001; van 't Land *et al*, 2005).

Those who enter QCT are mainly male long-term users of heroin and cocaine, who also use alcohol and cannabis. Their average age is over 30 years and they have a lot of problems besides the addiction. Their income (besides that obtained from acquisitive crime) is often obtained from dealing drugs and state welfare benefits. They predominantly commit non-violent offences against property (54% of their offences in 2005; van Laar *et al*, 2007); violent offences (24%), vandalism and public order offences (22%). Research showed that average criminal records comprised two offences and that the number of self-reported offences against property are 20 times more frequent than shown in official records (Koeter, 2002; Meijer *et al*, 2003). About 30% reported committing a property crime a least once a day in the year before detention. Violent offences were less frequently reported (van 't Land *et al*, 2005).

We must conclude that the mechanisms designed to push users from the penal system to a care programme have not been applied consistently. The rate of entry into QCT programmes is, as a consequence, quite low.

QCT in reality – step two: retention

The programme theory assumes that external pressure is maintained through positive and negative incentives while a switch to intrinsic motivation occurs. In practice, this mechanism is not consistent. The external negative incentive constituted by the imminent enforcement of a sentence – the 'last resort' – does not always appear to be present. Departure from a treatment programme before its completion is not always reported to the judicial system, or is not reported immediately. In this situation, the user in question is not actively traced by the police (Broër & Noyon, 1999; van Gestel, 1999). They remain free until they are arrested again. In this way, some considerable time may expire between violation of the QCT conditions and punishment of their violation in the form of the enforcement of a sentence. A problem in this context is that the treatment programme does not always know who is registered with the criminal justice system and does not register this. For those involved, 'quasi-compulsion' is not always a clear concept (Oosterhoff & Vermeulen, 1995; Korf et al, 2000).

Intrinsic motivation, the internal positive incentive, does sometimes develop (eg. in the intercultural motivation centre [Intercultureel Motivatie Centrum]; van Ooyen et al, 1993). However, sometimes it does not (eg. in a protracted, phased care programme and in a preparatory programme followed during detention; de Koning, 1998; Jongerius & Koeter, 1997).

Premature dropout percentages vary from 20% to even 100% (for outpatient programmes entered after pre trial assistance; Koeter, 2002). A percentage varying from 50% to 60% is most often encountered (van Ooyen et al, 1993; van Gestel, 1999; Schutte & Bleker, 2001; Drouven et al, 2001; Koeter, 2002). What is striking is the high dropout percentage found even at the end of care programmes, during the open and resocialisation phases.

QCT in reality – step three: social integration

It is assumed that the interventions made in care programmes address the broad problems experienced by users and that improvements are achieved that the user wishes to maintain. Literature on the subject shows that treatment programmes offer a broad range of interventions, varying from detoxification, relapse prevention, crisis intervention, motivation promotion, work, education, activities, help with financial problems, skills training, accommodation, social relationships and help adjusting to life in independent accommodation. It is not known whether all of the various components of an offer are implemented consistently. Nor do we know what happens to a user's intrinsic motivation after completion of a treatment programme.

In general, a user's situation after a care programme is better than their situation before it. Drug use decreases or stops (van Ooyen et al, 1993; Oosterhoff & Vermeulen, 1995; Vermeulen et al, 2000; Koeter, 2002; Bieleman et al, 2002). With some users, their physical condition, work situation and social relationships also improve. Some psychological progress can also be observed. Some users display less criminal recidivism. The studies vary on the extent of improvement: Oosterhoff & Vermeulen (1995) state that 45% had not reoffended one year after completion of the care programme. Vermeulen et al (2000) found that 64% of the users had not been re-arrested for an offence against property after leaving a care programme. Koeter (2002) found no offence-free users at all following ambulant care programmes and approximately 30% after clinical programmes. According to Bieleman *et al* (2002), two-thirds had not reoffended after completion. For some users, the improvement is maintained for a number of years, while others relapse. Several studies observe that most users remain in the care programme and fail to achieve any independent or regulated existence without drugs (Bröer & Noyon, 1999).

However, the difference between the situation before and after a care programme does not reveal whether the improvements achieved are the result of a QCT-programme. The rare Dutch studies that do allow conclusions to be made on effectiveness do not show any uniform findings. It would seem that there could be a limited effect on alcohol and drug use and on several aspects of the problem. The effect on recidivism is unclear. A recent study in five European countries (not the Netherlands) by Uchtenhagen *et al* (2006) suggested that QCT participants do as well as voluntary clients in the same treatment centres.

The general picture that emerges is that of a filter. ***Figure 1*** (adapted from Koeter & van Maastricht, 2006) illustrates this. Only a small part from the target-group is reached by QCT and profits from QCT.

Figure 1: The filter from QCT target group to successful completion of QCT

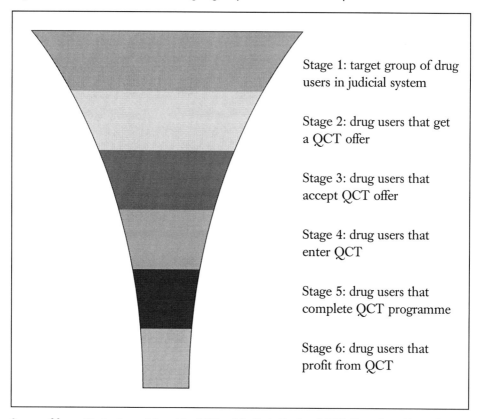

Stage 1: target group of drug users in judicial system

Stage 2: drug users that get a QCT offer

Stage 3: drug users that accept QCT offer

Stage 4: drug users that enter QCT

Stage 5: drug users that complete QCT programme

Stage 6: drug users that profit from QCT

Source of figure: Koeter & van Maastricht, 2006, originally in Korf *et al*, 2000. Text adapted by author.

LESSONS TO BE LEARNED

From the available evidence, we have to conclude that, so far, QCT in the Netherlands has not been very well implemented. This is a general picture. But let us look more closely at the results and concentrate on conditions in which things work out well. These elements of good practice show us what we can do to improve QCT.

There are certain user characteristics and also characteristics of the judicial and the care context that relate to high entry rates. These characteristics are important for QCT. As regards users, the general picture is that higher entry is achieved if basic motivation is present. It seems as if those who want to change something about their lifestyle and are fed up of a life revolving around drugs, are motivated to grasp the QCT offer. We see, for instance, a relatively high entry rate for users that want to change and who have not been successful in doing so in the past, for users with a strong need for help, just as for users with serious problems in many areas and a history of numerous offences (van Ooyen *et al*, 1993; Jongerius & Koeter, 1997; van Gestel, 1999; Korf *et al*, 2000; Bieleman *et al*, 2002; Koeter, 2002). However, de Koning (1998) reports higher entry into care programmes where users have been less involved in crime. Entrants to the care programmes would appear to be mainly a group of users with serious problems who have not been successful in care programmes before, but who now are motivated. Sometimes younger ones enter, who have been addicted for a shorter period of time, often primarily to cocaine, and who have not been admitted before.

It should be noticed, however, that the quasi-compulsion has not been strongly enforced, as noted above, so it is not surprising that only those who are motivated actually enter treatment. This might change now following the introduction of longer prison sentences by placement in an Institution for Frequent Offenders (ISD). There is not yet any evidence on the effect of this measure.

Before ISD, a large group of users remained who did not receive a treatment offer, did not choose treatment or did not end up in treatment. This would appear to apply especially to users who have lower motivation for changing their drug use.

However, there are other factors in the decision to enter treatment, besides motivation, or associated with motivation. For example, higher treatment entry rates are achieved where users are actively and intensively approached, advised and canvassed for entry into a treatment programme (Schutte & Bleker, 2001; Oosterhoff & Vermeulen, 1995; Korf *et al*, 2000). Various studies show that the greater the threat of punishment, and the more severe the penalty (eg. a longer prison sentence), the higher the entry rate achieved (Jongerius & Koeter, 1997; de Koning, 1998; van den Hurk, 1998; Broër & Noyon, 1999; Korf *et al*, 2000; Koeter, 2002). The threat of three months' detention proved effective with detainees in the study conducted by Jongerius & Koeter (1997). The time at which the quasi-compulsory process is introduced also plays a role. The later this takes place in the judicial process, the higher the entry rate seems to be. The available evidence suggests that programmes during detention have a positive effect on entry into care programmes after detention, compared to imprisoned drug users who did not have access to a programme while in prison (Jongerius & Koeter, 1997; van den Hurk, 1998.

Conditions in the treatment programme also matter. If low-threshold care programmes are available, which are not of a psychotherapeutic character and are not immediately geared towards detoxification, but offer users the opportunity to reduce the use of methadone slowly and at their own pace, higher entry rates tend to be achieved (van Ooyen *et al*, 1993; van Gestel, 1999; Drouven *et al*, 2001; Bieleman *et al*, 2002).

Last but not least, collaboration between the various agencies has been found to be important. Collaboration is often a problem, leading to insufficient use of facilities (Terpstra & Bakker, 2002; van 't Land *et al*, 2005; Snippe & Ogier *et al*, 2006; Biesma *et al*, 2006). The closer the collaboration and the better the information exchange, the higher the entry rate achieved (Oosterhoff & Vermeulen, 1995; de Koning, 1998; van Gestel, 1999; Korf *et al*, 2000; Drouven *et al*, 2001; Miedema *et al*, 2005; Snippe & Ogier *et al*, 2006). Various factors would appear to be conducive to collaboration between agencies:

- working with fixed consultation procedures and fixed staff-member lists and mutual familiarity between institutions
- the proper guidance of users moving from the criminal justice system to the care programme
- one party is in charge and collaboration is not limited to certain projects or contact persons
- judicial authorities give priority to the use and enforcement of quasi-compulsion
- judicial authorities gain positive experience with treatment referrals
- institutions are willing to give up some of their autonomy
- treatment centres can arrange admissions in direct contact with referrers
- online web-based applications for information exchange.

Characteristics that lead to improved retention have also been identified. Users with a high level of initial motivation tend to stay in treatment longer (van Ooyen *et al*, 1993; van Gestel, 1999; Bieleman *et al*, 2002), as do older users, users without a record of violent offences and users whose criminal behaviour began after their addiction (Vermeulen *et al*, 2000; Schutte & Bleker, 2001; Bieleman & Kroes, 1991; de Koning, 1998). As for rates of entry to treatment, recent addicts on the one hand and very long-term addicts on the other appear to remain in care programmes longer (Drouven *et al*, 2001). In addition, users who attend a preparatory programme during detention subsequently remain in treatment programmes for a longer period of time (Koeter, 2002).

The likelihood of punishment also plays a role here: the greater it is, the higher the level of retention. This is the case, for example, when legal proceedings or a charge is pending or when detention under a hospital order remains in force for a longer period of time (Oosterhoff & Vermeulen, 1995; Broër & Noyon, 1999; van Gestel, 1999; Vermeulen *et al*, 2000; Schutte & Bleker, 2001).

Retention is higher when a treatment programme is better able to address users' motives and tailor the approach adopted to the problems of the individual user (van Ooyen *et al*, 1993; van den Hurk, 1998). A clinical programme that is geared towards skills, sport, relaxation and useful activities (work programmes, daytime activities) holds users longer (Schutte & Bleker, 2001; Koeter, 2002; Koeter & van Maastricht, 2006). Higher retention can also be seen where more and better skilled staff are present and a more intensive approach is offered. Staffing is a regular problem, both in terms of staff numbers and staff expertise (Jongerius & Koeter, 1997; Drouven *et al*, 2001; Bieleman *et al*, 2002; Miedema *et al*, 2005). Staff have often not been prepared for the difficulties involved in dealing with this problematic group. This also holds true for SOV (van 't Land *et al*, 2005) and for recent approaches in the framework of the Safety Programme (Snippe & Ogier *et al*, 2006). Good protocols for coping with aggression and psychiatric problems help. A clear, uniform and shared approach must be adopted and programme integrity is vital.

As for predictors of eventual outcomes on drug use and crime, it has been suggested that users who stay in a treatment programme for a longer period of time and complete it make more progress. Stayers do better than quitters (van Ooyen *et al*, 1993; Vermeulen *et al*, 2000; Drouven *et al*, 2001; Bieleman *et al*, 2002). Better results are also achieved by users who do not suffer from serious mental disorders and whose offences were committed only after their addiction began (van den Hurk, 1998; Bieleman & Kroes, 1991; Bieleman *et al*, 2002). However, the available studies conducted are inconclusive on outcomes. A recent meta-study shows that certain interventions involving heroin and cocaine addicts may be effective. Success is more difficult to achieve among polydrug users (Rigter *et al*, 2006). Several studies observe that more aftercare is required (van den Hurk, 1998; Bieleman *et al*, 2002; Snippe & Stoep van der *et al*, 2006).

SO WHAT HAVE WE LEARNED?

In the Netherlands, quasi-compulsion is used with criminal problematic drug users who are persistent offenders. This policy aims at diverting users from the judicial system into treatment programmes. In theory, this approach looks very promising. It is a way of guiding drug users towards improving their lives, in an ethically accepted way, without direct compulsion. The approach, however, is poorly implemented in practice.

Users who belong to the target group of long-term problematic drug users with high criminal recidivism should get a choice between a penal sanction and a treatment programme. That choice is not always given to them. Only a fraction of the target group is offered the opportunity to take part in QCT. Users are not approached actively, they are not canvassed, pushed or pulled into treatment. Users that are given the choice often prefer imprisonment. For users that choose to participate in a treatment programme, this care is sometimes not actually available. The threat of punishment is often limited and so is not a strong incentive. As a consequence, only a limited group enters QCT. These are the people with the strongest motivation.

During the treatment programme the threat of enforcement of the sentence, which ought to follow a user's violation of the conditions stipulated by the judicial authorities, should act as an external incentive for retention. This is a core element of QCT, referred to as 'the stick behind the door'. But this threat is not immediately fulfilled. Users that leave a treatment programme before its completion are not immediately reported and traced by the police. The external pressure is therefore weak. Improvement is sought in strengthening of the supervision of probation services, who can signal non-compliance to conditions.

The intrinsic motivation of the user should grow and act as a motor for the change process during treatment. However, we found no rigorous Dutch research findings on this topic. When the users come out of the treatment programme, they should find themselves in a better living situation, with less drug use and less criminal behaviour. This is mostly the case, especially for the people who finish the programme and do not drop out prematurely. Dutch studies on effectiveness of QCT are scarce and they do not report consistent findings. QCT seems to lead to less use of alcohol and drugs and a better physical condition, but the effects on criminal behaviour are not clear. The available Dutch studies are often methodologically inadequate to give insight into effectiveness. There is international evidence, however, that shows that QCT is as effective as care on a voluntary basis, provided in the same facility. This might hold true for the Dutch situation, because our QCT system is comparable to those involved in the international study.

There are certain conditions in which QCT does relatively well. From these conditions, we can learn lessons. They show us the way towards improvements of QCT. It is clear that drug users can be stimulated to enter treatment. This is most likely if they are canvassed actively and intensively, and if they can enter low-threshold facilities that are non-therapeutic, skills-based and not immediately geared towards detoxification.

The motivation of users can be developed. If intensive and practical care is offered to them, which fits well with their individual problems and is implemented by sufficient numbers of skilled staff, users will remain longer in treatment. Motivation is not a static characteristic, it can grow and change under the right conditions (Prochaska & DiClemente, 1984; DiClemente, 2003; Spriggs, 2003; Soulet & Oeuvray, 2006; Stevens *et al*, 2006). There are approaches – like motivational interviewing – that enhance motivation and influence users' willingness to be treated, to abstain or reduce their drug use (Rigter *et al*, 2006).

The capacities of the target group should not be forgotten. New findings from biomedical research show that brain functions of long-term addicts often are very damaged and altered in a way that enhances the risk of relapse (ZonMw, 2005; de Jong *et al*, 2006). Mental illness is very common in the group of long-term hard drug users (van der Stel, 2006). This would mean that the possibilities of interventions and motivation are limited. Long-term aftercare is necessary and low-threshold, long-stay facilities should be available for this group. More QCT efforts could be directed towards younger drug users with criminal behaviour, whose chances for improvement might be better, instead of focusing solely on long-term users with a large number of problems (Berghuis, 2005). These views are finally getting through to policy makers.

The external pressure of a threat of a sentence operates as the stick behind the door. The more imminent the threat, the more drug users are inclined to choose a treatment programme and the longer users would appear to remain in the care programme. According to recent experiences in the field of addiction care, the threat of a two-year imprisonment under the new measure ISD might even work as a stimulus for voluntary entry into a care programme, before the drug user comes into the judicial system; we might call this 'pre-QCT'.

The pressure can be enhanced by offering QCT at a moment that the threat of punishment is felt strongly, for instance just before court hearings or when legal proceedings are pending. The later quasi-compulsion is used in the criminal justice process, the higher the rate of entry would appear to be. Research findings show that entry into care is also high for users who have participated in diversion trajectories inside prison.

The threat of a sentence should be real, of course. If the sentence is not executed when the conditions for QCT are violated, the threat is an empty gesture. That was usually the situation in the Netherlands, and so it could be stated that quasi-compulsion has been, in practice, very much like voluntary placement.

Residential programmes seem better for retention than outpatient programmes. In addition, staff should be well equipped to cope with a highly problematic group. Retention is important, because users who complete treatment make more progress than users that fail to complete the programme. Aftercare would appear to be important to the long-term sustainability of outcomes.

In QCT, concerted collaboration is needed between judicial authorities (the police, the public prosecutions department, the prison system) and treatment and care programmes (facilities for addicts, housing agencies, municipalities). This is particularly important during the entry stage and the stage of social integration and aftercare. The fact that criminal behaviour is but one of the many problems of chronic hard drug users, and the belief that improvement is dependent from a multidisciplinary chain-co-operation, resulted in local structures in several municipalities in the Netherlands: 'veiligheidshuizen' (*safety houses*) in which professionals from different fields co-operate. The new viewpoint is that besides an approach for drug using repeat offenders prevention and treatment for younger at-risk groups should be a relevant part of a total course-of-life approach. However, the collaboration often leaves much to be desired. This is also true for compulsory admissions to treatment. Collaboration may be a systemic problem. The collaboration problem seems to be as persistent as the criminal recidivism of the problematic drug users. Efficient steering of the network of agencies is essential.

Recently, there have been relevant and positive developments. More low-threshold facilities aiming at chronic hard drug users with multiple problems and criminal recidivism have been established. These facilities do not demand abstinence, instead they offer shelter and guidance. Recently, in February 2007, a first so-called long-stay facility opened its doors, which offers long-lasting domicile. The measure of placement in an Institution for Frequent Offenders (ISD) was implemented in 2005. This enables diversion to care under a greater external judicial pressure than in the preceding years. Co-ordination between judicial and treatment trajectories is being improved and problematic drug users with high criminal recidivism are now more systematically screened and assessed. Considerable efforts have been made to improve collaboration and aftercare through a person-centred approach. Results from recent studies show that this might work out well, but also point to continuing problems in exchange of information and in collaboration. Also, it is suggested that the psychological and psychiatric problems of the target group are not yet adequately dealt with. Although the new developments are promising and go in the right direction, serious attention still needs to be paid to the problems that have previously been identified.

The Dutch government and the European Union both encourage the use of QCT. QCT will continue to develop. The middle ground position between voluntary and compulsory care is a difficult one. However, with improvements it can work better. The transition from the criminal justice system to the treatment system can happen more smoothly than it has until now. QCT can be applied more firmly and more convincingly in order to improve outcomes.

References

Berghuis AC (2005) *De Aanpak van Veelplegers Tussen Nuttig Investeren en Verjubelen.* The Hague: Public Prosecutor Office.

Bieleman B, Biesma S, Jetzes M, Jong A de & Valk V de (2002) *Opgevangen onder Drang. Evaluatie SOV-drang in Rotterdam.* Groningen/Rotterdam: Intraval.

Bieleman B & Kroes L (1991) *Door Regelen in de Maat. Reacties van druggebruikers op maatregelen van overheid en burger.* Groningen: Intraval.

Biesma S, Zwieten M van, Snippe J & Bieleman B (2006) *ISD en SOV Vergeleken. Eerste inventarisatie meerwaarde Inrichting voor Stelselmatige Daders boven eerdere Strafrechtelijke Opvang Verslaafden.* Groningen: Intraval.

Broër C & Noyon R (1999) *Over Last en Beleid, Evaluatie Nota Overlast en Vijf Jaar SVO-beleid Tegen Overlast van Harddruggebruikers.* Amsterdam: Regioplan Stad en Land.

Commissie Vrijheidsbeperking (2003) *Vrijheidsbeperking onder Voorwaarden.* Den Haag: SDU.

DiClemente CC (2003) *Addiction and Change: How addictions develop and addicted people recover.* New York: Guilford Press.

Drouven L, Schutte S & Kingma M (2001) *Eindrapportage Evaluatie IMC's.* Enschede: Hoeksma, Homans & Menting.

European Monitoring Centre for Drugs and Drug Addiction (2003) *Treating Drug Users in Prison – A critical area for health-promotion and crime-reduction policy.* Lisbon: European Monitoring Centre for Drugs and Drug Addiction, Drugs in Focus, 7.

Farrington DP & Welsh BC (2001) What works in preventing crime? Systematic reviews of experimental and quasi-experimental research. *The Annals of the American Academy of Political and Social Science* **578** (1).

Farrington DP, Gottfredson DC, Sherman LW & Welsh BC (2002) The Maryland Scientific Methods Scale. In: LW Sherman, DP Farrington, BC Welsh & D Layton MacKenzie (Eds) *Evidence-Based Crime Prevention.* London: Routledge, 13–21.

Gestel B van (1999) *Tussen Straat en Kliniek. Evaluatie van vier intramurale motivatiecentra voor harddrugsverslaafden.* Amsterdam: Regioplan Stad en Land.

Hurk A van den (1998) *Tussen de Helpende en de Harde Hand. Een studie naar mogelijkheden van succesvolle zorg voor verslaafde gedetineerden.* Nijmegen: Catholic University Nijmegen.

Jacobs M, Kalmthout A van & Bergh M von (2006) *Toepassing van Bijzondere Voorwaarden bij Voorwaardelijke Vrijheidsstraf en Schorsing van de Voorlopige Hechtenis bij Volwassenen.* Tilburg: IVA.

Jong CAJ de, Schellekens AFA, Ellenbroek B, Franke B & Verkes R-J (2006) *The Course of Addiction. Neurobiological predictors of chronicity.* Den Haag: ZonMw.

Jongerius J & Koeter M (1997) *Drang tot Verandering? Haalbaarheid en effecten van een drang- en dwangbenadering van drugverslaafden in detentie. Eerste fase.* Amsterdam: Amsterdam Institute for Addiction Research (AIAR series 3).

Justitiële Verslavingszorg (in preparation) *Een analyse van het Beleid Voor Verslaafde Justitiabelen.* The Hague: Ministry of Justice & Ministry of Health, Welfare and Sports.

Koeter M (2002) *Vroeghulp aan Verslaafden. Het effect van de vroeghulp interventie aanpak op criminele recidive en verslavingsgedrag.* Amsterdam: Amsterdam Institute for Addiction Research (AIAR series 6).

Koeter M & Maastricht A van (2006) *De Effectiviteit van Verslavingszorg in een Justitieel Kader. Verslaving deel 6.* The Hague: ZonMw.

Koning P de (1998) *Resocialiseren onder Drang: Verslag van het Rotterdamse experiment met de strafrechtelijke opvang van verslaafden.* Rotterdam: EUR.

Korf DJ, Wijngaarden B van, Koeter M, Riper H & Seeman C (2000) *Vroeghulp aan Verslaafden. Evaluatie van de vroeghulp interventie aanpak (VIA) van de justitiële verslavingszorg.* Amsterdam: Amsterdam Institute for Addiction Research and the Bonger Institute of Criminology (AIAR series 6).

Laar MW van, Cruts AAN, Verdurmen JEE, Ooyen-Houben MMJ van & Meijer RF (2007) *Nationale Drug Monitor. Jaarbericht 2006.* Utrecht: Trimbos-instituut.

Land H van 't, Duijvenbooden K van, Plas A van der & Wolf J (2005) *Opgevangen onder Dwang. Procesevaluatie strafrechtelijke opvang verslaafden.* Utrecht: Trimbos-instituut.

Leeuw FL (2003) Reconstructing program theories: methods available and problems to be solved. *American Journal of Evaluation* **24** (1) 5–20.

Lower House of the States General (1988) *Dwang en Drang in de Hulpverlening aan Verslaafden.* The Hague: Lower House of the States General, TK 20, 415.

Lower House of the States General (1993) *Nota Inzake het Beleid Gericht op het Verminderen van de Door Verslaafden Veroorzaakte Overlast.* The Hague: Lower House of the States General, TK 22 684, 12.

Lower House of the States General (2002a) *Naar een Veiliger Samenleving.* The Hague: Lower House of the States General, 28 684, 1.

Lower House of the States General (2002b) *Drugbeleid.* The Hague: Lower House of the States General, TK 24077, 112.

Lower House of the States General (2003) *Wijziging van het Wetboek van Strafrecht het Wetboek van Strafvordering en de Penitentiaire beginselenwet (plaatsing in een inrichting voor stelselmatige daders). Motie van het lid Vos.* The Hague: Lower House of the States General, TK 28980, 15.

Lower House of the States General (2006) *Vaststelling van de Begrotingsstaten van het Ministerie van Justitie (VI) voor het jaar 2006.* The Hague: Lower House of the States General, TK 30300-VI, 164.

Meijer R, Grapendaal M, Ooyen M van, Wartna B, Brouwers M & Essers A (2003) *Geregistreerde Drugcriminaliteit in Cijfers. Achtergrondstudie bij het Justitieonderdeel van de Nationale Drugmonitor: Jaarbericht 2002.* Meppel: Boom Juridische uitgevers (WODC series on research and policy, 204).

Miedema F, Mensink C, Eppink M & Woldringh C (2005) *Verslaafde Justitiabelen op Hun Plaats? Evaluatie van de pilots justitiële verslavingszorg.* Nijmegen: ITS.

Ministry of Justice (2004) *Gedragsinterventies voor Veelplegers.* The Hague: Ministry of Justice.

Oosterhoff S & Vermeulen K (1995) *Tussentijds Evaluatieonderzoek naar de Effecten van en Samenwerking Binnen het GAVO-project.* Utrecht: CVO.

Ooyen M van, Walraven M & Mensink C (1993) *Hulpverlening (z)onder Drang. Het intercultureel motivatie centrum geëvalueerd.* Utrecht: NIAD.

Pawson R (2002) Evidence-based policy: the promise of realist synthesis. *Evaluation* **8** (3) 340–358.

Pawson R & Tilley N (1997) *Realistic Evaluation.* London/Thousand Oaks/New Delhi: Sage Publications.

Prochaska JO & DiClemente CC (1984) *The Transtheoretical Approach. Crossing traditional boundaries of therapy.* Homewood, Il: Dow-Jones-Irwin.

Rigter H, Gageldonk A van, Ketelaars T & Laar M van (2006) *Hulp bij Probleemgebruik van Drugs. Stand van de wetenschap voor behandelingen en andere interventies.* Utrecht: Bureau National Drug Monitor (update).

Schutte SJM & Bleker RW (2001) *Vooronderzoek Evaluatie Forensische Verslavingskliniek.* Enschede: Hoeksma, Homans & Menting.

Snippe J, Ogier C & Bieleman B (2006) *Lokale Aanpak zeer Actieve Veelplegers: Justitieel traject.* Groningen-Rotterdam: Intraval.

Snippe J, Stoep R van der, Zwieten M van & Bieleman B (2006) *Lokale Aanpak zeer Actieve Veelplegers: Nazorgtraject.* Groningen-Rotterdam: Intraval.

Soulet M-H & Oeuvray K (2006) *QCT Europe: Final report: Constructing, producing and analysing the qualitative evidence.* Fribourg: University of Fribourg.

Spriggs M (2003) Can we help addicts become more autonomous? Inside the mind of an addict. *Bioethics* **17** (5–6) 542–554.

Stb 2004/351 (2004) *Wet van 9 Juli tot Wijziging van het Wetboek van Strafrecht, het Wetboek van Strafvordering en de Penitentiaire Beginselenwet (plaatsing in een inrichting voor stelselmatige daders).* The Hague: SDU Uitgevers.

Stel JC van der (2006) *Co-morbiditeit. Verslaving plus een psychische stoornis.* Den Haag: ZonMw.

Stevens A, Berto D, Frick U, Hunt N, Kerschl V, McSweeney T, Oeuvray K, Puppo I, Santa Maria A, Schaaf S, Trinkl, Uchtenhagen A & Werdenich W (2006) The relationship between legal status, perceived pressure and motivation in treatment for drug dependence: results from a European study of quasi-compulsory treatment. *European Addiction Research* **12** 197–209.

Terpstra J & Bakker I (2002) *Met Recht Lokaal. Evaluatie van justitie in de buurt.* Enschede: IPIT.

Tollenaar N, Harbachi S el, Meijer RF, Huijbregts GLAM & Blom M (2006) *Monitor Veelplegers. Samenvatting van de resultaten. WODC-recidivestudies.* The Hague: WODC: Fact sheet 2006–12.

Uchtenhagen A, Schaaf S, Bock I, Frick U, Grichting E & Bolliger H (2006) *QCT Europe. Quasi-compulsory and compulsory treatment of drug-dependent offenders in Europe. Final report on quantitative evaluation.* Zürich: Research Institute for Public Health and Addiction, Zürich University.

Vermeulen K, Hendriks V & Zomerveld R (2000) *Drangbehandeling in Den Haag: Evaluatieonderzoek naar de effectiviteit van het behandelprogramma triple-ex voor justitiabele verslaafden.* The Hague: Parnassia Addiction Research Centre.

ZonMw (2005) *Het Programma Verslaving: Van wetenschap tot zorg op straat.* The Hague: ZonMw.

CHAPTER 7
Quasi-compulsory treatment in Europe: an evidence-based response to drug-related crime?

Alex Stevens

In many countries, increasing attention is being given to the link between illicit drug use and crime. Few believe that imprisonment is an effective response to drug-related offending (EMCDDA, 2003) and drug treatment has been shown to be more effective in enabling dependent drug users to change their lives. Treatment alternatives to imprisonment for drug dependent offenders offer a way to reduce the health and criminal harms of drug use, while avoiding the costs and other harms that prison incurs.

The vast majority of studies in this area are from North America, which has different patterns of drug use and a very different penal response to drug users than most European countries. If policies and programmes are to continue and expand in Europe on the promise that they will cut crime and improve health, then we need to test whether this promise can be fulfilled.

The QCT Europe project aimed to provide such a test. In this project, we used the term quasi-compulsory treatment (QCT) to describe treatment of drug dependent offenders that is motivated, ordered or supervised by the criminal justice system and takes place outside regular prisons. This chapter looks in particular at three questions about QCT that are often debated in the absence of evidence.

1. Are people who are ordered into treatment by the courts less motivated to change than people who come into treatment in other ways?
2. Does being ordered into treatment harm the prospects of the person engaging in treatment and being retained?
3. Are outcomes from treatment any worse (or better) for people in QCT?

PREVIOUS RESEARCH ON QCT

There is consistent evidence of high levels of drug use among offenders, even though *'little support can be found for a single specific and direct causal connection'* between drugs and crime (Lurigio & Schwartz, 1999). However drug use is linked to crime, there is now a growing consensus that various forms of drug treatment can help dependent drug users reduce their offending. A meta-analysis of 78

American studies, including therapeutic communities, detoxification, methadone maintenance and outpatient drug-free treatment, found that people in the treated groups consistently had larger reductions in their drug use and offending than similar people in untreated comparison groups (Prendergast *et al*, 2002). Outcomes were similar across the various types of treatment. Large-scale treatment studies, such as the Drug Abuse Treatment Outcome Study in the USA (Hubbard *et al*, 2003) and the National Treatment Outcome Research Study in the UK (Gossop *et al*, 2002), have also produced evidence that these forms of treatment produce reductions in drug use and offending. Newer forms of treatment, such as heroin-assisted treatment, have also shown significant reductions in offending (see **chapter 3** of this book).

The vital question is whether these positive outcomes can be produced among clients who are diverted into treatment from the criminal justice system. The biggest trial of this idea is taking place in the USA, where there are now over 1,200 drug courts in operation. These courts typically deal with non-violent drug offenders. They differ from traditional courts by attempting to build a relationship between the offender and the judge, who can use treatment, drug tests, personal encouragement, threats and sanctions (including time in prison) to push the offender towards abstinence and a crime-free life. Early studies of the drug court approach were overwhelmingly positive, but suffered from serious methodological flaws, such as reporting results only for those people who complied with treatment and ignoring those who dropped out from the drug court programme (Belenko, 2001). These flaws were so great that an American judge described the rapid expansion of drug courts throughout the USA as a 'scandal' (Hoffman, 2000). However, more recent and rigorous research has increased confidence that drug courts do reduce drug use and offending (General Accountability Office, 2005).

There are problems in comparing drug courts to the European situation, as many offenders entering USA drug courts would not be considered eligible for QCT in most European countries. For example, the original Dade County Drug Court – which was taken as a model by many others – only dealt with people charged with drug possession or purchasing. It explicitly excluded people who were charged with drug dealing or who had more than two previous non-drug convictions (Nolan, 1998). By contrast, the English Drug Treatment and Testing Order was targeted at persistent acquisitive offenders and several European QCT systems explicitly aim to replace prison with therapy for more serious offenders. USA drug courts rely on the enhanced, therapeutic role of the judge – a role that has not yet been taken by judges in Europe (Nolan, 2002). A more direct comparison could be made to the New York Drug Treatment Alternatives to Imprisonment Programme (DTAP, National Center on Addiction and Substance Abuse, 2003). This programme limited eligibility to drug dealers who would have been sentenced to imprisonment and showed that those who entered the residential treatment programme had lower rates of recidivism than similar offenders who went to prison.

Diversion to treatment has been taking place in some European countries (including Italy, Austria, Netherlands, Belgium, Switzerland and Germany) for several years, but in the absence of a solid base of evidence. The Dutch research is perhaps the most developed in this area and is covered in **chapter 6** of this book. Germany has a variety of QCT approaches, and these accounted for 20% of men and 11% of women undergoing treatment in 2000 (Welsch, 2001). German research is generally less encouraging than the American studies regarding the effectiveness of coerced treatment. Several studies have shown that legal pressure can reduce the prospects for successful treatment (Projektgruppe Rauschmittelfragen, 1991; Sickinger, 1994). Schalast (2000) showed a strong correlation between entering treatment under legal coercion and relapse, a link that was also highlighted by a German study of Swedish compulsory treatment, which showed that only 10% of clients were drug-free at follow-up (Heckmann, 1997).

Swiss results are more similar to those from American reviews. An evaluation of 2,793 clients found no significant differences in outcome at treatment exit between voluntary and court-referred clients (Grichting et al, 2002). Court-referred clients stayed significantly longer in treatment. Another study of residential drug treatment clients found no significant differences in drug use and social integration between voluntary patients and court referrals after the first 18 months following discharge (Uchtenhagen et al, 1997).

QCT is a more recent development in the UK, and early results seemed inconclusive. The Drug Testing and Treatment Order (DTTO) was introduced in 1998. It has since been replaced for adults in England and Wales by the Drug Rehabilitation Requirement (DRR). Both the DTTO and DRR provide courts with the option to sentence an offender to receive a course of treatment for their drug dependence, under the supervision of the probation service and with regular drug testing. Both require that the offender consents to entering treatment in order for the sentence to be given. If there is no such consent, offenders face the usual range of sentences for their offences. The court regularly reviews offenders' progress in treatment. If offenders fail to comply, they can be resentenced for the original offence. In England, three pilot DTTO projects showed high dropout, but significant falls in crime and drug use for those who stayed on the programme (Turnbull et al, 2000). There were difficulties in establishing coherent programmes. In Scotland, the order was introduced differently, and pilot results were more encouraging, with lower dropout (Eley et al, 2002). The two-year reconviction rate for those who started on a DTTO in England in 2001 was as high at 85%, but in a group that would have been expected to have an even higher rate (Spicer & Glicksman, 2004).

THE QCT EUROPE PROJECT

When it started in 2003, the QCT Europe project entered a field that was characterised by uncertainty over the process and effects of quasi-compulsory treatment, with conflicting results from various countries, and a paucity of evidence from Europe. It aimed to build the evidence base on the European use of QCT, with funding from the European Community's Fifth Framework Research and Technological Development Programme. It included partners in Austria, Germany, England, Italy, the Netherlands and Switzerland. The project started by reviewing the literature (Stevens & Berto *et al*, 2005) and describing the QCT systems operating in these countries (Werdenich *et al*, 2004). We concentrated our research on QCT structures as an alternative to prison or to avoid law enforcement procedures, requiring the consent and co-operation of the offender. As noted by the EMCDDA (2005) special report on alternatives to imprisonment, QCT can start at three stages of legal proceedings: pre trial (eg. by deferral of prosecution), trial/court stage (eg. by imposition of a sentence to treatment) or post trial (by substitution of treatment for part of the prison sentence). This third type is more common in Italy and Austria than in the other countries included in the project.

In England, we examined the process and effect of the DTTO. In Germany, Austria and Switzerland, our focus was on sections of the penal code that allow for 'therapy instead of punishment', either during prosecution or at the trial stage. It was not possible to randomly allocate drug dependent offenders to QCT or another sentence. We decided that it would be appropriate to compare people who undergo QCT with a sample of people who enter treatment without formal legal pressure, whom we called the 'volunteers' (the inverted commas are there because, as discussed below, many people who come into treatment without legal compulsion do experience some form of pressure). If we assume, from previous research, that these people are likely to experience greater reductions in drug use and offending than similar people who are imprisoned or who get no treatment, and if the QCT group experience similar or greater reductions in crime and drug use to these 'volunteers', then it seems reasonable to assume that QCT is also producing effects that are superior to imprisonment or no treatment (although this assumption needs to be tested in future, randomised studies).

A common problem in existing research on QCT is that it tends to ignore the person's experience of coercion and to assume that a person feels pressured just because they have arrived in treatment under some form of order from the court. The existing studies also tend to ignore the interplay between legal status, coercion, motivation, treatment engagement and outcome (Wild, 2006). This chapter highlights these issues.

METHODS
We carried out structured interviews with 845 people who were entering treatment and then contacted them for follow-up at six-month intervals until 18 months after treatment entry. The composition of our sample by country and legal status group is shown in *table 1*, opposite.

We used a questionnaire based on the European Addiction Severity Index (EuropASI) (Kokkevi & Hartgers, 1995) with the addition of EuropASI crime module (Öberg *et al*, 1999), the questions on perception of pressure from Simpson

Table 1: Composition of sample by country and group

	Sample size (*n*)	% in QCT group
UK	157	57%
Italy	300	48%
Austria	150	35%
Switzerland	85	59%
Germany	153	60%
Total	845	51%

and Knight's (1998) initial assessment form for correctional residential treatment, the Readiness to Change Questionnaire (Rollnick *et al*, 1992) and an adapted version of the Treatment Perceptions Questionnaire (Marsden *et al*, 2000). We also carried out 218 qualitative interviews and four focus groups with people who were going through QCT in these countries, and the judges, lawyers, probation officers and treatment staff who were working with them.

The sample

At entry to treatment, the sample members tended to report high levels of drug use and crime. These levels tended to be higher in the QCT group. For example, the members of the English intake sample who were on DTTOs reported an average expenditure on drugs in the previous month of £3,580, compared to £1,059 among the 'volunteers'. The most common pattern of drug use was daily heroin use, often involving injecting and combined with use of other drugs; 64% of the sample reported that heroin was their main problem drug, with another 24% reporting that poly-substance use was their main problem. Crack use was more commonly reported in England than elsewhere. The average age of the sample was 31 in both groups.

There was a high level of mental health problems in the sample. At entry to treatment, 60% of the sample reported a history of serious depression, and 61% reported that they had ever experienced serious anxiety. Also, 50% of the sample reported that they had current, chronic physical health problems. These included asthma, bronchitis, HIV, hepatitis C and deep vein thrombosis. Women were significantly more likely than men to report both mental and physical health problems. Only 7% of the QCT group, compared to 11% of the 'volunteers' were female. There is a potential problem of gender equity in channelling more resources to drug treatment through the criminal justice system. As most offenders are men, this implies that treatment becomes more available for men, without any necessary improvement for women.

The treatment that people entered in QCT tended to differ between England and the other countries. In England, members of our sample were mostly in day programmes and receiving opioid substitution treatment (mostly methadone). In the other countries, larger proportions of the sample entered residential treatment.

There were interesting differences between the countries in our sample in the type of offences that led to people entering QCT. **Figure 1** shows that, in England, it was predominantly property offenders who got a DTTO in our sampled sites. Shoplifting was by far the most commonly reported offence. In other countries, it was more common for people who had committed more serious offences, such as violence and drug dealing, to enter QCT. It may be that less serious offenders are more likely to get more serious sentences in England than in these other countries, which have lower rates of imprisonment (Council of Europe, 2006). However, it also suggests that the introduction of the DTTO may have led to 'net-widening' (Cohen, 1985), with DTTOs being given to people who would not have gone to prison if this sentence had not been available. This suggestion was backed up by qualitative interviews with some English probation officers. The National Probation Service uses the Offender Assessment System (OASys) to give offenders a score for how likely they are to cause harm and to be reconvicted. Probation offices that we interviewed in one of our English sampled areas reported that the minimum OASys score that they used to distinguish likely candidates for the DTTO was reduced during the period of our research. This was done in order to meet challenging targets for the number of DTTO commencements.

Figure 1: Proportions of the QCT sample by offences that led to QCT in each country

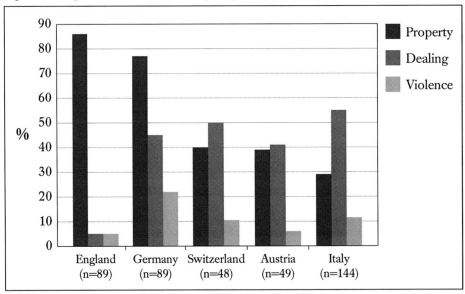

Are QCT clients less motivated?

It is often assumed that, because people in QCT are under pressure from the criminal justice system, they will have less intrinsic motivation to change and will therefore be less likely to succeed in treatment. It has been found in other studies that people who are more motivated at the start of treatment are more likely to be retained and to do well (eg. Joe *et al*, 1998; Simpson & Joe, 1993; Sung *et al*, 2004). However, the effect of legal pressure on motivation is less well known.

In interviews with our sample members we asked them about the pressure they felt they were under and about their feelings towards their drug use and their readiness to change. Members of the QCT reported feeling significantly more pressure to be in treatment than the 'volunteers'. But, interestingly, 65% of the 'volunteers' reported feeling some pressure, including pressure from their families and – for parents who were afraid of having their children taken from them – from social services. Also, 22% of the QCT group reported feeling no pressure. Not all people who are in QCT experience a feeling of compulsion from legal or other sources and many people who do not enter treatment under formal legal supervision nevertheless feel under pressure to be there.

Despite feeling, on average, more pressure to be in treatment, members of the QCT sample were not significantly less motivated to change. In order to test whether there was a link between feeling more pressured and feeling less motivated, we split the sample into groups according to where they fitted on Prochaska & DiClemente's (1983) 'cycle of change' (eg. pre contemplation, contemplation, action) when they entered treatment. The members of the QCT group were not generally at a lower level of motivation. Also, there was no link between feeling pressure from the police or courts and the stage of change that people were at. The results did not support the assumption that legally coerced treatment clients have poorer motivation.

We explored this finding in qualitative interviews. Many of the people in the QCT group reported that, even though they were under legal pressure to be in treatment, they still saw their entry to treatment as being something they had chosen. Many had been in treatment before. Also, others tended to report that they had often considered going into treatment but had not done so. For these people, QCT can be seen as providing a helpful push to get over the threshold of the treatment service. One English DTTO client said,

I mean I say "I'll do it today, not tomorrow", but before you know it that day's leading to a week, that week's leading to a month, and I suppose if you do get arrested and you've got that chance to do something about it then you'll take it.

We also found that motivation is often mixed, ambivalent and subject to change. Variations in motivation may come from changes in the person's feelings about the treatment they are offered and the circumstances they are in. Treatment providers can therefore enhance retention and outcome. They can do this by using methods such as motivational interviewing (Miller *et al*, 2002) which are known to increase motivation, by providing a warm and welcoming environment for service users, and by attending to other issues such as welfare benefit and housing problems that may otherwise damage motivation.

There are some limitations to these findings. For example, there were a large number of people who entered QCT at our sampled sites, but did not take part in interviews. This was often because they did not stay in treatment long enough to be contacted by our researchers. These people are likely to have been those who were least motivated to change. Their early exit from treatment points to the need to improve assessment and engagement processes for all clients, including those referred from the criminal justice system (see also Stevens *et al*, 2007). Full details of the findings and limitations on coercion and motivation have been given in a journal article (Stevens *et al*, 2006).

DO QCT CLIENTS ENGAGE IN TREATMENT?

The best chance of successful outcomes from drug treatment come when clients are successfully engaged and retained (Joe *et al*, 1999). So if there are differences between the engagement and retention of QCT and 'voluntary' clients, then this will have important implications for the targeting and delivery of drug treatment. We used the adapted treatment perceptions questionnaire to explore engagement in treatment at the six-month follow-up stage. This questionnaire had 18 questions in it. We used principal component analysis to identify three factors that were closely associated with different patterns of response to these questions.

The first factor we named 'treatment engagement'. People who scored highly on this factor tended to give positive responses to questions on whether they had been well informed about decisions on their treatment, whether staff had always been available to talk, whether staff helped to motivate them to sort out problems, whether staff were good at their jobs and whether they received the help they were looking for. The other factors were named 'treatment disdain' (which was associated with not having their needs understood, having different ideas to staff about their treatment objectives and with not liking the rules of treatment) and a weaker factor that we named 'non-committal'. This final factor seemed potentially contradictory, as it was associated with reporting not having had time to sort out problems and not being understood by staff, but was also associated with support for the treatment rules and with having had a choice between treatment options. From experience of interviewing, it seemed that there was a group of clients who saw it as their own responsibility to sort out their problems and so were less likely to place this responsibility onto the treatment agency.

We created scores that indicated how highly each person rated on these factors. These scores were not significantly different between QCT and 'voluntary' groups. This suggests that those who entered treatment under QCT did not have different perceptions of treatment or different levels of engagement in treatment.

When comparing retention in treatment between the two groups, we found that the average time that the QCT group stayed in treatment was 8.9 months. For the 'volunteers', it was 9.6 months. This difference was not statistically significant. We checked whether there was a relationship between the factors of treatment perception and the retention of clients in treatment. Unsurprisingly, those who reported higher than median scores for 'treatment engagement' were, on average, retained for significantly longer than those who reported lower scores. Also, those who reported high scores for 'treatment disdain' were retained for significantly less time. Those who had high scores on the 'non-committal' factor also had lower average retention times, but this last finding was not statistically significant in bivariate analysis.

We carried out a multivariate analysis (logistic regression) to examine the influences on whether people were retained in treatment at the six-month follow-up stage. This retention was not significantly more or less likely depending on whether the person entered treatment under QCT, on whether the client reported feeling pressure to be in treatment, or on what stage of motivation they were in at the start of treatment. Retention was related to the client's perceptions of treatment. In this analysis 'treatment engagement' was again significantly related to increased chances of retention, while both 'treatment disdain' and being 'non-committal' were significantly related to being less likely to still be in treatment at the follow-up stage.

These results again suggest that treatment outcome is not destined to be worse for people who enter treatment under QCT, or even for those who enter with lower levels of motivation. If treatment can be provided that accords with the needs and aims of the clients, in ways that make them feel supported and motivated to deal with their problems, than prospects for success are enhanced, whatever their route into treatment.

ARE OUTCOMES DIFFERENT FOR QCT CLIENTS?

There are a number of different outcomes that drug treatment can produce. The most visible concern for politicians and others who are not themselves engaged in problematic drug use is the potential for reductions in offending. There is also political and public interest in reducing levels of drug use. Drug users themselves normally enter treatment with the aim of at least reducing, and often eliminating their drug use. There are also potential benefits in terms of improved health (both mental and physical) and increased integration into society (eg. improved housing and employment). We were able to check progress in all these domains.

There is an important limitation to our findings, which is that there were many people whom we interviewed at intake whom we did not interview at subsequent stages. This is a common problem in studies of drug treatment. In our study, we interviewed 393 (46.5%) of the original sample at the 18-month follow-up stage. In order to check the influence of the missing respondents on our findings on outcome, we used the technique of last observation carried forward (LOCF). This assumes that the data for a missing follow-up stage will be identical to the previous stage when the person was interviewed. For example, if a person reported spending £1,000 per month on drugs at intake, and was then not re-interviewed, the figure of £1,000 per month was included in the analysis of follow-up stages of this person.

This is considered to be a conservative method, as it assumes no improvement for people who are not followed up. The results of the LOCF analysis showed very similar patterns to the results reported below.

We asked our interviewees to tell us about their offending. Of course, we can be sceptical about how truthful their replies may have been, but previous studies have found that trends in self-reported offending are corroborated by other indicators, such as arrests and convictions (Nurco, 1985; Thornberry & Krohn, 2000). Before starting treatment, members of our sample – and especially those in the QCT group – reported very high levels of offending. **Figure 2** shows how these levels changed after treatment entry.

Figure 2: Changes in offending by group

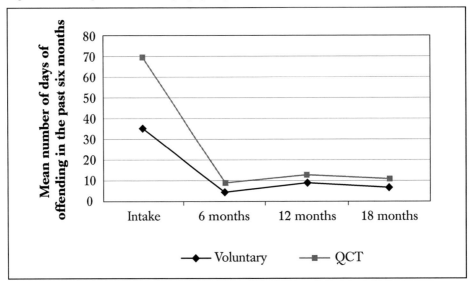

There were large and significant reductions in the frequency of offending in the first six months after treatment entry. At the 18-month follow-up, 76% of the QCT group and 83% of the 'volunteers' reported that they had committed no offences in the previous six months.

As a measure of drug use, we used the EuropASI composite drug use score (Koeter & Hartgers, 1997). **Figure 3**, opposite, shows the reductions in these scores.

Before entering treatment, most of the members of both groups in the sample were using drugs in various combinations every day. They reported experiencing a lot of problems with their drug use. Over the first six months of treatment, they tended to make significant reductions in their drug use and the level of problems they experienced with it. The changes were again mostly maintained over the next 12 months. The QCT group started treatment with slightly heavier patterns of drug use than the 'volunteers', but were able to achieve similar reductions.

Figure 3: Changes in composite drug use score by group

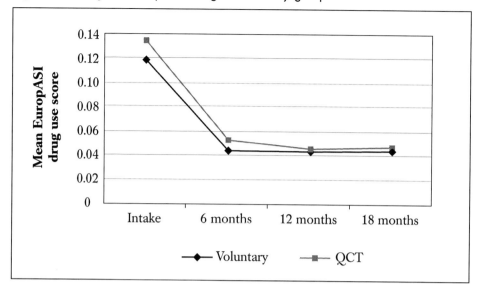

Thirty-five per cent of people who were interviewed at 18-month follow-up reported that they were abstinent from all drugs. The remainder reported an average of 14 days of drug consumption in the month before that interview. However, their patterns of drug use tended to have changed, with many fewer of them injecting heroin, and many more restricting themselves to cannabis, with some taking prescribed methadone.

The most commonly reported mental health problems in our sample were anxiety and depression. There were similar reductions in both QCT and 'voluntary' groups in the proportions of people who reported serious depression or anxiety in the month before the interview. For depression, this reduction was from 36% of the combined sample to 24% at the 18-month follow-up and was statistically significant. The reduction for anxiety was smaller, from 39% to 34% and was not statistically significant. **Figure 4**, overleaf, shows that there was reduction in both groups in the mean number of days that people reported experiencing mental health problems in the past month. This reduction was statistically significant.

There was a different pattern for self-reported physical health problems. These were less frequently reported than mental health problems. **Figure 5**, overleaf, suggests that there was a reduction in both groups in the average number of days out of the past 30 that members of both groups reported experiencing physical health problems. This reduction was larger and statistically significant for the 'voluntary' group. The small reduction for the QCT group was not significant.

There were significant reductions in homelessness for both groups. At entry to treatment, 21% of the QCT group and 14% of the 'volunteers' reported that they were homeless. At the 18-month follow-up, these proportions had reduced to 4%

Figure 4: Changes in number of days experiencing mental health problems by group

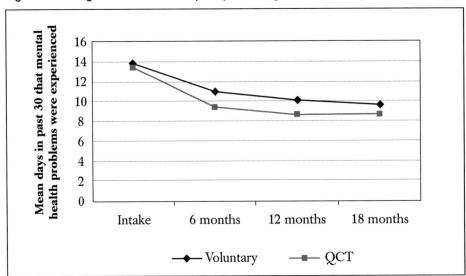

Figure 5: Changes in number of days experiencing physical health problems by group

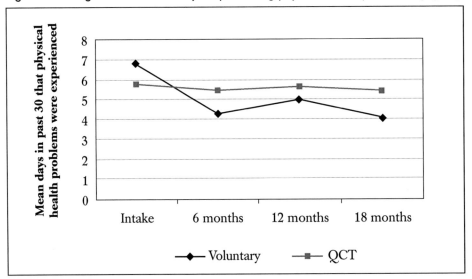

and 3%. There were also significant improvements in the employment status. The proportion of the sample who were in employment increased from 18% to 56% for the 'volunteers' and from 24% to 49% for the QCT group.

However, these improvements in employment were not seen in the English sample, whose level of employment stayed resolutely low. This may partly be due to the English sample generally having a worse employment record at intake. It may also be due to other countries' treatment systems putting more emphasis on helping people into work. The Italian sample were especially successful in finding employment, despite poor employment records in the QCT group. Their treatment tended to include work placements, which they were able to use to find jobs. The problem of employment integration for English drug users in treatment has been recognised as very difficult to solve (McSweeney *et al*, 2004), but there would seem to be scope for borrowing methods such as job brokering and employment support from other fields (eg. mental health services) in order to help drug users overcome disadvantage and stigma in the labour market. One English man who had completed a DTTO programme said in a qualitative interview,

'I mean I don't know what I'm meant to be doing, right. I'm not committing crime. I'm not taking Class A drugs. Alright, I might be smoking a bit of hash, I might be drinking too much. But that's all I'm doing wrong though. Apart from that I'm practically isolating myself… when I was on the DTTO I thought I had things going for me. You know, things seemed to be moving on. But they've stopped now…. We can all be cosy, right, sitting in the bedsit. I've got me tin, I've got me video. I've got credit up the offy. But I want to fucking do better. I want a nice flat, I want a girl, I want a motor. I want to be working'.

Overall, these results suggest that there were positive outcomes in the various ways in which drug treatment can help people who have drug problems to change their lives. These outcomes were not achieved by every person who entered treatment. Many dropped out and went back to prison or to a life dominated by drugs and the need to commit crimes to buy them. However, on average, there were similar reductions in drug use and offending, and improvements in health and social integration. These outcomes were similar for people who entered treatment on QCT or as 'volunteers'. The pattern of outcome was also similar across countries, except for employment. This suggests that a variety of QCT approaches are capable of helping problematic drug users to achieve positive outcomes.

LEGAL STATUS, PRESSURE, MOTIVATION, ENGAGEMENT AND OUTCOME

As well as looking at differences in outcome according to the route of entry into treatment (which seem to be small), we can look at differences associated with different levels of legal status, perceived pressure, motivation and treatment engagement. The EuropASI drug use score will be used, as this measures the drug use which is targeted by treatment.

In order to explore the relationships between these issues, a multivariate, logistic regression analysis was carried out to test the influence of these variables on the likelihood that a person reported higher than median EuropASI drug use scores at the 18-month follow-up stage. The intake level of the EuropASI drug use score was included in this analysis, as it is likely that the level of initial drug use would otherwise confound the influence of other variables. The results of this analysis were that whether the person was in QCT, the amount of pressure they felt and whether they were in the action stage of motivation at intake were not significantly influential in predicting whether they would have high levels of drug use at 18-month follow-up. On the other hand, their level of treatment engagement was influential. Those who reported high levels of the 'treatment engagement' factor were about a third less likely to report high levels of drug use at 18 months.

This again suggests that, even though the QCT group were more likely to report feeling pressured to be in treatment, this did not damage their prospects for succeeding in drug treatment. It also suggests that success is not limited to those people who have already decided to change their drug use. Initial motivation did not have a significant impact on this measure of treatment success. Success was most likely for those people who reported positive experiences of treatment, including feeling that the staff were good at their jobs, understood their needs, motivated them to change and were there for them when needed.

ENABLING AND HINDERING ENGAGEMENT AND CHANGE

In an article based on the qualitative interviews and focus groups, Oeuvray *et al* (under review) have highlighted some aspects of the QCT process that can support or obstruct the process of change. In a list of 'commitment enabling' conditions they include the process of entry, the provision of security, having an ally, and linking to people and roles that have nothing to do with drugs and treatment.

The process of entry should logically follow a sequential order of deciding whether the person is eligible for QCT, whether they have the opportunity to benefit from QCT (is the time right, are the practicalities in place?), and finally what sort of treatment they should enter. In practice, the process is often messier than this. One example is the use of central targets and quotas to decide who will get QCT, rather than the assessment of local and individual need. Another is making the treatment that QCT clients receive dependent on local contracts for service provision, rather than the assessed needs and wishes of the client. In Germany, QCT clients were funded by their own state health insurance and so could, and often did, choose to move between treatment modalities, while staying in QCT. In England, in contrast, the treatment modality was often decided by pre existing agreements between probation and treatment service providers. In one of our English research areas, QCT clients found it very hard to access residential treatment (which was the usual mode of treatment outside England). In one town, all QCT clients were sent to a 12-step, abstinence-based day programme. Many of them had difficulty adjusting to its demands for abstinence from all drugs (including cannabis and alcohol). The dropout rate was high.

Treatment clients are more likely to stay and engage in treatment when they can participate in a safe and predictable routine. Many treatment centres attempt to provide such a routine for their clients by setting rules and expectations for attendance and acceptable behaviour. However, many people, especially in the early stages of treatment, have difficulties in adjusting to these expectations. This is especially difficult if they have other areas of their life that are not safe and predictable. If they are unable to eat because they have no income or welfare benefits, if they are unable to sleep because they have nowhere to live, and if they are unable to live without pain because they have untreated medical needs, then their participation in the routine of treatment will be compromised. This is why it is important for treatment agencies to pay attention to the wider needs of their clients, including help with benefits, housing and medical care.

In interviews with people who were doing well in QCT, many of them mentioned the importance of having an ally in assisting them to enter and stay in treatment. This was someone who 'really listened' and who helped to remove obstacles that were in their way. The importance of the alliance between therapist and client is well known (Ashton & Witton, 2004). In this study, the concept of the ally was broader than the relationship with the treatment worker. The ally could be a probation officer, a prison officer, a lawyer or even a judge. The person's profession seemed less important than the fact that they took an interest in the person's situation and helped them move through the difficulties that faced them.

If it was important to have people and processes that helped drug users into treatment, it was also important that people were linked back into the non-drug world. Once people had used treatment to reduce and stabilise their drug use, they tended to be keen to move on (as seen in the quote from the English bedsit-dweller above). Work was often mentioned in this context. This is seen as symbolising reentry to the normal world. It is also the predominant path out of poverty (Smith & Middleton, 2007). However, for many of our respondents, employment seemed little more likely at the end of the project than it had at the start, even when they had made progress in other areas of their lives. Many of them had spent several years developing contacts in the underground drugs economy and had no remaining contacts in the legitimate world of work. In England, it seemed that it was only those who had relatives with businesses who were able to find jobs. Our interviewees told us that they were screened out early from more formal recruitment processes. As mentioned above, some of the treatment agencies in our study (particularly in Italy) made deliberate attempts to link their clients into the world of work. This presumably helped to both improve their CVs and to create the kind of informal contacts that are often as necessary in the labour market as they are in the drugs market.

CONCLUSION

Quasi-compulsory treatment is not a panacea, either for problems of drug-related crime, or for the personal problems of problematic drug users. However, the evidence gathered by the QCT Europe does suggest that it has a place in the range of services that should be provided in countries that have significant numbers of drug users who commit criminal offences. It should not be seen as a substitute for providing access to high-quality drug treatment for all those who need it, regardless of their offending behaviour. Such services are needed by problematic drug users and have been shown to be cost-effective (NICE, 2007a, 2007b, 2007c, 2007d). It does offer a valuable alternative to imprisonment, which has been shown to be ineffective in helping drug users to reduce their drug use and offending in the long term (Hough, 1996).

In a context where policies of compulsion and punishment seem to be spreading rapidly (Pratt *et al*, 2005), it is important to reflect on the nature of coercion in QCT, and especially on the importance of the quasi-compulsory element. Undiluted compulsion, with no element of choice, is likely to lead to reduced feelings of autonomy and so to feelings of anger and resistance (Deci & Ryan, 1985). Such feelings are likely to damage motivation and treatment engagement. However, people who enter QCT retain some autonomy. They know that they could have chosen to face the alternative sentence for the crime that led to their prosecution. Many of the QCT Europe sample saw their entry to treatment as being freely willed, and it is suggested that this is why the compulsory element of QCT did not seem to damage their motivation and engagement in treatment. This does not mean that these findings can be expanded to cover compulsory treatment for drug users, especially for those who have committed no other crimes. It seems that such compulsion has hindered treatment engagement in the Dutch SOV trial (van 't Land *et al*, 2005). In addition, it would breach principles of human rights if drug users were forced to participate in treatments that are lengthier and more intrusive than the sentences that they would otherwise have got for their crimes (Gostin & Mann, 2004; Porter *et al*, 1986).

There are limits to the uses of quasi-compulsory treatment, and there are also limits to its potential effects. The man who has been credited with inventing the DTTO warned in 1994 that it would not be capable of producing major reductions in the crime rate. This is because of the 'funnel of crime'. Those offenders who are caught and convicted (and can therefore be coerced into treatment), represent only a small proportion of the total 'universe' of criminals; in Britain only three in 100 offences result in an offender being convicted or cautioned (Russell, 1994). People who enter QCT may be frequent offenders who commit more than their fair share of crime, but there is still a large and constantly replenished reservoir of unarrested, unconvicted offenders. Wider solutions to drug-related crime will require wider attention to the social problems that are associated with the onset and maintenance of offending (Stevens *et al*, 2005; Straw & Michael, 1996; Wikström & Sampson, 2006).

The QCT Europe project added to the available evidence for the use of treatment as an alternative to imprisonment in Europe. This study had its limitations, and there should be more research, including randomised trials and ethnographic studies of the outcomes and processes of QCT. The main implications of the QCT Europe project are that QCT for drug dependent offenders can be successful in helping them to reduce their drug use and offending. It is not inevitable that people who are ordered into treatment by the courts feel less motivated and will do worse than others in treatment. Prospects for success may be damaged where systems do not allow for the creation of supportive relationships between professionals and drug users, and where it is assumed that one size fits all. They are enhanced where time is taken to listen to people's needs, to help them with the full range of needs that they express, and to support them out of treatment into employment.

Acknowledgements

The author wishes to acknowledge the invaluable contribution of the QCT Europe project partners to this research. They were:

- Neil Hunt, EISS, University of Kent, UK
- Paul Turnbull and Tim McSweeney, ICPR, King's College London, UK
- Dr Daniele Berto, Barbara Tabachi and Morena Tartari, ULSS No. 16, Padova, Italy
- Marianne van Ooyen, WODC, Ministry of Justice, Netherlands
- Professor Marc-Henry Soulet and Kerralie Oeuvray, Université de Fribourg, Switzerland
- Professor Dr Ambros Uchtenhagen, Susanne Schaaf and Ulrich Frick, Insituts für Sucht und Gesundheitsforschung, Switzerland
- Dr Wolfgang Werdenich, Gabriele Waidner and Barbara Trinkl, University of Vienna, Austria
- Professor Dr Wolfgang Heckmann, Elfriede Steffan and Andrea Viktoria Kerschl, MISTEL/SPI Forschung, Germany.

The QCT Europe study was funded by the European Community's Fifth Framework Research and Technological Development Programme.

References

Ashton M & Witton J (2004) *Engaging and Retaining Clients in Drug Treatment.* London: NTA.

Belenko S (2001) *Research on Drug Courts: A critical review 2001 update.* New York: National Centre on Addiction and Substance Abuse.

Cohen S (1985) *Visions of Social Control.* Cambridge: Polity Press.

Council of Europe (2006) *European Sourcebook of Crime and Criminal Justice Statistics.* The Hague: WODC, Ministry of Justice.

Deci EL & Ryan RM (1985) *Intrinsic Motivation and Self-determination in Human Behavior.* New York: Plenum.

Eley S, Gallop K, McIvor G, Morgan K & Yates R (2002) *Drug Treatment and Testing Orders: Evaluation of the Scottish pilots.* Edinburgh: Scottish Executive Central Research Unit.

EMCDDA (2003) *Treating Drug Users in Prison – A critical area for health-promotion and crime-reduction policy. Drugs in Focus No. 7.* Lisbon: European Monitoring Centre for Drugs and Drug Addiction.

EMCDDA (2005) *Annual Report 2005: Selected issue 2. Alternatives to imprisonment – targeting offending problem drug users in the EU.* Lisbon: European Monitoring Centre on Drugs and Drug Addiction.

General Accountability Office (2005) *Adult Drug Courts: Evidence indicates recidivism reductions and mixed results for other outcomes. GAO-05-219.* Washington, DC: General Accountability Office.

Gossop M, Marsden J, Stewart D & Treacy S (2002) Change and stability of change after treatment of drug misuse two-year outcomes from the National Treatment Outcome Research Study (UK). *Addictive Behaviors* **27** (2) 155–166.

Gostin L & Mann J (2004) Toward the development of a human rights impact assessment for the formulation and evaluation of public health policies. In: K Malinowska-Sempruch & S Gallagher (Eds) *War on Drugs, HIV/AIDS and Human Rights.* New York: International Debate Education Association.

Grichting E, Uchtenhagen A & Rehm J (2002) Modes and impact of coercive inpatient treatment for drug-related conditions in Switzerland. *European Addiction Research* **8** (2) 78–83.

Heckmann W (1997) Schwedische Gardinen: Zur Tradition der Zwangsbehandlung Suchtkranker und gefährdeter in Schweden. *SUCHT. Zeitschrift für Wissenschaft und Praxis* **43** (3).

Hoffman MB (2000) The drug court scandal. *North Carolina Law Review* **76**.

Hough M (1996) *Drug Misusers and the Criminal Justice System: A review of the literature. Drugs prevention inititiative paper 15.* London: Home Office.

Hubbard RL, Craddock SG & Anderson J (2003) Overview of five-year follow-up outcomes in the drug abuse treatment outcome studies (DATOS). *Journal of Substance Abuse Treatment* **25** (3) 125–134.

Joe GW, Simpson DD & Broome KM (1998) Effects of readiness for drug abuse treatment on client retention and assessment of process. *Addiction* **93** (8) 1177–1190.

Joe GW, Simpson DD & Broome KM (1999) Retention and patient engagement models for different treatment modalities in DATOS. *Drug and Alcohol Dependence* **57** (2) 113–125.

Koeter M & Hartgers C (1997) *European Addiction Severity Index: Preliminary procedure for the computation of the EuropASI composite scores.* Amsterdam: Amsterdam Institute for Addiction Research.

Kokkevi A & Hartgers C (1995) Europe ASI: European adaptation of a multidimensional assessment instrument for drug and alcohol dependence. *European Addiction Research* **1** (4) 208–210.

Lurigio AJ & Schwartz JA (1999) The nexus between drugs and crime: theory, research and practice. *Federal Probation* **63** 67–72.

Marsden J, Stewart D, Gossop M, Rolfe A, Bacchus L, Griffiths P, Clarke K & Strang J (2000) Assessing client satisfaction with treatment for substance use problems and the development of the treatment perceptions questionnaire (TPQ). *Addiction Research* **8** (5) 455–470.

McSweeney T, Herrington V, Hough M, Turnbull PJ & Parsons J (2004) *From Dependency to Work: Addressing the multiple needs of offenders with drug problems.* Bristol: Policy Press.

Miller WR, Rollnick S & Conforti K (2002) *Motivational Interviewing: Preparing people for change* (2nd ed). New York: Guilford Press.

National Center on Addiction and Substance Abuse (2003) *Crossing the Bridge: An evaluation of the Drug Treatment Alternative-to-Prison (DTAP) Program. A CASA white paper.* New York: National Center on Addiction and Substance Abuse, Columbia University.

NICE (2007a) *Psychosocial Management of Drug Misuse. Draft for consultation.* London: National Institute for Health and Clinical Excellence.

NICE (2007b) *Opiate Detoxification for Drug Misuse. Draft for consultation.* London: National Institute for Health and Clinical Excellence.

NICE (2007c) *Naltrexone for the Management of Opioid Dependence. NICE technology appraisal 115.* London: National Institute for Health and Clinical Excellence.

NICE (2007d) *Methadone and Buprenorphine for the Management of Opioid Dependence. NICE technology appraisal 114.* London: National Institute for Health and Clinical Excellence.

Nolan JL (1998) *The Therapeutic State: Justifying government at century's end.* New York: New York University Press.

Nolan JL (2002) *Drug Courts: In theory and in practice.* New York: Aldine de Gruyter.

Nurco DN (1985) A discussion of validity. In: BA Rouse, NJ Kozel & LG Richards (Eds) *Self-Report Methods of Estimating Drug Use: Meeting current challenges to validity. NIDA research monograph 57.* Rockville, Maryland: National Institute on Drug Abuse.

Öberg D, Sallmén B, Kaplan C, McMurphy S, Ackerson T, Krantz L, Martens P, Schlyter F & Turner T (1999) *ASI Crime Module.* Höör: Karlsvik Rehabilitation Center.

Oeuvray K, Soulet M-H, Hunt N & Stevens A (under review) Court ordered commitment: enabling (or hindering) conditions of commitment emergence in quasi-compulsory treatment for drug using offenders. *European Addiction Research.*

Porter L, Arif A & Curran WJ (1986) *The Law and Treatment of Drug and Alcohol Dependent Persons – A comparative study of existing legislation.* Geneva: World Health Organisation.

Pratt J, Brown D, Brown M, Hallsworth S & Morrison W (2005) Introduction. In: J Pratt, D Brown, M Brown, S Hallsworth & W Morrison (Eds) *The New Punitiveness: Trends, theories, perspectives.* Cullompton: Willan Publishing.

Prendergast ML, Podus D, Chang E & Urada D (2002) The effectiveness of drug abuse treatment: a meta-analysis of comparison group studies. *Drug and Alcohol Dependence* **67** (1) 53–72.

Prochaska JO & DiClemente CC (1983) Stages and processes of self-change of smoking: toward an integrated model of change. *Journal of Consulting and Clinical Psychology* **51** 390–395.

Projektgruppe Rauschmittelfragen (1991) *Forschungsprojekt 'Amsel'.* Abschlussbericht Band 1. Frankfurt/Main: Jugendberatung und Jugendhilfe e.V.

Rollnick S, Heather N, Gold R & Hall W (1992) Development of a short 'Readiness to Change' questionnaire for use in brief, opportunistic interventions among excessive drinkers. *British Journal of Addiction* **87** (5) 743–754.

Russell J (1994) *Substance Abuse and Crime (some lessons from America). Harkness Fellowship report.* New York: Commonwealth Fund of New York.

Schalast N (2000) Rückfälle während der Behandlung im Maßregelvollzug gemäß 64 StGB. *SUCHT. Zeitschrift für Wissenschaft und Praxis* **46** (2).

Sickinger R (1994) *Ausstieg aus der Heroinabhängigkeit.* Freiburg: Lambertus Verlag.

Simpson DD & Joe GW (1993) Motivation as a predictor of early dropout from drug abuse treatment. *Psychotherapy* **30** 357–368.

Simpson DD & Knight K (1998) *TCU Data Collection Forms for Correctional Residential Treatment.* Fort Worth, Texas: Christian University, Institute of Behavioral Research.

Smith N & Middleton S (2007) *A Review of Poverty Dynamics Research in the UK.* York: Joseph Rowntree Foundation.

Spicer K & Glicksman A (2004) *Adult Reconviction: Results from the 2001 cohort. Home Office online report 59/04.* London: Home Office.

Stevens A, Berto D, Frick U, Hunt N, Kerschl V, McSweeney T, Oeuvray K, Puppo I, Santa Maria A, Schaaf S, Trinkl B, Uchtenhagen A & Werdenich W (2006) The relationship between legal status, perceived pressure and motivation in treatment for drug dependence: results from a European study of quasi-compulsory treatment. *European Addiction Research* **12** 197–209.

Stevens A, Berto D, Heckmann W, Kerschl V, Oeuvray K, van Ooyen M, Steffan E & Uchtenhagen A (2005) Quasi-compulsory treatment of drug dependent offenders: an international literature review. *Substance Use and Misuse* **40** 269–283.

Stevens A, Radcliffe P, Sanders M, Hunt N, Turnbull P & McSweeney T (2007) *Early Exit: Estimating and explaining early exit from drug treatment.* London: Department of Health.

Stevens A, Trace M & Bewley-Taylor DR (2005) *Reducing Drug Related Crime: An overview of the global evidence. Report five.* Oxford: Beckley Foundation.

Straw J & Michael A (1996) *Tackling the Causes of Crime: Labour's proposals to prevent crime and criminality.* London: Labour Party.

Sung H-E, Belenko S, Feng L & Tabachnick C (2004) Predicting treatment noncompliance among criminal justice-mandated clients: a theoretical and empirical exploration. *Journal of Substance Abuse Treatment* **26** (1) 13–26.

Thornberry TP & Krohn MD (2000) The self-report method for measuring delinquency and crime. In: JE Samuels (Ed) *Measurement and Analysis of Crime and Justice. Criminal Justice 2000. Volume 4.* Washington, DC: National Institute of Justice.

Turnbull PJ, McSweeney T, Webster R, Edmunds M & Hough M (2000) *Drug Treatment and Testing Orders: Final evaluation report.* London: Home Office Research, Development and Statistics Directorate.

Uchtenhagen A, Gutzwiller F, Dobler-Mikola A & Stephen T (1997) Programme for a medical prescription of narcotics: a synthesis of results. *European Addiction Research* **3** (4) 160–163.

van 't Land H, van Duijvenbooden K, van der Plas A & Wolf J (2005) *Opgevangen Onder Dwang Procesevaluatie Strafrechtelijke Opvang Verslaafden.* The Hague: WODC, Ministry of Justice.

Welsch (2001) Suchthilfestatistik 2000 in Deutschland. *SUCHT. Zeitschrift für Wissenschaft und Praxis.* Geesthacht: Neuland Verlag.

Werdenich W, Waidner G & Trinkl B (2004) Quasi-compulsory treatment of drug dependent offenders – a description of existing systems. *Verhaltenstherapie und Verhaltensmedizin* **1** 71–78.

Wikström P-OH & Sampson RJ (2006) *The Explanation of Crime: Context, mechanisms and development.* Cambridge: Cambridge University Press.

Wild TC (2006) Social control and coercion in addiction treatment: towards evidence-based policy and practice. *Addiction* **101** (1) 40–49.

CHAPTER 8

Involved, represented, or ignored: the place of user involvement in British drug treatment

Daren Garratt

'If you do something the patient doesn't want, you're going to fail.' (Dr Chris Ford, 2007)

INTRODUCTION

Although the treatment of an individual's illicit drug use has been a part of the British medical landscape for over a century, the quality and efficacy of this potentially life saving intervention has, arguably, only become of strategic national importance as the socio-political dimension of drugs has grown over the last 10 years or so. This chapter will, therefore, explore how the integral role of users in drug treatment has developed on policy and practice levels over the last decade, how its effectiveness is supported by an increasing body of research evidence and best practice examples, and how it continues to face and overcome strategic and operational barriers in its attempt to be accepted as a valuable, indispensable social and medical intervention as opposed to a cynical act of political tokenism.

The arrival of a new Labour government in 1998 also brought with it *Tackling Drugs to Build a Better Britain: The government's 10-year strategy for tackling drug misuse*, and it would prove to dominate the drug treatment field for the next decade as drug action teams up and down the country reviewed and revised their services in order to help the government achieve its target of helping problematic drug users *'reduce and overcome their problems and live healthy and crime-free lives'* by increasing the *'participation of drug misusers in treatment by 100% by 2008'* (UK Anti-drugs Co-ordination Unit, 1999 p17).

The problem, though, was that there was no standardised quality of treatment in the UK at that time. It was evident that serious investment was needed to ensure that users received appropriate levels of well-researched, planned and implemented interventions in order to support them in their desire to bring stability and order to previous, frequently chaotic and damaged lives. Noted UK author, service user and activist Peter McDermott explains that this was a period when,

'Drug treatment in the UK was often extremely poor, and was often based upon the prejudices and whims of those involved, rather than being based upon the available evidence.

Long waiting times and sub-optimal dosing for patients receiving pharmacotherapy were the rule, rather than the exception in many areas' (McDermott, unpublished).

This view was not exclusively held by service users. Even the General Medical Council acknowledged and stated that it is,

'unethical for a doctor to withhold treatment from any patient on the basis of a moral judgement that the patient's activities or lifestyle might have contributed to the condition for which treatment was being sought' (DoH, 1999 p2).

Yet this was still common practice among some members of the medical community, and further advancements were going to be needed if treatment was to be improved to the point where users and government could both achieve their desired outcomes.

Help arrived in 1999 when the Department of Health published *Drug Misuse and Dependence – Guidelines on clinical management*, which is more commonly referred to as the 'Orange Guidelines' (due to its distinctive, bright orange cover). This document comprehensively revised the previous 1991 guidelines and can be subsequently viewed as a veritable 'year zero' for drug treatment in Britain. It quickly became established as an indispensable cornerstone in developing standards and quality of care in the appropriate treatment of drug users. Further, it acknowledged that,

'Drug misusers have the same entitlement as other patients to the services provided by the National Health Service. It is the responsibility of all doctors to provide care for both general health needs and drug-related problems, whether or not the patient is ready to withdraw from drugs' (DoH, 1999 p1).

In order to attempt to redress inequity of provision and bring a wider strategic and clinical coherence to drug treatment both in primary and secondary care settings, the government established the National Treatment Agency (NTA) in 2001. The NTA was a special health authority whose remit was, *'to improve the availability, capacity and effectiveness of treatment for drug misuse in England'* (NTA, 2008a).

It was needed. Earlier, in February of the same year, the Audit Commission published its own report, *Changing Habits*, which identified that many drug users struggle to get appropriate help because of:

- limited treatment options
- lengthy delays
- under-developed care management
- poor service planning
- different views about 'what works'
- poor collaboration between treatment providers and other key stakeholders (Audit Commission, 2002).

It proved timely, therefore, that the NTA published their *Models of Care for Treatment in Adult Drug Misusers* document in December 2002, which set out a national framework required to achieve the equity, parity and consistency in the commissioning and provision of drug treatment and related care that the Audit Commission called for.

Crucially, *Models of Care* acknowledged the central role that users and carers played in drug treatment by outlining the right of users to be actively involved in interventions and *'activities that affect their health and well-being'*, while valuing and respecting *'the unique expertise and experiences of drug users and carers and... health, esteem and other personal benefits which involvement can bring...'* (NTA, 2002 p190).

The government was by now investing unprecedented amounts of public money into the development of an equitable, national framework that would:

- provide 'more treatment, better treatment, fairer treatment'
- closely monitor public authorities to ensure that treatment services were commissioned to appropriate standards
- place individual users as central to their own care and the decision-making process.

However, time has taught us that despite undeniable advancements in drug treatment and user involvement since the inception of the NTA, the admirable rhetoric still too frequently betrays the reality of most users' inability to be respected or accepted as active partners and decision-makers in their own care.

This is, admittedly, a very forthright and some may say cynical, possibly even unfair, statement to make, but it is based on 10 years of experience of being an illicit drug user (although admittedly never a service user) working in the harm reduction and user involvement field as a coal-face worker, strategic co-ordinator and, presently, manager of a national charity. The overarching methodology used in this chapter is, therefore, individual viewpoint presented by peers, colleagues, and myself, but supported by a robust understanding, reflection and critique of national policy and other relevant, related documentation and research.

THE ROLE OF USERS IN DECIDING INDIVIDUAL TREATMENT
'Only the wearer of the shoe knows where it pinches' (Weale, 2006).

Although the advent of the NTA and *Models of Care* highlighted the importance of user involvement in improving the process and outcomes of drug treatment, acknowledgment of the crucial role that users had to play in the planning and delivery of services was already well established.

Indeed, by the dawn of the new millennium, 'user involvement' had virtually become a statutory responsibility following the publication of such documents as the *NHS Patients' Charter* (DoH, 1991) and the Community Care Act (1990), which highlighted the increased consumer rights awarded to NHS patients and the increased obligations of local authorities to consult and consider the views of their clients respectively.

Furthermore, in July 2000 the newly published *The NHS Plan* was even more direct when it acknowledged that,

'Patients are the most important people in the health service. It doesn't always appear that way. Too many patients feel talked at rather than listened to. This has to change. NHS care has to be shaped around the convenience and concerns of patients. To bring this about, patients must have more say in their own treatment and more influence over the way the NHS works' (DoH, 2000 p88).

However, six years after the plan was published, two research studies suggested that this principle still hasn't extended to the treatment of drug users. Walsall Drug Action Team conducted a survey (2006) of current service users to gauge if the theory of the treatment journey process differed from the reality of experience. The vast majority of the sample were very happy with improvements they had seen around waiting times, dosing levels and flexibility around areas such as supervised consumption. However, of the 52 users interviewed, 65% were unaware of what a care plan was and the importance it had in making them active partners in deciding their own treatment. Comments from the semi-structured interviews conducted included,

'What is a care plan? I was never involved in any thing like this. I was never asked what I wanted out of my treatment, but now I know this is something that is meant to happen. I am going to ask my key worker about having it explained by her and for a review of this process',

and,

'I have never been involved in drawing up a care plan in the six years I have been coming to the service. However, I am going to ask to be involved in this process'.

These figures are worryingly comparable to those revealed in a recent study of 100 heroin users, commissioned by pharmaceutical company Schering-Plough. In this survey, only 47% of users felt that they had decided their own treatment regime, while the other respondents reported that their choice of medication had been decided by either their GP (27 respondents) or their key worker (24 respondents).

However, if the fundamental right of an individual to be involved in deciding and shaping their own treatment is such a crucial tenet of the new NHS, why does it appear to be taking so long to influence the culture and practice of some areas of the drug treatment field?

Maybe it is because traditionally, as soon as an individual presents with problematic drug use they immediately become the 'client' of a service rather than a 'patient'.

And while this may, on the surface, seem like a pedantic point about semantics, let us not forget that the way we, as a society, chose to label and define our citizens will inevitably influence the way they are viewed and treated. This was acknowledged by social services in the 1980s when the term 'client' was deemed 'patronising and stigmatising', yet somehow, it appears that the stigma, fear, ignorance and morality issues that still prevail around illicit drug users and their lifestyle choices systematically result in them becoming exempt from the basic rights and privileges afforded other NHS stakeholders.

Even the otherwise admirable Audit Commission report falls short of acknowledging the central role that users can play in developing and deciding their own treatment options. In the section on care management within community drug services, it is rightly stressed that,

'individual clients receive an integrated package of care that offers a holistic response to their problems. Clear care plans can promote effective co-ordination between services, taking account of each client's changing needs over time. Ideally, the plan should reflect the contributions of all relevant agencies and copies of individual plans should be given to users' (Audit Commission, 2002 p46).

But surely, the one missing ingredient here is the role of the individual user as a 'relevant agency' and their fundamental right and need to *agree* their care plan before being presented with it?

This may seem a rather petty observation considering the developments made, but the truth is, at this point, although many individual users and user groups were cautiously optimistic about the validity and respect being afforded them by the NTA and other agencies, there was still a suspicion that they were largely having things done to them not with them, and although 'user involvement' was becoming an increasingly ubiquitous term, the conditions of involvement were always on someone else's terms and never their own.

Take the April 2001 edition of *Monkey* magazine, *'a quarterly newsletter for hardcore drug users, ex-users and carers'*, which was developed by Trafford User Forum and edited by Ian Smith. By the time of publication, the NTA was not even formally established, yet here was a user-led magazine cautiously welcoming any agency that has *'the power to make sure that the new money that's coming down for treatment will actually end up being spent on treatment'*, but astutely observing that,

'There is the small matter of user consultation. Not a word about the consumers of drug services in any of the consultation documents. This, despite all the stuff in NHS documents about patients first and the 'best value' approach in local government that says consumers of public services should be consulted. Never mind. We can help make up for that as time goes by' (Monkey, 2001).

Herein lies another important historical and political observation: users had been mobilising, organising and gathering a voice long before the arrival of the NTA (who were, incidentally, preempted in issue four of *Monkey* via the circulation of rumours of a new agency that would *'buy all residential beds centrally'* (Monkey, 2000)). The NTA though, quickly established itself as the catalyst of local, regional and national activity and soon began to shape and control the way 'user involvement' was viewed, planned, funded and delivered.

In truth though, the NTA first had to find a way to appease, accommodate and utilise an underground movement that had already begun to galvanise, support and promote itself regardless of any mainstream, governmental support or financial backing. *Black Poppy* magazine – Britain's unique, pioneering and premier drug users' health and lifestyle magazine – was first launched in winter 1998 and already featured an article on work to establish the National Drug Users' Development Agency (NDUDA) earlier in October. This fledgling agency had arisen because,

'User groups are feeling that they are, at best, patronised by being superficially consulted on decisions made after the event rather than included in the complete developmental process' (Black Poppy, 2000).

Therefore, although Britain already had a strong, emergent user voice, it was very much entrenched in an understandable and necessary culture of political activism, which required drug users and harm reductionists to work together and challenge the prevailing stigmas and discriminatory policies and practices that only worked to exacerbate negative consequences for drug users and their families.

However, as McDermott (unpublished) points out, while the NDUDA established itself over time as an umbrella lobbying group that sought to bring about legal and constitutional change, in reality,

'Objectives of groups like this cannot be reconciled with the objectives of a government-funded organisation whose aims are to increase the capacity of the drug treatment system, and to improve the quality of the treatment provided'.

These tensions that grew between the needs of users and the needs of government will be explored later in this chapter, but back in 1998 there were three other user-led agencies that were beginning to raise the profile of the crucial role that individual users played in their own health and associated care.

Mainliners was originally established as a self-help and advocacy organisation for intravenous drug users living with HIV as far back as 1990. Its pioneering work in providing safer-injecting workshops for users enabled individuals to review their practice, reduce mortality by reducing the risk of contracting blood-borne viruses and helped establish the profile and role of harm reduction as an invaluable, effective treatment modality.

Perhaps more influential though, was the formation of the United Kingdom Harm Reduction Alliance (UKHRA) in 1998. UKHRA is a campaigning coalition of drug users, health and social care workers, criminal justice workers and educationalists that aims to put public health and human rights at the centre of drug treatment and service provision for drug users. The organisation formed as a response to rising concerns that the prevention of individual and public health problems arising from drug use did not feature prominently in the national drug strategies of the UK, and called for an additional fifth aim to be included in the 10-year drug strategy: individual and public health – to minimise harm to the health of individuals and communities arising from drug use.

The increasing power and voice that users were having in influencing government policies was evident in 2002 when the government's 'updated strategy' appeared with a new, enhanced section on 'treatment and harm minimisation' (Home Office, 2002), which incorporated the targets originally proposed by UKHRA as a 'key element' within it.

Also in 1998, the Methadone Alliance was founded by a group of committed drug users and professionals working together as equals to improve the quality and availability of treatment in the UK. The original aims and objectives of the Methadone Alliance were as simple as they were direct:

- to ensure that drug users are actively involved in the debate about their treatment and care at every level – locally, regionally, and nationally
- to provide advocacy and representation to people receiving poor care, and to help improve their situation and their experience of 'treatment'
- to educate users about their rights to effective treatment so that they could take an informed role themselves in the treatment debate.
- to show that a 'user-led' service is possible – our company rules state that the majority of our board must be either current or former users (Methadone Alliance, 1998).

The overarching vision of the Methadone Alliance's founder, Bill Nelles, and staunch allies such as Dr Chris Ford (Royal College of General Practitioners or RCGP) and Gary Sutton (Release) was simply to support people either in treatment or seeking help for drug dependency, and enable them to access the most appropriate help to meet their individual needs through the provision of training, a peer-run helpline and a unique, specialist, independent advocacy service. The Methadone Alliance believed that when users of drug services and professionals work together as equals, it creates a powerful voice to help set high standards for drug treatment, and influences change in policy development and operational delivery. The Methadone Alliance felt it was essential to demonstrate and evidence that this change cannot only bring immeasurable benefits to the health and mental well-being of individuals, but also to the wider socio-economic factors that influence and shape social exclusion.

Over time, the Methadone Alliance earned a deserved reputation as a professional body that placed the voice and choice of individual patients as central to service delivery, and its credibility was further enhanced when it relaunched itself simply as the Alliance. Nelles was concerned that the organisation was becoming too closely related to only one treatment modality, and despite the invaluable role that the organisation had undoubtedly played in raising the profile, understanding and provision of effective, evidence-based methadone prescribing, it was time to reinforce the message that advocacy was available to support *anyone*, regardless of their presenting drug of choice or favoured treatment option.

In 2003, in a bold attempt to further improve and solidify the advancements already made in user involvement and drug treatment, the Alliance broadened their work in assisting service users to learn more about the process of treatment and how they can ensure that the services they receive match the new standards of care by initiating an important project to develop patient knowledge and advocacy skills.

The key to this was the support given to the organisation by the Royal College of General Practitioners. The College made 12 places available on their year-long Part 2 diploma course in Management of Substance Misuse in General Practice to people from the Alliance and from other user organisations. Originally, the course was only open to practitioners who had completed the College's Part 1 certificate and were interested in developing their skills to become GPs with a special clinical interest or practitioners with a special interest. By expanding the eligibility criteria to include users and patient advocates, it ensured that user participants were the first group of 'expert patients' to gain this particular qualification.

This programme was so successful that it has subsequently been opened up to a larger group of user advocates with experience of many different treatments, and the Alliance's own Basic Advocacy Course has now been approved by the RCGP as a valid entrance exam for users wishing to complete the Part 2 certificate.

While the NTA were still primarily interested in developing networks of user involvement that improved broader treatment options and systems (to be discussed in the next section), their next major strategic development would begin to firmly place users as indispensable pilots of their own individual treatment journey and would, somewhat ironically, be adapted and influenced by programmes initiated in the traditionally punitive USA.

On 30 June 2005 the NTA launched their new *Treatment Effectiveness Strategy* in London. This new strategy aimed to build upon existing work but with a slightly different emphasis, namely it was,

'designed to deliver a more dynamic treatment system by focusing on service users' "treatment journey", together with a focus on an individual's holistic needs (including housing, employment) to maximise the benefits of treatment'.

The key areas identified by the NTA that will impact on the client's journey are:

- treatment engagement
- treatment delivery
- treatment completion and/or community integration.

'Care planning' is acknowledged as being an integral component in ensuring successful treatment outcomes.

This was hardly earth-shattering news, as the development of care plans that matched client need to appropriately tailored interventions had always been a theoretical part of structured treatment.

Now though, there was a government-led national strategy that placed an operational expectation on all providers to engage with their clients on an equal footing and ensure, where possible, that the specific needs of a client were listened to and respected.

As the NTA's own subsequent *Care Planning Practice Guide* acknowledges,

'One of the critical success factors in delivering improvement in clients' lifestyles and drug-related behaviour, as identified in the Treatment Effectiveness Strategy, is effective care planning. This should include frequent reviews of care plans, with clients as partners in their drug treatment' (NTA, 2006 p9).

Drug users are not a homogenous group, and just because 70mls of oral methadone linctus works for a substantial number of users, why should it be assumed that it's applicable to all? Some will prefer and respond better to buprenorphine due to its less sedatory effects. Some may know that only injectable diamorphine or morphine sulphate will help reduce the chaos. Some may need the complete antagonist security blanket of naltraxone. The knowledge that comes with experience – of one's own body and how it responds to previous treatment episodes – *should* be respected.

Further, if a service user is in full-time employment, or is a parent with a young family, and they find that getting across town to be supervised taking their medication is inconvenient, inappropriate and actually jeopardising and disrupting essential parts of their increasingly stable life, then that should be negotiated and more appropriate, supportive arrangements should be put into place. People's circumstances change, and indeed *should* change as they progress through treatment. So an effective package of care is one that responds appropriately and makes a user's life easier and more manageable and does not put unnecessary, inflexible obstacles or procedures in place that undermine this process.

This was acknowledged by the NTA 12 months prior to the launch of the *Treatment Effectiveness Strategy*. In the fifth of their research-into-practice briefings, *Engaging and Retaining Clients in Drug Treatment*, it is noted that,

'Client choice is the ultimate in responsiveness and can be an effective tactic when what the service user wants is feasible and likely to correspond to what is needed... In other words, what is key is flexibility and responsiveness in pursuit of shared goals, not in whose hands the decision nominally lies' (NTA, 2004 p6).

The growing voice, role and influence of users have successfully brought into focus some of these unnecessary, inflexible and undermining procedures. Take for example, the practice of 'blind reductions', when a key worker – not the GP – can decide to reduce scripts involuntarily after a failed urine test but 'top up' the remaining methadone with water so that users don't become suspicious. If users then complain that their script isn't holding them, the notion is often dismissed as 'imagination', and if they do finally get an admission, they're informed of a waiver they signed while withdrawing and desperate for support at their first appointment.

There are no demonstrable, clinical benefits to this procedure, and no robust evidence to support its efficacy, yet it was common practice among some agencies; one NTA regional manager even tried to justify it as an intervention in an edition of *Drink and Drug News* magazine (Bradbury, 2006).

However, by working together, users, with the support of their GP colleagues, have been instrumental in raising and challenging, and fundamentally ending this potentially damaging piece of bad practice. Maybe that in itself is evidence of why effective, targeted user involvement is so essential to improving treatment journeys.

THE ROLE OF USERS IN DECIDING WIDER TREATMENT OPTIONS

'Solutions to improving the health and well-being of drug users should develop both from a grass roots level and a top down strategic level, whereby users have ownership and understanding on the intentions of how commissioners and drug services alike are going to distribute public funding and improve services alike' (Garratt & Foster, 2005).

Maybe it's because this interpretation of truly proactive, targeted, measurable user involvement only really started to creep into policies and practice guidance after a long period of 'fumbling in the dark'.

It is fair to say that, in the main, user involvement has often been insufficiently goal-orientated and over ambitious in its aims. It proceeds without really knowing where it's going. Although there have been many successful user involvement projects, the knowledge gained is not shared widely enough. Most attempts to develop effective user involvement have, to a large degree, been unstructured, undefined and insufficiently audited, and as a result, the integration of users into the treatment arena remains unco-ordinated, unfocused and largely ineffective.

That is not to say that there has not been a concerted effort to involve users at local, regional and national levels, but it has, arguably, been a very process-and target-led development, and not a generic, flexible and needs-specific advancement that has been directed by, and responsive to, users' expressed needs.

From their inception, the NTA have striven to work in accordance with Section 11 of the Health and Social Care Act 2001, which places a duty on NHS organisations to make arrangements to involve and consult patients and the public in:

a) planning services that they are responsible for
b) developing and considering proposals for changes in the way those services are provided
c) decisions to be made that affect how those services operate.

To enable this process, the NTA established a national, regional and local network that:

- established a national user advisory group
- established a user forum in each of the nine NTA regions
- ensured that service user involvement is a component of each of the NTA's activities at every level, including representation on the NTA board
- issued guidance to local providers and drug action teams on how to implement user involvement projects
- made progress on user involvement – one of their performance indicators for local drug action teams.

On an operational level, this culminated in an influx of locally established user groups that were financially and strategically supported by their relevant drug action teams (DATs), often via the co-ordination of a recently appointed user involvement worker. The minimum requirement that the NTA expected from these localised set-ups was *'the involvement of users in the design of the local treatment system and their involvement throughout the implementation, monitoring, review and evaluation processes'*, (NTA, 2005b) and this would be assessed via measuring a DAT's progress against the following criteria.

1) Service users who are representative of the diverse communities within the partnership area are involved in needs assessment, setting partnership plan priorities, and are consulted on plan at draft stage and throughout the process with evidence that the involvement has resulted in action at partnership and provider level.
2) Partnership service user involvement strategy, which includes current, ex- and potential service users.
3) Resources and investment, including user involvement expenses and remuneration arrangements, child care and transport costs, grant aid/funding to local user groups.
4) Network of advocacy and support services aimed at drug users, which involves,

where appropriate, PALS (NHS Patient Advice and Liaison Service), local authority and independent sector.

5) Service level agreements require services to display a service user charter, include user consultation in service reviews, and promote access to advocacy for users.

As a measure to ensure DATs *'make sure users and carers are involved and consulted from the very beginning of any process to develop services or change how they operate'* (NTA, 2008b), this directive should have proved an unqualified success in the drug treatment sector, but there are still some questions to be raised. Although the quality of effective, measurable involvement will undoubtedly change from area to area, it is worrying that only 47% of DATs in England have drug user representation at a commissioning level, while 36% evidenced no strategic user involvement. However, the involvement of drug users in identifying gaps in current service delivery, and in making decisions that redress these imbalances in the quality, quantity, creativity, accessibility and range of wider treatment provision, should have become such an invaluable, ingrained part of the local commissioning culture by now that one can only hope that it will continue, regardless of the changing whims of local and national government.

On a regional level, the NTA established user forums in each of its nine regions, with a view to bringing representatives from all the relevant DATs together in order to *'make sure that the NTA and local partnerships have up-to-date, accurate views of what is happening in each area'* (NTA, 2008b) via the provision of formalised, structured opportunities for networking, consultation and treatment planning and reporting.

Regions responded to utilising user involvement in various ways. One notable example is in the south east region, which contracted with Oxford User Team (OUT) to sit in and review each of the region's DATs' draft plans from a 'best practice' user perspective, as part of the draft treatment planning review process.

Effectively though, the main role of the regional fora were to act as a bridge between local action and central NTA activity, and therefore, two democratically elected representatives from each region were invited along with members of national user-led organisations to attend the NTA's own National User Advisory Group (NUAG). Part of the role of the NUAG, as identified in the group's terms of reference, was to provide service user perspectives on NTA policy, research and performance management issues and provide a pool of interested service users to assist the NTA in developing new policies or research.

However, despite the noble aims of the NTA, individual members were often critical of a forum that often seemed directionless and unresponsive, appeared insensitive to the user (as opposed to NTA) agenda, and became increasingly viewed as a tokenistic exercise in being seen to invite user input, but failing to act upon key suggestions; an observation not only drawn from personal conversations with other group members, but also reflected in the official notes from a meeting held on 8 November 2005, which posed the question, *'Big question is – what happens as a result of being here?'*

As a result, membership became inconsistent and erratic, proactive networking became derailed by a seemingly endless round of meetings that discussed and debated the same process-related issues, and members were informed that the group would finally be wound down during a meeting on 11 April 2006 with the minutes stating,

'As the focus for the future will be on the regions, in order to sufficiently develop them before their move into the strategic health authorities, there is now no role for the NUAG as a group that meets regularly'.

Sadly, and despite all the strides taken by the NTA and numerous user groups and individual activists to get the user voice heard and established as a key tenet of improving treatment planning and service delivery, many users viewed the dissolution of the NUAG as confirmation of their long-held suspicion that user involvement had failed in this country.

This was largely because the nature and aims of user involvement had become, on the one hand, so prescriptive and target focused, yet conversely confused and directionless, that it was not really about them anymore. Ironically, it could be argued that by trying so hard to establish a hitherto unknown cultural framework of user involvement that DATs and users had to respond effectively to, but despite no national guidance being produced until 2006, the NTA were ultimately setting both sides up to fail; users responded to 'involvement' as a right, DATs and the NTA as a responsibility. But did they both fully understand what each party wanted or needed? Were the NTA aware that true user involvement would inevitably lead to conflict and them giving away some of their power? If not, they should have been.

Services and strategic infrastructures tend to be developed from a top down process in which policy makers and providers identify what they perceive to be users' problems and then provide solutions that they hope users will concur with; solutions that tend to be overtly ambitious and poorly focused towards the problems as users perceive them. Across the field, many professionals fail to empower users to define their own issues and develop their own solutions. Thus, user empowerment is ultimately under the control of the state. Professionals are often unwilling or afraid to relinquish the power conferred by their expert role and equally fail to see that service users have expertise of their own. On the one hand, users are often socially excluded, and on the other, professionals fail to deliver socially inclusive services. Service user involvement is often located within a judgemental, discriminatory class system, which does not support users' rights and freedoms, and views users as the problem and not the solution. Is this not – in essence – just a further extension of the blame culture that still underpins whole swathes of drug treatment provision in the UK; the 'problematic' drug user, the 'chaotic' lifestyle, the 'difficult' client, the 'hard-to-reach' group? Perhaps only when we begin to talk of the 'problematic' treatment regime, the 'chaotic' bureaucracy, the 'difficult' provider and the 'hard-to-access' service in equal measures will we be at a point where we can work effectively and constructively to redress this balance.

Let's not make any bones about this – involving current users in delivering initiatives is risky and difficult to manage. However, if managers believe in the benefits that can be achieved and have the patience, energy and flexibility to develop a collaborative partnership with users and see a project through, the positive results can be immeasurable.

In truth though, many local partnerships, regional management structures and national government bodies may have spoken of involvement, and many have probably genuinely thought they were being sincere in their expressed desire, but this grew to be increasingly at odds with the needs and wants of their user populations. What they *meant* was user *representation* and what they *wanted* was merely to be informed by users; they did not appear to want users actually integrated and doing things.

Examples of this include DATs who identify money to establish a local user group or even employ their own user involvement worker, but fail to ensure that individual users/members have access to appropriate travel and accommodation expenses, petty cash, childcare, subsistence or training/conference opportunities. Organisationally and individually, I have received many requests for help from users who have found themselves in the situation where they have had to withdraw from user involvement as it is no longer economically viable for them, or they feel that their group only exists to serve the DAT's needs and not their own. Indeed, many a potential talent has been lost to this field because policy makers have not thought about the financial implications that true involvement places on users, thus restricting many individuals to only participating in local, no-cost events – like DAT meetings.

In short, this ongoing difference of interpretation of what user involvement actually is has inadvertently set people up to fail because many areas have started involvement work that could not be sustained but has still raised people's expectations, and only resulted in further disappointment, disillusionment and distrust. Furthermore, it is important to not put the responsibility for the successful completion of any work on the shoulders of one key individual. All work should be firmly based within a workable system. One that does not rely on personalities, otherwise it only takes one relapse, argument or relocation to see all best intentions of both parties wasted.

This dichotomy was recognised and highlighted by the National Consumer Council (2001) in October 2001 as part of their *Involving Patients and the Public in Healthcare – A discussion document*, in which they identified that, *'Involvement and representation are not the same thing and both are required'.*

The National Consumer Council (2001) defined 'involvement' thus:

'The public will only invest their time when they feel directly affected by an issue and when they trust that their input will make a difference. As a result, involvement cannot be relied on for ongoing input in standing structures. It is a method more suited for issue-specific and time limited initiatives'.

Whereas 'representation',

'means being well informed by individuals or groups who have a strong policy analysis, which is based on high quality research of patient and public experience and the realities of the NHS'.

Therefore, it has become apparent that, in England at least, the more that government bodies have tried to empower users by encouraging them to become more involved and take more control over the drug treatment issues that affect them, the more they have ended up distanced from each other. The inherent power imbalance that still exists ensures that users are only allowed to become involved on certain, policy-defined levels rather than on their own terms.

THE ROLE OF USERS AS PROVIDERS
Users as workers

For many users, one of their ultimate goals is to re-engage with the workplace, often in the drug treatment sector. The *National Treatment Effectiveness Strategy* (NTA, 2005a) states both that long-term maintenance is a viable treatment modality and that provision of employment options is an essential component of a holistic treatment journey.

However, many provider agencies have long held policies that will not accept users as employees unless they have been out of treatment for at least two years. Historically, this emerged as a misapplication of guidance first published by SCODA (later DrugScope) in 1998, but rectified in the later *Enhancing Drug Services* document, which categorically stated that,

'People with experience of drug use and drug treatment can be effective workers in drug services, particularly when they have support and backup from their management.... Current and former drug users should not be considered or rejected for employment in a drug service solely on the basis of their drug use' (DrugScope/NTA, 2003 p22).

One could argue, therefore, that any agencies insisting that users have to have been out of treatment for a minimum of two years before they will even consider them for employment are unable to fulfil their required therapeutic duties, and should be decommissioned. However, until a swift, final, definitive statement or gesture to put this unethical, discriminatory bad practice to bed is issued, many users may be unable to escape the cycle of crime and dependency and find the required outcomes of their treatment journey unfulfilled.

Although there is no suggestion here that 'a drug user doth a good drug worker make', if one follows the discourse around effective user involvement to its logical conclusion, there is an argument to support the notion that although the right user/employee will by no means have a greater understanding of what is best for their client, they may have a greater understanding, desire and empathy for why their client needs to be central to their own treatment planning, based on their own experiences – be they positive or negative.

Thankfully, there is some anecdotal evidence to suggest this is starting to occur more regularly, although conversely, the same anecdotal evidence also suggests that some workers who have previously shielded their service user status have suddenly found themselves dismissed or suspended once they have 'outed' themselves, despite, in some cases, feeling safe in the knowledge of a hitherto faultless employment history and an imminent promotion. Unfortunately, for one observer, this is indicative of the mistrust that still permeates many 'therapeutic relationships' wherein,

'Professionals are often uncertain about the Expert Patients' Programme. They "fear" expert patients as a challenge to their own expertise' (Cayton, 2006 p22).

Specialist independent advocacy
'To harness the potential to change behaviour, service providers must appreciate a user's own view of the future and allow informed choice and opportunity. Advocacy services are important for drug users in complicated situations, and users say that frontline staff need to be more aware of this, as well as being proactive in promoting them.' (Audit Commission, 2004).

One area in which users have become increasingly involved as providers and helped shape and improve treatment outcomes for other users is in the field of specialist independent advocacy.

What is advocacy?
Advocacy is about taking action to help people say what they want, secure their rights, represent their interests and obtain the services they need. All service users have the right to be heard and for their views to be respected, but although many service users have the capacity to contribute to their own care, they may need help to overcome the problems that prevent them from doing so.

It is often the most vulnerable members of society who find themselves in circumstances where they need advocacy, but with the right support, everyone can communicate more effectively and gain more control over their own lives.

Why is it needed in drug treatment?
Advocacy fits within the drug treatment system as an independent way of resolving problems where it has not been possible to resolve the problem informally between

the client and the provider or agency. In *Drug Misuse and Dependence – Guidelines on clinical management*, (DoH, 1999) it is clearly documented that if users seeking substitute prescribing want to achieve a stabilised, well-functioning quality of life, the optimum maintenance dose of methadone should be *'up to a total of between 60 and 120mg'* (p47).

Unfortunately, the reality of UK drug treatment still paints a very different picture. In the third NTA research-into-practice publication (2004) it was found that:

- in British methadone treatment, doses are on average less than 50mg daily and only just over a quarter of service users receive over 60mg
- higher doses have been consistently shown to encourage treatment retention and reductions in illicit drug use in methadone maintenance regimes
- lower dose levels may be undermining the provision of optimal services and compromising the therapeutic relationship between service user and key worker
- recent research shows that responsive and flexible individualised dosing can help foster the therapeutic relationship and may lead to improved outcomes and reductions in illicit drug use.

Furthermore, as we move swiftly into a new era of 'treatment effectiveness', it is important to note that this new NTA initiative is largely underpinned by a public service agreement (PSA) target to,

'increase year on year the proportion of users successfully sustaining or completing treatment programmes' (NTA, 2004 p1).

It could be argued, then, that if the *Treatment Effectiveness Strategy* is to work, then advocacy needs to be a central component, because:

a) 'success' equates with higher retention
b) 'higher retention' is better achieved when users receive higher doses (NTA, 2004).

One of the primary goals of specialist, independent advocacy in the drug treatment sector is to maximise the impact of treatment interventions, and there have been anecdotal reports from the NTA's NUAG and regional user forums that care planning and users' experiences of treatment vary throughout the country and in some instances have required advocacy to resolve some of these issues.

Further, and to their credit, the NTA acknowledged (2007) the need for advocacy in their *Treatment Planning Guidance* for 2006/07, which places an expectancy on local partnerships to develop:

- **networks of advocacy and support services aimed at drug users**, which involves, where appropriate, PALS (NHS), local authority and independent sector

- service level agreements that require services to display a service user charter, include user consultation in service reviews, **and promote access to advocacy for users**.

Their annual report for 2004/05 also states,

'Service users can act as advocates on behalf of other service users. Their knowledge of treatment and the systems that monitor them can enable other users to get a better service.' (NTA, 2005a)

Perhaps more significantly though, this was also acknowledged by the Department of Health in 2005, who awarded the Alliance a grant to establish a national model of peer-led, independent specialist advocacy.

Independent specialist advocacy services are developed by current/ex/non-service users or carers to help service users participate fully in care planning, make informed decisions around treatment options and take control of their own treatment journey. The provision of independent specialist advocacy services is in line with the *Models of Care*, update 2005 (NTA, 2005a), focusing on reducing harm to individuals and communities, improving clients' journeys through treatment, predicting client flow through local treatment systems and improving the effectiveness of local drug treatment systems, because it can provide an alternative source of constructive intelligence and feedback about how well services are meeting the needs of their client groups and inform future needs and priorities while protecting the confidentiality of individuals.

The Department of Health money has allowed the Alliance to appoint nine regional advocates, in each of the nine NTA regions, to support the development of localised autonomous advocacy and other user involvement initiatives. At the time of writing all nine advocates have been employed, seven of whom are current service users, one no longer uses services, and the ninth is the carer of a user.

For the government to show faith and belief in a drug-user-run advocacy system, and for the Department of Health to pledge three years of funding to ensure it happens, is unprecedented. There have been a number of justifiable concerns expressed lately around Britain losing its place in the vanguard of harm reduction, and the undeniable shift of government policy from public health to criminal justice. The need to respond effectively to the emergence and spread of HIV in the mid-1980s meant that the state-sanctioned establishment of formal needle exchange schemes in 1987 could co-exist with street level, 'guerrilla' exchanges like those typified on Merseyside, because Britain had always historically worked within an effective, public health focused drug policy, and harm reduction slipped into an amenable existing framework. During the next 10 years, there were a number of pragmatic, innovative harm reduction interventions pioneered in the UK, including, but not restricted to, the 'Break The Cycle' campaign that worked to prevent the initiation of non-injectors to injecting practice, localised ambulance and police protocols that discouraged police presence at overdose scenes and maximised emergency health service responses, the 'Up Your Bum' campaign that promoted non-intravenous modes of heroin ingestion, and the increasing provision of single-use injecting paraphernalia, which was still technically illegal under the Misuse Of Drugs Act 1971.

However, the last 10 years have seen UK drug policy resort to a punitive, crime-led agenda, and the once pervasive harm reduction aesthetic reduced to a couple of overdose prevention and blood-borne virus outputs in the NTA's treatment planning grid. I have observed many practitioners express concerns that both harm reduction and user involvement in this country have become increasingly tokenistic. Nevertheless, the establishment of a designated national model of advocacy gives the Alliance the opportunity to achieve something truly exceptional, exciting and unique as they've been given the chance to not only work towards securing better scripts and doses for heroin users, but better treatment and support programmes for all drug users. Theoretically, the political go ahead has been given to help develop and support a potential user-workforce of between nine and over 100 salaried or volunteer advocates nationwide, but whether this will be achieved, supported or sustained in practice is another question entirely.

FUTURE DEVELOPMENTS

The future of drug treatment in this country is now more difficult to predict than in recent history. Following virtually a decade of unprecedented growth in the field, DATs are preparing to face a future of no financial uplifts, and possibly even disinvestments as a result of the financial crisis engulfing the NHS. As Britain bids farewell to one 10-year drug strategy, what surprises will the new one bring? Will we see a return to a cross departmental, public health driven agenda that focuses on the wider socio-economic issues that affect and exacerbate problematic drug use, and that places the health and well-being of the individual as central to their holistic package of care, or will we see an increasingly punitive, stigmatising policy that views drug use as purely a crime issue and drug users as antisocial deviants who should be punished?

Whatever the future holds in store, it is essential that the voice of the individual user is still heard, particularly in regard to the decisions that affect their health and their future.

One contemporary example is that users, with the support of the Alliance, National Addiction Centre and Action on Addiction, are assisting in the development, implementation and dissemination of a randomised controlled trial of injectable opioid treatment for heroin dependence (RCT-IOT) which, should the findings prove favourable, may finally open the doors to a new heroin-assisted treatment model in this country.

Furthermore, users have proved that by mobilising themselves, getting involved in strategic planning, service delivery and direct action, they can help influence change that not only benefits the health of individual users, but that of wider society.

However, this cannot be achieved alone. Historical issues surrounding the very public implosion of the NDUDA and the subsequent demise of the NTA's NUAG possibly led some observers to conclude that the end of the nationally co-ordinated user movement was nigh. However, the recently formed National User Network (NUN) could prove to provide the umbrella framework that users need to continue their forward trajectory.

Truly independent, NUN, in its mission statement, aims *'to promote and support user involvement in all aspects of care, treatment and service development'* and will hopefully grow to be a formidable and essential body, but issues remain about where it will attract political and financial support. As one senior NTA official informed the discussion group in an online forum,

'Previously, we have encouraged the creation of NUN because a national users' network would help both service users and non-service users to make comments about treatment services. However, because NUN will cover a range of issues outside treatment issues, the NTA has declined to fund its activities'.

Hopefully, regardless of whatever system replaces the NTA, there will be some champion to ensure that the rights of individual patients are not eroded, and the work and commitment evidenced by groups such as NDUDA, the Alliance, OUT, UKHRA, NUN and the RCGP has not been in vain.

References

Audit Commission (2002) *Changing Habits: The commissioning and management of community drug services for adults.* London: Audit Commission.

Audit Commission (2004) *Drug Misuse 2004: Reducing the local impact.* London: Audit Commission.

Black Poppy (2000) The National Drug Users' Network. *Black Poppy* **4** 6–7.

Bradbury C (2006) Kingdom of the blind. *Drink and Drug News* **27** (Feb) 6–7.

Cayton H (2006) Patients as entrepreneurs: who is in charge of change? In: E Andersson, J Tritter & R Wilson (Eds) *Healthy Democracy: The future of involvement in health and social care.* London: Involve & NHS National Centre For Involvement.

Department of Health (1991) *The NHS Patients' Charter.* London: DoH.

Department of Health (1999) *Drug Misuse and Dependence – Guidelines on clinical management.* London: DoH.

Department of Health (2000) *The NHS Plan: A plan for investment, a plan for reform.* London: DoH.

DrugScope/National Treatment Agency (2003) *Enhancing Drug Services.* London: NTA, p22.

Ford C (2007) In: *Substance Misuse Management in General Practice. Modern Maintenance Therapy: Prescriber imperative or patient choice? Report of a socratic dialogue.* London: Schering-Plough.

Garratt D & Foster J (2005) Fumbling in the dark. *Druglink* **20** (3) 12.

Home Office (2002) *Updated Drug Strategy.* London: Home Office.

McDermott P (unpublished) *A Brief Overview of the History of Drug User Involvement and Activism in the UK.* (contact author for access)

Methadone Alliance (1998) *The Alliance. Taking treatment forward* [online]. Available at: http://www.m-alliance.org.uk/index.html (accessed March 2008).

Monkey (2000) National Treatment Agency to be set up: Rehab? Forget it. *Monkey Users Magazine* **4** 5.

Monkey (2001) Junkies to fund National Treatment Agency. *Monkey Users Magazine* **5** 3.

National Consumer Council (2001) *Involving Patients and Public in Healthcare. A discussion document.* London: National Consumer Council.

National Treatment Agency (2002) *Models of Care for Treatment in Adult Drug Misusers.* London: NTA.

National Treatment Agency (2004) *Engaging and Retaining Clients in Drug Treatment.* London: NTA.

National Treatment Agency (2005a) *National Treatment Effectiveness Strategy.* London: NTA.

National Treatment Agency (2005b) *Adult Drug Treatment Plan 2006/7.* London: NTA.

National Treatment Agency (2005c) *Models of Care for Treatment in Adult Drug Misusers.* London: NTA.

National Treatment Agency (2006) *Care Planning Practice Guide.* London: NTA, p9.

National Treatment Agency (2007) *Treatment Planning Guidance 2006/07.* London: NTA.

National Treatment Agency (2008a) *Introduction* [online]. Available at: http://www.nta.nhs.uk/about/default.aspx (accessed March 2008).

National Treatment Agency (2008b) *User Involvement* [online]. Available at: http://www.nta.nhs.uk/areas/users_and_carers/user_involvement.aspx (accessed March 2008).

UK Anti-drugs Co-ordination Unit (1999) *First Annual Report and National Plan.* London: The Stationery Office.

Walsall Drug Action Team (2006) *Your Journey: An audit of drug user experience and drug treatment.* Walsall Drug Action Team.

Weale A (2006) What is so good about citizens' involvement in health care. In: E Andersson, J Tritter & R Wilson (Eds) *Healthy Democracy: The future of involvement in health and social care.* London: Involve & NHS National Centre For Involvement, p38.